WORLD ECONOMIC

HISTORICAL

STATISTICS

WORLD ECONOMIC
HISTORICAL
STATISTICS

Carlos Sabillon

Algora Publishing
New York

© 2005 by Algora Publishing
All Rights Reserved
www.algora.com

No portion of this book (beyond what is permitted by
Sections 107 or 108 of the United States Copyright Act of 1976)
may be reproduced by any process, stored in a retrieval system,
or transmitted in any form, or by any means, without the
express written permission of the publisher.
ISBN: 0-87586-352-3 (softcover)
ISBN: 0-87586-353-1 (hardcover)
ISBN: 0-87586-354-X (ebook)

Library of Congress Cataloging-in-Publication Data —

Sabillon, Carlos, 1962-
   World economic historical statistics / Carlos Sabillon.
      p. cm.
   Includes bibliographical references and index.
   ISBN 0-87586-352-3 (pbk. : alk. paper) — ISBN 0-87586-353-1 (hard cover
: alk. paper) — ISBN 0-87586-354-X (ebook)
      1. Statistics. 2. Economic indicators. 3. Economic history. I. Title.

HA155.S225 2004
330.9'002'1—dc22

2004017622

Printed in the United States

Dedication

This book is dedicated to the few men and women who over the centuries dedicated their lives to improving the lot of humanity by making scientific and technological progress. Throughout time, technology and science have been the only real and effective mechanisms for creating wealth and delivering benefits to society. Therefore, it is those people who made progress on this front who deserve to be classified as the most relevant benefactors of humanity.

ACKNOWLEDGMENTS

This book is the culmination of a four-year research project undertaken to analyze the long-term historical development of the nations of the world. The work was funded in part by the Swiss National Fund for Scientific Research, the Graduate Institute of International Studies in Geneva, Switzerland, by the Geneva Business Institute, and by private contributions.

The author wishes to thank several academics in particular for having revised and commented on the different parts of the research: Professor Norman Scott of the Graduate Institute of International Studies in Geneva, Switzerland; Professor Karlhans Sauernheimer of the Ludwig Maximilians University in Munich, Germany; Professor Peter Tschopp of the University of Geneva; Professor George Viksnins of Georgetown University in Washington D.C.; and Professor Gilbert Etienne of the Graduate Institute of International Studies in Geneva.

The author thanks Pablo Aviles for his contribution to the calculation of growth rates; and Carlos Roberto Montoya, whose regular complaints about the scarcity of long-term statistics to a great extent motivated the author to fill that vacuum.

TABLE OF CONTENTS

INTRODUCTION

Human beings have since the earliest of times endeavored to uncover the causes of prosperity. Due to this question's overwhelming importance, over the millennia some of the best thinkers have dedicated their lives to pondering the matter and they have progressively formulated ever more complex ideas. In the 16th century economic ideas began to take a more elaborate form and evolved into theories. In the following centuries the number of books on economics rapidly grew and economists' knowledge did likewise. By the early 21st century, economists understood vastly more than their counterparts of past centuries, but still none of the theories they produced could provide clear guidelines on how to attain fast and sustained economic growth. Below, a quick review of some of the more accepted theories shows that there are perhaps more exceptions than not, and none of the theories alone can account for much of history.

Economic growth is the key to prosperity and by the early 2000s several countries enjoyed a very prosperous existence relative to other nations. Living conditions in these nations had improved enormously; famines and epidemics had disappeared. However, relative to the aspirations of the average person, prosperity had not been attained. Even the most developed countries were enduring high levels of unemployment or underemployment. In the nations that were less developed, the situation had not improved much, over all.

History is the best tool that society possesses for identifying and analyzing the factors that have made human existence so painful. Living conditions worldwide were miserable and largely stagnant up to the 18th century, but there were small fluctuations of the economy. Hundreds of variables interplayed simultaneously and it is the task of scientists to discover which among those variables most contributed to, or allowed for, the small improvements in living conditions — and which delivered the opposite result. In the 19th and in particular the 20th century, the fluctuations became much larger and information by which to judge events was more abundant. This expanded the possibilities for identifying a common denominator that may have been present whenever there was progress, and absent when there was not.

The research that led to this book concentrated on analyzing the economic history of several nations. At first, the research focused on East Asia because by the early 1990s this region was attracting attention worldwide for its fast economic growth in the preceding decades. In 1991 the World Bank undertook a major research effort intended to find out why this region had grown faster than all others since the end of World War II. The fact that the World Bank failed to uncover a common denominator induced several academics to claim that even if a denominator would be found for the case of East Asia, it did not guarantee that the causality of growth had been found, because it was just one region from a total of ten.

The author therefore began to research other regions. Western Europe and North America were chosen because of their developed status. By the 1990s these two regions were the wealthiest in the world, having attained the fastest economic growth in the preceding two centuries. After having analyzed most of the developed world, the author turned his attention towards Russia and Eastern Europe. Once that was completed, it was the developing nations' turn. South Asia, Southeast Asia, Latin America, Sub-Saharan Africa, the Middle East and Southeast Asia were analyzed.

A few countries were selected from each region for detailed analysis. The countries were selected based on their economic performance and their importance in international affairs. That meant selecting those which had attained the fastest rates of growth during the 19th and 20th century and/or which had the greatest impact on world politics. For East Asia, emphasis was placed on Japan and China; but South Korea, Taiwan and Hong Kong were also investigated with relative depth. For Western Europe, the accent fell on Germany, France and Great Britain. For Eastern Europe, priority was given to Russia and for North America on the United States. India was at the core of the research on South Asia but Pakistan and Bangladesh were also covered. For Latin America priority was given to Mexico, Brazil and Argentina. For Sub-Saharan Africa the emphasis fell on South Africa, Nigeria, and to a lesser extent on Botswana and Equatorial Guinea. In the Middle East the accent was placed on Egypt and Iran but Libya,

Israel, Saudi Arabia, the United Arab Emirates, Qatar and Bahrain were also covered. For Southeast Asia the priority was set on Indonesia, Thailand, Vietnam, Singapore, Malaysia and the Philippines. Practically all of the remaining countries from all regions were also analyzed, albeit not as thoroughly.

This book is divided into two parts. The first part analyzes the most compelling ideas and theories on what have been considered causal variables of growth. It summarizes these ideas pedagogically and tests them against the historical data. The results of these analyses are troubling, because they reveal a weak or very inconsistent correlation between theory and reality. Even ideas that are considered ultimate truths by mainstream economic schools are easily shaken by contrary examples.

The second part of the book presents a collection of statistics. After a review of hundreds of books and documents on economics, economic history and history, it became evident that economic statistics had never been elaborated in an orderly and consistent fashion. Even academics who specialize in individual countries almost never present a set of statistics covering the whole 20th century — and for the previous centuries, the data is even more chaotic. The World Bank in its yearly World Development Report presents the most organized set of statistics for the vast majority of countries in the world, but interested readers must have at their disposal several of these Reports in order to compare the statistics of the last four decades of the 20th century. For the 1950s and previous decades, the World Bank has nothing to offer. The World Bank data is also problematical in that it provides too many economic variables. Most specialists and non-specialists, who want to look at the fundamental variables, tend to get lost in the mass of data.

The second part of this volume seeks to fill that gap. It presents long-term, medium-term and short-term statistics of all the nations of the world. They cover periods of ten years, fifty years and one hundred years. The fundamental economic variables such as GDP, manufacturing, agriculture, services, exports, inflation, unemployment and population are covered. The charts display the variables that have been more frequently presented as determinant for the attainment of prosperity. Most figures are presented on an average annual rate basis, which allows for easy comparison through time and space. Charts are structured chronologically and there is one for each nation. There are ten charts for each region of the world and two for the world as a whole.

The use of precise numbers is becoming more common in economics and in the social sciences because figures are fundamental for the harnessing of ideas. Statistics supply at a glance a general idea of what took place and people no longer have to speculate in a vacuum. The conclusions extracted from the analysis of these statistics are highly unorthodox and iconoclastic. They are a clear example of what takes place when ideas are solidly based on the facts. When the facts are clearly known, a whole new world of possibilities emerges.

The history of science shows that without an adequate knowledge of the facts it is impossible to establish cause and effect linkages for any given phenomenon, and when the causality of a situation is not known it is very hard for society to progress. The progress of humanity is the result of science and technology, and these two (in particular science) cannot move forward if they are not supplied with organized data that reflects the development of events in the world.

METHODOLOGY FOR PREPARING THE CHARTS

The data used to prepare the historical charts came from numerous sources. For the period running from the 16th century to the mid-20th century, it was extracted from economic, history and economic history books. For the second half of the 20th century most came from the publications of international organizations such as the World Bank, the Organization for Economic Cooperation and Development, the International Monetary Fund, the World Trade Organization, the United Nations' specialized agencies, research institutes and country statistical publications. Books and journals also supplied a considerable amount of data for this last period.

Although international standards of coverage, definition, and classification apply to most statistics reported by international agencies, governments and other sources, there are inevitably differences in timeliness and reliability arising from differences in the capabilities and resources devoted to basic data collection and compilation. Competing sources of data required review to ensure that the most reliable data available were presented. In some instances, where available data are deemed too weak to provide reliable measures of levels and trends or where they did not appear to adequately adhere to international standards, the data are not shown. Because data quality and inter-country comparisons are often problematic, readers are encouraged to consult the notes in the charts.

Even though some territories such as Hong Kong are not politically independent, they were presented in a similar way as sovereign countries because authorities report separate economic statistics and because of their relevance to the main goal of this book. This book's priority is to present information on economic growth; and economies such as Hong Kong attained an impressive rate of growth in the 20th century.

There is a chart for practically every country in the world except the smallest, many of which were not included because of the scarcity of information, their lack of relevance in world affairs, and their unimpressive economic performance. The charts concentrate fundamentally on showing the long-, medium- and short-term development of the main economic indicators of the world, as a whole, by region and by country.

The variables that are of most interest are gross domestic product, manufacturing and agriculture. Data on population, inflation, unemployment, exports, services, construction and life expectancy are also compiled, although in a less time-consistent way. Charts are structured chronologically and there is one for each nation. Each nation's chart was constructed by compiling data extracted from numerous statistical sources and assembling it in an organized and coherent way.

The charts are offered in an effort to display the variables that have been most frequently presented as determinant for the attainment of prosperity. Most figures are presented on an average annual rate basis in order to make them more amenable to comparison. One variable is presented as a proportion of the total workforce, which also allows for easy comparisons among nations of different size and over different periods of time. For reasons of simplification, manufacturing is abbreviated as *Man*, gross domestic product as *GDP*, agriculture as *Agri*, population as *Pop*, inflation as *Inf*, exports as *Ex*, services as *Serv* and construction as *Const*. The one variable that is not measured on an average annual rate basis is unemployment; it is abbreviated as *Unem*. Unemployment is measured as a share of the total workforce. Life expectance is not abbreviated.

Gross domestic product is gross value added, at purchaser prices, by all resident producers in the economy plus any taxes and minus any subsidies not included in the value of the products. Agriculture is all farm activity, including also forestry and fishing. Manufacturing is similar to the traditional definition of industry but does not include mining and construction. Manufacturing is all production that takes place in a factory. Services are all intangible activities that do not fall into agriculture, manufacturing or construction. Construction is all building activity. Exports represent the value of all goods provided to the rest of the world. Population includes all residents living in a country, regardless of legal status or citizenship. Inflation is the increase in prices. Unemployment is the share of the workforce that is involuntarily jobless. Life expectancy is the amount of years that on average a population lived at a given time.

In order to structure chronologically consistent statistics for nations in Eastern Europe, the former USSR and South Asia as well as for several in East Asia, Southeast Asia, Latin America, Sub-Saharan Africa and the Middle East, merely assembling and organizing data was not enough. Because these countries distorted market forces in a very large way during much of the 20th century, the official figures were not representative of reality. Being highly inflated, these figures were not comparable with the nations that attained the highest levels of efficiency. In consequence the official figures were recalculated so that they would be compatible with the most market-driven economies in the world.

Figures were reconstructed in proportion to the differing levels of market distortion that were experienced. The figures were reduced the most for countries such as those in the former USSR, Eastern Europe and East Asia that practiced central planning. Despite the differences of view among particular Western specialists on communist countries, the large majority have stated that about half of the goods produced in those countries were not capable of being consumed due to their low quality. As a result the official figures were reduced by about half. The discounting was also done in proportion to the level of distortion through time. In the USSR the distortions were the highest in the 1930s and 1940s while for Eastern Europe and China they were the highest in the 1950s and 1960s.

For most developing countries the statistics were shrunken the most during the 1950s, 1960s and 1970s because these were the decades when the economy was most distorted by trade barriers, state enterprises and regulation.

The discounting for developing and for communist countries was so large that it was decided to present the discounted and the official GDP figures separately. The official statistics are presented in brackets. Only the GDP figures were reconstructed. Rates of output of manufacturing, agriculture and of all the other variables were left as the official figures presented them. The term "official figure" does not necessarily mean that the source was the government. In this essay information provided by the World Bank and similar sources were also considered "official."

Much effort was made to standardize the data, but full compatibility cannot be assured and care must be taken in interpreting the indicators. Many factors affect data availability, comparability and reliability. Statistical systems in many developing economies were still weak even in the 1990s and the further back we go in time, the less reliable is the information. Cross-country and inter-temporal comparisons involve complex technical and conceptual problems that cannot be resolved unequivocally. For these reasons, although the data are drawn from the sources thought to be most authoritative, they should be construed only as indicating trends and characterizing major differences among economies rather than offering precise quantitative measures of those differences.

Efforts at elaborating statistics for the 16th, 17th and 18th century are inevitably condemned to imprecision. With respect to the differences among nations and with respect to the statistics from the 19th and 20th century (which are endowed with a relatively high level of precision), all the figures presented in this book are compatible with the consensus agreed by practically all economic historians.

The vast majority of the growth rates presented in this book are derived from the compilation of existing published rates. When there were no available rates or when the existing ones did not appear to be consistent with the non-statistical information describing the economic situation of that period, rates were computed using the least-squares regression method. This method was used wherever a sufficiently long time series exists to permit a reliable calculation. The least-squares growth rate, r, was estimated by fitting a linear regression trend line to the logarithmic annual values of the variable in the relevant period. The calculated growth rate is an average rate that is representative of the available observations over the entire period. It does not necessarily match the actual growth rate between any two periods. The regression equation takes the form

$$\ln X_t = a + bt$$

The large majority of the compiled data had to be reorganized because it comprised periods that lacked significance. Even the World Bank was not capable of providing information for every decade in an organized form. Instead of supplying a figure for the 1960s, for example, they provide one that covers the period 1960-70. As for books of economic history, they usually provide periods such as 1947-58, 1918-38 or 1870-1914. Even economic historians wishing to see the big picture tend to present figures that are not very useful for cross-country comparisons. Angus Madison, for example, in *L'Economie Chinoise — Une Perspective Historique*, provides useful figures of the 18th century for China, India Japan, the US and Europe, but the time span is 1700-1820. The large majority of the mathematical work in this book consisted in adding, subtracting, stitching the pieces together, and calculating averages.

The World Bank's World Development Report was the only source that supplied data on several variables and on numerous nations, but even that is only for the period 1960-99. Other international organizations have provided information for numerous nations, but only for one particular variable presented in this book and at most covering the second half of the 20th century. For all the preceding time the great bulk of the information even for a particular country and for just a single variable, like GDP, usually came from numerous sources. Even short periods of time such as the 1940s, the 1910s or the 1850s were frequently not found in such a form in any particular book.

This book aims to assist people who are interested in measuring the effectiveness of policies. Therefore, to measure the average of every region, each economy was given the same weight. History shows that population size, geographic size, economic size or a combination of the three does not have an effect on the rate of economic growth. A wrong economic policy delivers the same negative effects in a country with an insignificant population as in one teeming with people; an effective policy delivers impressive results independent of the geographic location and size of the economy.

Only in one region (North America) were all of the countries belonging to that region included in the calculation of the regional average. Although in the other regions not all countries were included, the large majority of the economies in those regions were analyzed. For the region of Oceania however, only Australia, New Zealand and Papua New Guinea were averaged. In this region there are dozens of small islands that were not covered, and for a number of reasons. Nauru was the only of these islands to be analyzed, because of its impressive growth in the 1970s and 1980s. However, it was left out of the average because the evidence suggests that the numerous other islands attained modest rates of growth. Nauru's rates of growth in the second half of the 20th century are also considerably higher than those of the only three large countries in Oceania. Since Nauru's growth rate was not representative of those of the numerous islands that were not included, it was left out of the average of the region in order to avoid an obvious distortion.

For the region of Eastern Europe and the former Soviet Union, in the 1990s the average includes the fifteen countries that emerged out of the Soviet Union even though only Russia appears in the charts.

PART I

On Economic Growth

The Nature of Economics

Economics has been defined in numerous ways, but perhaps the most rational way of summarizing its nature is to describe it as the science that makes possible the improvement of living conditions. Since economics inquires into the causes of economic growth, and growth is the factor that most improves living conditions, it follows that this is the scientific discipline that seeks to supply society with material welfare. Through history, only when growth took place did nations reduce famine, improve housing, ameliorate health, improve education, diminish poverty, decrease unemployment or become wealthy.

Economic growth is the increase in the total production of goods and services that a nation attains. It can be measured in several ways, but measuring it in percentage terms most aptly renders the figures comparable over time and among different countries.

Government bodies such as the Ministry of Commerce, the Ministry of Economics or the Central Bank elaborate GDP statistics. Many government ministries work on a quarterly basis and every three months they publish the latest GDP statistics together with several others that measure unemployment, inflation and other macroeconomic variables. To measure the performance of an economy and the worthiness of policies, however, it is useless to look at a yearly figure or less still a quarterly statistic. Economists are interested in seeing the big picture and for that they need to analyze a longer period (such as a decade, or more) to appreciate the long-term effect of policies.

Economic growth is by far the most important matter for any nation, but growth in itself means little. If a nation grows by 0.1% annually, as Europe seems to have done from the tenth to the fifteenth century, it will never get out of poverty. The rate of growth must be much faster for it to deliver the desired results. Most nations of the world attained very slow rates of GDP during all of history up to the 18th century; and that is why living conditions remained primitive. Life expectancy for most of the populace was barely twenty years during all that time. It was only in the 19th century that a few nations started experiencing rates of 2% or more. The US, for example, was the fastest growing nation in the 19th century and the economy expanded on average by about 4.5% per year. In the 20th century the US grew by about 3.5% per annum. During the period 1800-2000, no other nation — with the exception of Luxembourg — managed to grow as fast as the US, and that is why by the year 2000 the US was the second wealthiest country in the world. Luxembourg was the wealthiest, on a per capita basis.

EFFICIENCY AND INFLATION

Economics also pursues goals other than deciphering the causes of growth. It looks for ways to increase efficiency as much as possible and to control inflation.

Raising efficiency is a relevant effort because resources are not unlimited. However, history does not give any indication that the prosperity of a nation is dependent on attaining high levels of efficiency. During the years 1920-39, in the Soviet Union, for example, efficiency decreased significantly and the quality of production also suffered considerably. In spite of that, the economy grew in an unprecedented way, averaging about 7% per year in real terms. (The official figures were much higher — 15%; but Western economists subtracted more than half in order to discount for the vast amount of goods and services that were of a quality too low to be accorded any value.) Even though the USSR had the lowest levels of efficiency in the world, the economy grew faster than in all other nations. [1]

Taking a long-term view of communism reveals as well how marginally useful is the enhancement of efficiency. During the seventy-year history of the

---

1. Clarke, Roger : *Soviet Economic Facts 1917-70*, Macmillan, London, 1972, p. 6-9.

Soviet Union, efficiency was lower than in any other similar period in Russia's history. In spite of that, the country's economy grew and living conditions improved more than ever before. [2]

Similarly, efficiency in China and Vietnam, during the second half of the 20th century, was lower than in any previous fifty-year period of their history due to the practice of central planning, import substitution and other competition-hindering practices. In spite of that, economic growth was unprecedented and living conditions improved more than ever before. By contrast, during the years 1900-49, competition in China and Vietnam was very high and efficiency was also high as a result of free trade and free market policies practiced by the foreign powers occupying China's coast. In Vietnam and in the rest of Indochina, the French colonial authorities practiced the same policies. In the non-coastal part of China under the control of the Manchu dynasty and the different governments that followed, policies were not as liberal as along the coast, but there were few regulations. In spite of that China, grew by a mere 0.5% annually and Vietnam by 0.8%. In the years 1950-99, the respective figures were 4.9% and 2.8% in real terms (the official figures were almost twice as high). Despite the massive waste of resources in the second half of the 20th century, the economy of China and Vietnam grew significantly faster. [3]

Also worth noting is that during the course of the second half of the 20th century, the large majority of countries in the world progressively exposed their economies to higher levels of competition. That was accompanied by a progressive increase of efficiency. However, the economic growth in the large majority of countries progressively decelerated, the rate of technological development diminished, and the pace by which living conditions improved slowed.

The above obviously must not be understood to mean that competition-hindering practices deliver positive results; there are countless examples in which countries practiced free trade and free market policies and attained faster growth GDP rates than the countries just mentioned. Throughout history worldwide, high efficiency has been more frequently accompanied by fast growth than low efficiency. However, the examples previously mentioned as well as others show that efficiency is not a fundamental factor in delivering prosperity to a nation. The evidence shows that its role is of a secondary importance.

2. Clarke, Roger & Matko, Dubravko: *Soviet Economic Facts 1970-81*, Macmillan, London, 1983, p. 6-15.
3. Perkins, Dwight (ed): *China's Modern Economy in Historical Perspective*, Stanford University Press, Stanford-CA, 1975, p. 46, 222.

Economics also covers inflation, which is the movement of prices in an economy. Fast-rising inflation is seen as an adverse situation because it increases income inequalities and delivers other effects that are generally considered undesirable. A high rate of inflation is usually defined as more than 3% per year and the ideal level is usually thought to be somewhere between 0% and 3%. In the 1990s, the US averaged a rate of inflation of about 3% per year, Germany 3%, and Japan just 1%. Not all nations, however, succeeded in controlling inflation so well. Some, like Russia, averaged a yearly rate of 414%. Under such conditions, prices for food, television sets, electronic equipment, automobiles, medical services, airplane tickets and everything else rise almost on a daily basis. It is indeed a highly problematic situation for consumers and producers alike. [4]

Many economists have asserted that low inflation is a precondition for growth. However, a correlation with fast growth cannot be found. During the roughly thousand-year period of the Middle Ages in Europe, there was absolutely no inflation and in spite of that there was no economic growth. Prices in the rest of the world also remained stable up to the 18th century; but the economy remained stagnant and, as a result, living conditions did not improve. [5]

In the 20th century the world experienced by far the fastest rate of inflation in history, and it was then that the world economy grew by far its fastest pace. Argentina makes this particularly evident; in the 20th century it attained one of the highest rates of the inflation in the world, averaging about 77% per year. In spite of that, it was in that century that Argentina's economy grew at the fastest pace. In the 18th century, when inflation was zero, the economy was stagnant while in the 20th century it grew by about 2.5% annually.[6]

When analyzing shorter periods and particular countries, the absence of a correlation becomes evident. South Korea during the 1970s experienced a high rate of inflation — about 18% per year; but the economy grew at the impressive pace of 10% annually, and as a result living conditions improved noticeably. Inflation in Saudi Arabia and Oman in the 1970s was even higher, averaging about 25%; but the economy grew by about 12% annually. In the 1970s inflation in Brazil was about 32% annually, but the economy grew by 8% and poverty

---

4. *L'OCDE en Chriffres* 2001, OCDE, Paris, 2001, p. 52.
5. Ramsey, Peter: *The Price Revolution in Sixteenth Century England*, Methuen & Co., London, 1971, p. 38-41.
6. Output and Population, *The Economist*, 31 December 1999, p. 147.

decreased like never before. In Japan, on the other hand, where inflation was just 1% in the 1990s, the economy grew by less than 2%. [7]

The above however must not be understood to mean that inflation delivers positive results; there are countless cases in the 20th century in which high inflation was accompanied by stagnation or recession. In Chile, for example, during the 1970s, inflation averaged about 243% per year and the economy expanded by less than 2%. In Bolivia in the 1980s inflation of 392% was accompanied by a widespread stagnation of the economy, and in Argentina during the same decade inflation of 335% was paralleled by a contraction of about -1% annually. In Russia during the 1990s triple-digit inflation was accompanied by a terrible recession, the worst in the country's history. Yugoslavia in the 1990s experienced hyperinflation of eight digits and the economy contracted by about -2%. [8]

History shows that low inflation or an absence of inflation is usually beneficial for a nation, but it is not fundamental or even important for the well-being of a population. That does not meant that governments should not seek to control prices; but it is evident that the priority for a country is attaining the fastest possible rates of economic growth and inflation plays practically no role in that.

History nonetheless shows that it is possible to attain the best of all possible worlds (fast growth with low inflation). Examples include the US during the last twenty years of the 19th century, when the economy grew by almost 8% per year and inflation was at 0%. In more recent times there is the case of Italy in the 1950s, where the economy averaged about 7% annual growth and inflation was at 3%. In Germany in the 1950s, growth was at 8% while inflation was only 2%. Hong Kong, Taiwan and Singapore grew in the 1960s by about 10% and inflation was just 2%. Even in the long term such double success is possible, as shown by the case of the US from 1850 to 1899, when there was zero inflation but the economy grew by 6%. In Singapore during the second half of the 20th century, inflation was at 2% while GDP expanded by 8%. [9]

---

7. *World Development Report 1981*, The World Bank, Washington D.C., 1981, p. 135-137.

8. *World Development Report 1981 & 2000 — Basic Indicators*, The World Bank.

9. Hardach, Karl: *Wirtschafts Geschichte Deutschlands im 20. Jahrhundert*, Deutschland, Vonden-hoeck und Ruprecht, 1979, p. 192.

FAST AND SUSTAINED

Fast and sustained economic growth is the bottom line for prosperity. The concept of "sustained" must be understood as a period of at least a decade. The concept of "fast" must also be clearly defined, because the term "economic growth" is often mis-used and misunderstood. On numerous occasions nations have attained sustained rates of 1%, 2% or even higher while living conditions deteriorated. Those situations have driven many people to conclude that growth in itself cannot solve the fundamental problems of a country.

However, it is a bit more complicated than that; and the reality is that even the most developed nations of the world need sustained rates of at least 3% in order for living conditions to improve for the majority of the population. If the rate is below 3% over a decade, there will generally be a rise in unemployment and/or underemployment. Income distribution will also worsen. As the rate falls farther below the 3% barrier, a larger share of the population is battered by unemployment and/or underemployment. The lower the rate, the larger also are the income inequalities.

Middle-income countries have much lower living conditions than developed nations; their levels of unemployment and underemployment tend to be higher, and their rates of population growth are faster. They therefore need a rate of growth of at least 5% on a sustained basis in order to see a noticeable decrease in poverty and unemployment.

The challenge facing the least developed nations is even more demanding because their levels of consumption are lower than all other countries, their levels of unemployment and underemployment are higher, and their population is growing faster. As a result they need a GDP rate of at least 7% for the majority of the population to experience noticeable improvements in living conditions.

If developed nations grow by 2%, their levels of unemployment will rise. They will have increased their total wealth by 2% every year but that will not be enough to reduce unemployment. Western European countries for example averaged a GDP growth of about 2.4% during the years 1980-2003 and unemployment increased from about 4% in the 1970s to about 10% by the early 2000s.[10]

In Latin America during the same period the economy grew by about 2.4%. There was overall progress, but the incidence of poverty increased and income

---

10. *German Unification*, International Monetary Fund, Washington D.C., 1990, p. 131.

inequalities rose. In Sub-Saharan Africa the average GDP figure was 2.2%; and even though such a growth rate was far higher than that which the region had attained up to the 1940s, it was nonetheless incapable of improving living conditions for the large majority of the population. Poverty, unemployment and income inequalities increased. [11]

Although history shows that the faster the economic growth the larger the benefits for the whole population, there are limits to the speed by which a country can grow. The evidence from numerous countries nonetheless shows that it is possible to attain sustained rates that are much higher than most economists and politicians think. In the 1990s, the large majority of countries in the world attained a GDP rate of just 2.5%. This was the average of the world economy and even though governments worldwide were not satisfied with such figures, practically all of them were convinced that it was not possible to attain rates that were dramatically higher. Most policymakers in developed countries believe that 3-4% is the limit of what they can attain and most economists believe that the limit for developing countries is 6%.

In developed nations economists usually argue that because demand is largely satisfied, production cannot increase rapidly (without creating idle inventories of unwanted goods). However, by the late 1980s, Singapore had attained a level of development that was at parity with that of Western Europe. And even though the population of the island showed the same levels of consumption as Europeans, in the 1990s the Singaporean economy grew by about 7.8% while that of Western Europe averaged only 2.6%. Many analysts argued that culture and the fact that Singapore was in the midst of the fastest growing region in the world made the faster growth possible. [12]

However, Ireland did not enjoy such "advantages" and it nonetheless grew by 7.9% in the same decade. Many argued that Ireland's fast growth resulted from its relative underdevelopment in the region and the aid from the European Union (E.U.). The problem with that argument is that, by the late 1980s Spain, Portugal and Greece were equally underdeveloped and in the next decade they received similar amounts of aid from the E.U. They all received aid accounting for about 3% of their respective GDPs. In spite of that, they averaged a growth rate of about 2.2%. Debunking even more this argument was the case of Luxembourg. This tiny nation was by the late 1980s the most developed in the world,

---

11. The Fight Against Latin Poverty, *Businessweek European Edition*, 1 May 2000, p.48.
12. *Trade Policy Review — Singapore* Vol. I, GATT, Geneva, 1992, p. 1-11.

outperforming even the US. Even though demand was more satisfied than in all of its neighbors and it received no aid from the E.U., growth was double that in the rest of Western Europe. In the 1990s, Luxembourg's economy grew by about 5.4%. [13]

For developing countries it has been claimed that demand is much higher due to the scarcity of everything, which means, in a sense, that the country has more "room" to grow. However, it has never been believed that demand could grow at an explosive pace. Nevertheless, the evidence shows that demand can grow at a breathtaking pace. South Korea for example grew by 10% per year in the 1970s while Japan grew in the 1960s by 11%, and Hong Kong by 12% in the 1950s. Even that is not the limit of what is possible; Botswana averaged 15% in the 1970s and Libya grew by 24% in the 1960s. Not even those impressive figures seem to be the limit, for Qatar and Nauru grew by 30% in the 1970s. [14]

Many have argued that it was easy for Libya and Qatar to attain impressive growth because they were endowed with vast oil deposits. However, Botswana and Nauru lack oil and all other resources that traditionally have been highly valued. This suggests that spectacular growth rates might be possible regardless of resources.[15]

ON THE VARIABLES THAT AFFECT GROWTH

Over the centuries numerous scholars have pondered the causes of prosperity and developed a wide array of theories and ideas that sought to explain the phenomenon of economic growth. Numerous variables have been posited as being fundamental or important for growth.

Culture

It has long been claimed that fast growth is largely determined by a nation's culture. Up to the late 19th century, many (European) scholars posited that only countries that possessed a European culture could grow rapidly. They claimed that this culture favored high levels of savings and investment. Although the argument of the superiority of European culture progressively lost ground

---

13. The Luck of the Irish, *Fortune*, 8 November 1999, 124-135.
14. *The Middle East and North Africa 2002*, Europa Publications, London, 2002, p. 876-884.
15. *The Far East and Australasia 2001*, Europa Publications, London, 2001, p. 945.

during the course of the 20th century, it still had adherents until fairly recently. In 1998, a Harvard professor published a book making such claims. [16]

However, during the first half of the 20th century the fastest growing economy in the world was that of Japan — long before the average Japanese had any notion of Western culture. In the second half of the 20th century, Japan was still growing faster than practically any country with a European-stock population. On top of that, several other countries in East Asia grew even faster than Japan. [17]

Events in other regions further weaken this argument. The fastest growing half-century for Western Europe was 1950-99, when the region's GDP averaged about 4.0% annually. But East Asia, which achieved a rate of 5.6%, was not the only region to grow faster — despite lacking a European culture. The Middle East grew by about 5.1% and Southeast Asia grew by about 4.4%. By the early 2000s there were countries in East Asia and the Middle East that had become more developed than the majority of countries in Western Europe. This situation suggests that culture at best played a marginal role in growth.

The fast growth of Japan since the late 19th century and the even faster growth in the post-World War II decades converted the country, by the 1980s, intoone of the most technologically advanced nations in the world. By then its superior goods had taken a large share of the world market away from Western producers. As a result a growing number of Western scholars began to claim that Japanese culture was superior to that of the West, because it drove the population to study more, work more, save more and invest more. Then, in the 1990s, Japan experienced a mayor deceleration and its GDP figures flirted with stagnation. After having grown much faster than practically any country with a predominantly European population from the 1950s to the 1980s, it grew slower than most of them in the following decade and continued its poor performance in the early 2000s. Once again, the pundits changed tack and claimed that it was Japan's culture what was hindering growth. [18]

Culture is not immutable and every country has experienced changes over time. However, culture is something that has long-lasting effects and the main characteristics of it usually prevail for centuries, if not millennia. If a nation's culture were fundamental or at least important for growth, at least some con-

---

16. Landes, David : *Wealth and Poverty of Nations*, W. W. Norton & Co., New York, 1998.

17. *Le Japon d'Aujourd'hui*, Tokyo, Ministere des Affaires Etrangeres, 1971, p. 37.

18. Morishima, Michio: *Why has Japan Succeeded?* Cambridge University Press, Cambridge, 1982, p. 22-52.

stancy would be expected in growth rates. There should also be some constancy in the growth gap among nations. But every nation in the world has experienced abrupt fluctuations; most have also seen their faster rates become slower, or vice versa, even though the culture of the country had not changed significantly.

The erratic behavior of GDP figures in numerous countries (particularly over short periods) suggests that culture at best plays a marginal role in growth. Japan, for example, averaged an economic growth of more than 11% in the 1960s, while in the 1990s growth was less than 2%. On top of that, its superior record relative to the West came to an end. Libya, for example, became Muslim in the seventh century and the country's adherence to Islam has remained uncontested until the present time. In spite of that, Libya's economy grew by 24% in the 1960s and by only 2% in the following decade. It also went from attaining one of the slowest GDP rates up to the 1950s to the highest in the world in the next decade, and then one of the lowest in the following decades. [19]

Even though Japan's culture was deprecated in the 1990s, many analysts began to claim in this decade that East Asian culture and in particular that of the Chinese was very important for growth. China attracted attention because of its unprecedented growth rates and its large size. Western scholars were particularly driven to use culture as an explanation due to the economic policies Beijing endorsed. China had practiced a centrally-planned system from the 1950s to the 1970s. Even though in the following decade the economy began to be liberalized, by the early 2000s China was still a communist state and one of the most regulated in the world. Since the greater part of Western economists believe market-oriented policies are fundamental for growth, only the culture variable could be invoked to spare them from falling into a contradiction with the facts. Only with the argument of culture was it possible to explain how one of the most distorted economies in the world managed to attain one of the fastest GDP rates. [20]

History has seen a series of countries that at one moment were classified as possessing a "superior culture" that made progress possible, only to be labeled later as having a culture that hindered development. From the 16th to the 18th century Britain was seen as possessing a superior culture, but by the late 19th century some began to claim that its culture was inferior to that of many coun-

---

19. Balta, Paul: *Le Grand Maghreb*, Editions la Decouverte, Paris, 1990, p. 36-40.
20. *China at the Threshold of a Market Economy*, International Monetary Fund, Washington D.C., 1993.

tries in continental Europe and North America. In the 20th century this idea pre-vailed and was actually reinforced. [21]

Every country that was classified as having a superior culture was noted for having the fastest or one of the fastest rates of economic growth in the world. In each one of these countries that, at some future moment, was no longer clas-sified as having a superior culture, the downgrade coincided with GDP rates that were no longer among the fastest. Great Britain attained the fastest economic growth in the world from the 16th to the 18th century, but in the following century several countries in continental Europe and North America grew faster. In the 20th century, even more countries from these and other regions grew faster than Britain. [22]

The countries or regions that have been classified as not possessing an enterprising culture are those that experienced the lowest GDP figures in the world. Up to the 19th century, Sub-Saharan Africa was seen as the region with the least enterprising culture and that coincided with the worst economic per-formance to that date. In the 20th century, this region continued to attain the slowest growth figures and its culture continued to be classified as the least dynamic. East Asia up to the 19th century grew slower than Western Europe, and for centuries it was seen as lacking a work-oriented culture. In the 20th century, and more particularly in the second half, it grew faster than Western Europe and all the other regions. Suddenly, its culture was seen as thrifty and industrious. [23]

History shows that culture does not determine growth. It also shows that the relationship of causality runs in the opposite direction. It is growth what determines culture. Technology is by far the most powerful factor affecting culture because it transforms living conditions in important ways. Throughout history the pace of technological development has run in parallel with the rate of cultural change. That would explain why the cultures of nations all over the world experienced the greatest change in the 20th century, for in this century more technological progress was attained than in all of the preceding history of humanity.

Technology has always moved in tandem with economic growth. The 20th century witnessed by the far the fastest rate of economic growth in history and

21. Musson, A. E.: *The Growth of British Industry*, B.T. Batsford, London, 1978, p. 28.

22. Gamble, Andrew: *Britain in Decline*, Macmillan, London, 1985, p. 11.

23. Munro, Forbes: *Africa and the International Economy 1800-1960*, J. M. Dent & Sons Ltd., London, 1976, 23.

that coincided with the fastest development of technology. The 19th century witnessed the second fastest rate of economic growth and it was then that the rate of patent registration was the second fastest. In the 18th century the world economy grew at the third fastest pace and technical progress was the third fastest in history. There are numerous examples of nations that attained fast economic growth even though new technology was not created; but every time technological innovation was prolific, it was accompanied by fast economic growth. This suggests that technology is an effect of economic growth, not the other way around.

Fast economic growth is thus what most profoundly alters customs and traditions, because it generates fast technological development.

Religion

Probably the most outstanding aspect of a culture is its religion, and religion, too, is largely determined by growth. All of today's mainstream religions (and even those that are no longer practiced) were created at a time when economic stagnation prevailed. For the centuries preceding the eras when Hinduism, Buddhism, Christianity and Islam appeared, the regions where these religions came into being had experienced no growth. The famines, malnutrition, epidemics, wars, violence and ignorance were unrelenting. Life expectancy was short and infant mortality was extremely high. Life was brutal and harsh, and people sought desperately to alleviate their plight. In their frustration over the constant absence of progress, they were driven to deposit their hopes in new religions that claimed to have the capacity to improve their lives or at least compensate them for their suffering. [24]

As Europe and more particularly Western Europe emerged from stagnation in the 16th century, it experienced record growth. That was accompanied by an unprecedented improvement of living conditions. The economic growth delivered new farm technology that increased agricultural output, which reduced the incidence of famine and the diseases linked to it. The decrease in famines and epidemics was accompanied by a reduction in the amount of time devoted to prayer and other religious activities. Growth also delivered the technology that led Europeans to speculate about the credibility of some of their religious dogmas. In the 16th century, shipbuilding technology advanced so much

---

24. Watson, Francis: *A Concise History of India*, Thames & Hudson, Great Britain, 1979, p. 30-87.

that it allowed Western Europeans to discover new continents. This brought them in contact with other religions that also claimed to have an exclusive bond with God. With so many claimants to the ultimate truth, it was inevitable that doubts would rise.

Simultaneous with the above, the unprecedented growth allowed for the creation of new printing and publishing technology, which increased many times over the production of books, allowing knowledge to be disseminated much faster. Growth also delivered more wealth, which allowed for unprecedented spending in education; and a larger share of the population became acquainted with scientific knowledge. Science does not set out to debunk religion, but science tends to invalidate ideas and propositions that are inconsistent and improbable. As more people acquired scientific knowledge, more people began to distance themselves from religion. [25]

In the 17th and 18th centuries, Europe experienced a further acceleration of GDP rates, coinciding with a faster improvement of living conditions, a faster development of science, and a faster development of education. Along with that, Europeans distanced themselves from religion at a faster pace. In these centuries Europe was the continent with the fastest rate of economic growth and the continent where religion was most questioned. Rates were nonetheless slow, by today's measure, and in Western Europe they are likely to have averaged only 0.5% per year in the 18th century. In most other regions of the world, the economy was growing by only a fraction of that rate. [26]

In the 19th century rates of growth accelerated dramatically in Europe and in particular in the west of the continent; this improved living conditions significantly. In Western Europe, GDP averaged about 2.5%. That was accompanied by a massive decrease in the level of religious belief. As hunger, disease and violence rapidly decreased, people found less impetus to pray for a better life. A better life is what people have always demanded from religion and when economic growth finally delivers it, the justification for religious ritual is diminished. Once the major threats to their lives have been conquered, people begin to use their free time for entertainment instead of for religious activities. [27]

---

25. Holderness, B.A.: *Pre-Industrial England*, J.M. Dent & Sons Ltd., London, 1976, p. 84-99.

26. Madison, Angus: *L'Economie Chinoise — Une perspective historique*, OECD, Paris, 1998, p. 44.

27. Heywood, Colin: *The Development of the French Economy 1750-1914*, The Macmillan Press, London, 1992, p. 13, 14.

Economies around the world grew faster in the 19th century, and in the North American region growth was even faster than in Western Europe. However, even so, most of the world failed to grow at even 1.0% per year. Religious adherence tended to wane, all around the world, with the exception of the United States and the Islamic world.

Islam was born in the seventh century in the Arabian Peninsula and since then its presence was more strongly felt in the peninsula. However, by the early 2000s religion's role in politics, the economy and society was lower in several countries of the peninsula than in countries further away. In the United Arab Emirates, Qatar, Bahrain and Kuwait, daily life was less impregnated with religion than in Muslim countries that were not of Arab ancestry (such as Pakistan). The economies of these four countries were among the fastest growing in the world, expanding in the second half of the 20th century by about 8.7% per year. In the remaining Muslim countries, GDP rates were growing a fraction as fast and per capita incomes were a fraction as high. The four had higher per capita incomes than most Western European countries. As of the mid-2000s, these four Arab countries were stll strongly imbued with religion; however, relative to their less developed Muslim neighbors and relative to their own past, the four countries in question became far more secular in the course of 50 years' of economic progress. By the early 2000s the United Arab Emirates (UAE) was the most tolerant Muslim nation in the world, welcoming thousands of people belonging to other religions. The UAE was the wealthiest Muslim country and was also wealthier than the nations of Europe. [28]

Language

Language is another aspect of culture that very strongly differentiates countries. The strength of a language is determined by the economic importance of the country or region that speaks it. England had a small population relative to many European nations, not to mention China and India. In spite of that, the international importance of its language grew fastest. That went hand-in-hand with the fastest economic growth in the world from the 16th to the 18th century. In the 19th century, the economy of Great Britain grew faster than that of many other countries, but several European nations with different languages did grow as fast or faster. The importance of English worldwide increased nonetheless.

---

28. Chapin, Helem: *Persian Gulf States — Country Studies*, Library of Congress, Washington D.C., 1994.

That coincided with fast economic growth in English-speaking countries such as the US, Canada, Australia and New Zealand. The US attained the fastest GDP rate in the world and it rapidly acquired a large population, exceeding that of most European countries. In fact, all of these countries attained growth rates that were among the fastest. And while all of these countries combined account for a much smaller population than that of China or India, those two mammoth countries' economies grew much more slowly. No other group of countries speaking a common language attained a faster growth GDP rate than the English countries. This was accompanied by a continued economic supremacy of English-speakers in the international arena. [29]

When nations experience low rates of economic growth (within a given region or in the world as a whole), they are vulnerable to language colonization by those coming from fast-growing countries. Foreign words are incorporated into the local tongue and when the growth gap between the two nations is vast, the "weaker" language can even disappear. On the American continents, numerous languages had prevailed for millennia, up to the fifteenth century — and during all that time, any economic expansion was limited primarily to the gains that might come from an expanding population. Western Europe grew much faster during that time and since the 16th century it accelerated its pace dramatically. That difference created a substantial technological superiority for Europe; the indigenous Americans were militarily, economically and culturally crushed. The religions and languages from Europe rapidly supplanted those of the local populations. [30]

In Oceania a similar phenomenon took place. The indigenous populations of Australia and New Zealand were coasting along in relative stagnation up to the 18th century. With the arrival of English-speaking Christian colonizers of European stock, an economic and cultural transformation propelled the country forward. Of course, peoples with a low level of economic development are vulnerable not only linguistically. The aboriginal cultures were practically wiped out, along with much of the aboriginal population. Those who survived adopted the language and the religion of the conquerors. Within a couple of generations, many of the aborigines left behind their language and religion voluntarily,

---

29. Kolko, Gabriel: *Main Currents in Modern American History*, Harper & Row, New York, p. 1976.
30. Merrill, Tim & Miro, Ramon (ed): *Mexico — A Country Study*, Library of Congress, Washington D. C., 1997, p. xvii-xxvii.

seeking to partake of the conquerors' superior economic position. The countries by now have attained the status of "developed" nations. [31]

In Sub-Saharan Africa and South Asia the growth gap with Western Europe was very large since the 16th century and enormous in the 19th century. That made possible the technologically superior weapons that allowed Europeans to easily conquer other regions. The overall technological superiority also generated admiration or awe from the local populations, which helped the Europeans to impose their languages and religions. In Africa and South Asia local languages and religions were not totally supplanted because of the much larger populations of these regions, but they were considerably modified and diluted. [32]

Ethnicity

Ethnicity is another factor that strongly affects a culture; and changes in the ethnic composition of a population are strongly affected by the rate of economic growth. When a nation has one of the fastest rates of economic growth in a region or in the world, over a long period of time, it attracts people from neighboring countries and even from further away, and those immigrants become an integral part of the population. The pace of migration often depends largely on the growth gap between the fast grower and the slowest growing countries. In the Middle East, for example, by the early 2000s the countries with the largest share of foreign population were the United Arab Emirates, Qatar, Bahrain and Kuwait. That corresponded to the experience of the countries with the fastest growth in the region and in the world during the preceding half century. About a third of the population was foreign, mostly guest workers from South Asia. This significantly altered the original Arab ethnicity of the population. [33]

In Europe the same phenomenon has been observed. By the early 2000s, foreigners accounted for a significant share of the total population in practically every country in Western Europe. This was, after all, the region that was the second most developed in the world. Within this region, Luxembourg and Switzerland had the highest share of foreign population. In Luxembourg foreigners accounted for about 35%, and in Switzerland 18%. And, these were the countries

---

31. *The Far East and Australasia 2001: Ibid.*, p. 96-103.
32. Kulke, Hermann & Rothermund, Dietmar: *A History of India*, Croom Helm Ltd., Great Britain, 1986.
33. *The Middle East and North Africa 2002, Ibid.*, p. p. 1109-1114.

that during the period 1800-2000 attained the fastest rate of economic growth in Europe. As a result, by the early 2000s they had the highest wages in the continent and were thus the most attractive destinations for foreign workers. The higher share of Luxembourg coincided with a faster GDP growth rate than Switzerland's. Both countries experienced a significant transformation of their ethnicity and culture due to the influx of foreigners. However, it was the culture of the foreign workers which changed most, for they admired their host country and were eager to adopt its practices. [34]

The US attained the second fastest GDP rate in the world in the last two centuries, while the vast and ever changing inflow of migrants during that period substantially changed (and changed again) the ethnicity of the population. In 1800, practically all of the European-stock population was of British origin, but a century later about half the population was of non-British origin, and by 2000 the proportion had shifted still further. Native Americans accounted for the largest minority up to the early 19th century; then African Americans became the largest minority. The immigration of Hispanics during the last several decades has been so great that they became the largest minority in the US by the early 2000s. [35]

Size of Population

The influence of a country's size has long been debated among scholars. Many social scientists have claimed that it is harder for countries with large populations to achieve fast growth because they must provide employment to many more people and because governments find it harder to apply policies over such large numbers. History, however, does not support that theory.

One of the fastest growing economies in the world in recent decades was China. It had the largest population in the world, about 20% of the total. In 1980-99, China averaged a growth rate of about 7.4% in real terms while most other countries grew by just 2.5%. Countries such as Nicaragua, Jamaica, Panama and Honduras grew by just 1.8% annually during that same period, even though China had some four hundred times more people. [36] India's economy also expanded rapidly in the 1990s, averaging about 5.0%, in spite of having the

---

34. Trausch, Gilbert: *Histoire du Luxembourg*, Hatier, Paris, 1992, p.225-227.

35. Kolko: *Ibid.*, p. 68-75.

36. South America, *Central America and the Caribbean 2002*, Europa Publications, London, 2002.

second largest population in the world. Denmark, Finland and Iceland had a population of about 3.6 million each while India had about 930 million people. Despite that supposed advantage, the average growth of the three Scandinavian countries was just 2.6%. [37]

From a long-term perspective, too, this idea fails to be reflected in the facts. The average economic growth of the US during the last two centuries was faster than that of practically every other nation, despite having one of the largest and fastest-growing populations in the world. On the other hand, many small countries in Africa, Asia and Latin America experienced slow growth rates during the last two hundred years in spite of having to provide for only very small populations.

Thus, a large population is not in itself a barrier to growth. While size can play a role in growth, it is by no means the determining factor.

Population Growth

Population expansion or contraction is another variable that experts have said affects economic growth, either positively or negatively. Originally, a fast rate of population growth was seen as a negative factor. In 1798, the British scholar Thomas Malthus for the first time formalized the idea of a demographic link. He raised an alarm over the unprecedented rate of population growth in Britain, fearing that hunger and poverty would be the result, as the production of food and other necessary goods could not keep up with the population.

In Malthus' time, statistical information was scarce or non-existent; he had poor data to work from. In the 18th century, the population had indeed grown dramatically in Britain and in Europe, but the production of goods and services had also expanded — even faster, in fact, than the population. As a result, living conditions improved (albeit only slightly). In the 19th century, population growth accelerated considerably more, but the European economy still grew faster and living conditions improved further. In the 20th century, population growth in Europe slowed down, but the economy burst ahead; hunger and poverty were drastically reduced. Elsewhere in the world the population exploded. The world economy nonetheless experienced an exponential acceleration and living conditions improved abundantly over the world. [38]

---

37. Black Days, *Asiaweek*, 26 March 1999, p. 39.
38. Bairoch, Paul: *Economics and World History*, Harvester Wheatsheaf, London, 1993, 94-127.

After the Malthusian theory proved wrong repeatedly, analysts began in the late 19th century to claim that fast population growth contributed to growth. In the second half of the 19th century population in countries such as the US, Canada, Argentina, Australia and New Zealand grew extremely fast as a result of a vast immigration from Europe and a high birth rate. Since these countries attained the fastest GDP growth rates in the world, many argued that it must be because population growth increased demand and allowed for greater specialization and efficiency, which propelled growth. [39]

The weakness in that argument is shown by the fact that several West European countries that experienced a large outflow of people attained similar rates of economic growth, even though their rate of population growth was only a fraction of that of North America and Oceania. Luxembourg and Germany, for example, lost numerous mature, trained workers to the new continents, but their economies grew just as fast. Australia experienced the fastest population growth among the new countries, but the US enjoyed faster economic growth — even though both had the same economic system and the US suffered a devastating civil war. Furthermore, population growth in 1800-49 in the US was much faster than in the following fifty years, but the economy grew more than twice as fast in the second period. Japan and Brazil present further inconsistencies. Japan experienced no inflow of migrants and its population grew by just 0.8% in 1850-99. Brazil witnessed a large influx of European migrants and its population grew by about 1.8%. In spite of that, Japan averaged an economic growth of 2.4% per year while Brazil managed only 1.1%. [40]

In the second half of the 20th century, the population in non-developed countries exploded. Since many of these countries' economies grew slowly, academics once again inverted the argument and began to posit that fast population growth hindered development. These arguments were more frequently heard for the case of Sub-Saharan Africa because the region had fast population growth and the second slowest GDP figures in the world. Again, it was hard to make the argument jive with the facts. [41]

Population growth in Sub-Sahara abruptly accelerated in the 1950s and in the following decades it further gained in speed. Since the region's GDP growth

39. Kenwood A & Lougheed, A.: *The Growth of the International Economy 1820-1990*, Routledge, London, 1992, p. 20-60.
40. Robock, Stefan: *Brazil — A Study in Development Progress*, D.C. Heath & Co., Lexington-Mass., 1976, p. 18-20.
41. Bairoch: *Ibid.*, p. 127.

then decelerated, since the 1970s, the parallelism suggested a relation of cau-sality. In 1970-89, population growth averaged about 2.8% annually and the economy grew by 2.1%. The gap, which translated into lower per capita incomes, gave further credence to this idea. However, the case of individual countries shows a number of inconsistencies in that argument. Botswana, for example, experienced a much faster rate of population growth, averaging about 3.6% in that same period. The country's economy expanded by the impressive figure of 13.2%. In the 1990s, Sub-Sahara's rate of population expansion slowed down to 2.6%, but the World Bank, the United Nations and numerous pundits still argued that the rate was too high to allow the economy to grow rapidly. They claimed that too many resources were deployed to take care of the young popu-lation and not enough was left for investment. That seemed to be corroborated by the 2.4% GDP growth rate in the region. However, Equatorial Guinea had the same rate of population growth, but that did not keep the economy from growing by the spectacular figure of 18.2%. [42]

In other regions of the world, several individual countries reinforced the idea that fast population growth is not a hindrance for high GDP growth. During the second half of the 20th century, population growth in the United Arab Emirates, Qatar, Bahrain and Kuwait was extremely fast because of the very high birth rate prevailing in Muslim countries and the importation of vast numbers of foreign workers. It was the fastest population growth in the world, averaging about 4% annually. Nevertheless, the average GDP growth of the four countries was almost 9%.

Analyzing specific decades, the situation becomes even more clear. In the 1960s, Libya's population grew by about 4% per year, but the economy grew by 24%. There was a 20% per capita improvement of living conditions, which showed that even extremely rapid population growth need not be a hindrance to massive progress in nutrition, housing, education and everything else. [43]

The fact that Qatar and the island of Nauru in the Pacific Ocean attained rates of economic growth of 30% per year in the 1970s further corroborates the idea that, independent of the rate of population growth, GDP can rise even faster and living conditions can improve substantially. [44]

---

42. Mafeje, Archie & Rodwan, Samir (ed): *Economic and Demographic Change in Africa*, Oxford University Press, Oxford, 1995, p. 108-129.
43. *L'etat du Monde-Annuaire Economique et Geopolitique*, La Decouvert, Paris, 2002.
44. Paradise well and truly lost, *The Economist*, 22 December 2001, p. 67.

The desire of the World Bank and others to reduce population growth in Africa and other developing regions is rational from certain perspectives. By the year 2000, the world already had a population of six billion people, while two thousand years earlier the total was just 200 million. That thirty-fold increase exerts a high level of pressure on the environment, and on top of that the people of the early 21st century expect to enjoy a very high level of consumption.

However, from the perspective of the purported link between population growth and GDP growth, the argument is very weak. During the 1990s, the region of the world with the slowest rate of population was Eastern Europe and the ex-Soviet Union. This was actually the only region with negative figures, averaging about -0.2% due to emigration and low birth rates. In spite of such a theoretically advantageous situation, this was also the region with the worst GDP rates. The economy contracted by about -1.7%. Unemployment, underemployment, poverty and income inequalities increased. [45]

The evidence shows that slow or even negative population growth do not have a straight-line effect on economic growth. Nothing in all of history, much less recent history, supports the notion that population growth or reduction plays a determinant role in economic growth. An abundance of evidence, on the other hand, suggests that the GDP rate plays a decisive role in the rate of population growth.

When the GDP rate accelerates in a nation mired in rampant poverty, it translates into faster population growth because health improves and mortality rapidly decreases. Then, once nations attain a relatively high level of development and the basic necessities are met, the birthrate begins to fall. This last has a dynamic of its own. For one thing, once per capita incomes have risen to a level in which contraceptive technology becomes easy to buy. Once life becomes less precarious, there is less need to have large families in order to ensure posterity and a comfortable old age. In addition, wealth brings rising levels of education, and better educated people tend to have smaller families.

The evidence shows that draconian measures like those enforced in China and India are not the best mechanism for reducing the rate of population growth. Neither is that goal best addressed by birth control campaigns like those promoted by the United Nations. The best mechanism is fast and sustained economic growth. The faster the growth, the sooner a nation reaches a level of

---

45. *World Development Report 2000: Ibid.*, p. 279.

development in which the population spontaneously takes successful measures to reduce the birth rate. [46]

Natural Resources

Economists have long considered that wealth in natural resources was important for economic growth; and the impressive rise of numerous oil producing countries during the second half of the 20th century is seen by many as the ultimate evidence supporting this idea.

Without land, water, minerals, oil, etc. it would seem that the creation of wealth would be difficult, if not impossible. However, during the 20th century two of the economies with the least resources were Hong Kong and Singapore. They had very limited territories crammed with the highest population density in the world. They were so poor in natural resources that they even had to buy a large share of the water they consumed (from their neighbors, China and Malaysia, respectively). In spite of that they grew faster than 99% of all the countries in the world. The economies of Hong Kong and Singapore expanded on average by about 5.9% annually, while the average for the world was half of that. As a result, by 2000 both were among the wealthiest places in the world. The US, on the other hand, with its vast natural resources, grew by just 3.5% in the 20th century and Russia, which had by far the largest territory in the world and also has vast deposits of oil and other resources, grew by only 2.4%. [47]

During the longer period of 1800-2000, the US enjoyed a faster rate of growth on average than Hong Kong and Singapore, and that is why in the early 2000s it was still slightly wealthier (per capita). By then, per capita incomes in the US were about $32,000. Luxembourg, however, had higher incomes, averaging about $40,000, despite having one of the smallest territories in the world. Luxembourg had only one traditional resource in significant amounts, iron ore; but the ore deposits were of low quality and by the early 20th century they were largely depleted. That did not prevent the country from growing faster than all others in the last two centuries. [48]

---

46. Kulke & Rothermund: *Ibid.*, p. 324.
47. Huff, W. G.: *The Economic Growth of Singapore*, Cambridge University Press, Cambridge, 1994.
48. *Europe du Nord — Europe Mediane, Geographie Universelle*, Belin-Reclus, Paris, 1996, p. 460-462.

Oil, since the mid-20th century, has been considered a vital raw material; and the US has vast deposits. Luxembourg, however, has never possessed a drop of oil and nevertheless it outperformed all other nations of the world. Hong Kong and Singapore also lack oil but grew impressively fast. On the other hand, some countries with stunning oil reserves, such as Nigeria and Angola (which also possesses large deposits of numerous other minerals, ample fertile land, and vast forests), were by the early 2000s among the least developed in the world. On top of that, these Sub-Saharan countries benefited from some of the lowest oil extraction costs in the world and the collaboration of multinational oil companies from developed countries, which used the best technology. In spite of that, growth was slow. Nigeria averaged 2.8% in the second half of the 20th century and Angola 1.2%. Prior to the 1950s, stagnation prevailed in both. The case of Saudi Arabia further substantiates the weakness of traditional arguments. During the late 20th century it was by far the largest exporter of oil in the world, with the largest proven reserves on the planet. In spite of that, in the last two decades of the century the economy grew by less than 1% annually. The evidence clearly shows that a country's abundance or scarcity of natural resources, even oil, is not relevant to its own economic growth.[49]

The subject of natural resources is also linked to the possession of a sea outlet. The majority of international trade is conducted by sea, and economists see foreign trade as very important for growth. Logically, countries without an outlet to the sea would find it hard to conduct trade. As a result, many researchers have concluded that a landlocked country would face an obstacle to rapid growth. The World Bank and the IMF have repeatedly claimed, in numerous reports, that one cause of Africa's poverty is the fact that more than a dozen countries lack access to the sea.[50]

That argument overlooks the fact that Luxembourg, Switzerland and Austria were among the fastest growing countries in the world during the period 1800-2000, despite being landlocked. It also neglects the fact that the country with by far the fastest growing GDP in Sub-Saharan Africa during the second half of the 20th century was Botswana. It grew by about 7.5% annually, while the average for the region was of just 2.8%. Botswana, however, has no oil, is

---

49. *Africa South of the Sahara 2002*, Europa Publications, London, 2001.
50. *Sub-Saharan Africa—From Crisis to Sustainable Growth*, The World Bank, Washington D. C., 1989, 27.

largely a desert, and has no outlet to the sea. It is evident that being landlocked does not prevent growth. [51]

An analysis of what makes each of these a special case could fill another book. However, the very fact that there are so many special cases shows that under certain circumstances fast economic growth can be attained, regardless of a nation's culture, size, endowment of natural resources and access to the sea.

Politics and Economic Growth

Many social scientists claim that the socio-political environment significantly affects the economic performance of a nation. War, civil war and lawlessness are frequently presented as major hindrances to growth.

War is usually seen as the worst of evils and human history is full of its horrors. Historians have frequently presented religion, ethnicity, language and culture as causal factors of conflicts. They have posited the notion of a culture of violence that supposedly characterized certain countries. The fact that war, civil war, communal violence, ethnic cleansing, tribal conflicts, coups, crime and other forms of violence have been rampant in all regions of the world for millennia despite the large differences in culture shows the weakness of such an idea. The fact that, in practically every region, violence in its numerous forms considerably decreased for perhaps the first time in the 19th century further corroborates the thesis that the culture argument is incapable of explaining the phenomenon of violence. Still, there were significant differences among the regions and the ones that experienced the largest decrease in violence in the 19th century were the ones that experienced the fastest rates of economic growth. These were Western Europe, North America, Oceania and Eastern Europe.

In the 20th century violence decreased, throughout the world, notwithstanding the large differences in culture. This coincided with the establishment of the "balance of terror" between the great powers, but also with unprecedented growth in all regions. The world economy attained an average growth of about 0.2% annually in the 18th century, of 1.2% in the 19th century, and of about 3.0% in the 20th century.

Many people suggest that the bloodbaths of World War I and World War II invalidate the above thesis, and war has indeed become more industrialized and large-scale; but it is a fact that in the 20th century the Western world has

---

51. Carter, Gwendolen & O'Meara, Patrick (ed): *Southern Africa—The Continuing Crisis*, Indiana University Press, Bloomington-US, 1982.

had fewer wars than in previous centuries. Germany for example experienced two wars in the 20th century, but in the 19th century it had to endure four. In the 20th century it warred for about ten years while in the 19th century, when the economy grew slower and when the level of per capita wealth was much lower, it warred for about twenty years. The wars of the 20th century also caused less suffering to the civilian population. During World War II, for example, about 8% of Germany's total population perished while during the Thirty Years War in the 17th century the share that died was of about 36%. In the 17th century the German economy was almost stagnant, in the 19th century in was of about 2.7%, and in the 20th century the figure was 3.7%. [52]

History shows that cultural variables such as religion, language and ethnicity are not the cause of violence. It also suggests that violence alone does not prevent growth. The events of the 20th century are particularly illustrative. The fact that some countries attained the fastest rates of growth in their entire histories at the moment when they were enduring their highest levels of violence strongly supports the thesis that violence is an effect of an absence of growth — and not the cause. Great Britain attained one of the fastest rates of growth in the world during the period 1800-2000, averaging almost 3% annually. Despite its success relative to most other nations, such a rate was insufficient to eliminate unemployment and underemployment. As a result the country almost constantly endured uncomfortable levels of both. There were only two brief moments in all its history in which Britain eliminated unemployment and significantly reduced underemployment, and those were during the first and the second world wars. It was precisely at the moment when it was enduring the most encompassing wars of its history that it attained its fastest GDP rates. It is also worth mentioning that the first time Britain attained rates that were not sclerotic was during the Napoleonic Wars (1793-1814), the largest scale war up to that date. [53]

The US attained the fastest growth in the world in the 19th century and in particular in the last decades of that period, but not even then did the economy grow as fast as it did during World War II. Canada also enjoyed unprecedented growth during the war years. In Britain, the US and Canada, the economy was distorted and became more regulated in the first half of the 1940s than ever before. On top of that, international trade had collapsed. Even with these addi-

---

52. Bramsted, Ernest: *Germany*, Prentice-Hall, US, 1972, p. 76-84.
53. Floud, Roderick & McCloskey, Donald(ed): *The Economic History of Britain since 1700* Vol. I, Cambridge University Press, Cambridge, 1994, p. 13, 121.

tional hindrances, these countries grew faster than at any other moment in their histories. There is much to suggest that war in itself does not preclude growth. The US experience in the 1950s and 1960s offers further proof of this. These decades saw two large conflicts: in Korea and Vietnam. In the 1980s and 1990s, the US was involved in relatively minor military skirmishes. Even so, the US economy grew much faster during the 1950s and 1960s. [54]

Economists and social scientists have also claimed that civil war hinders growth, but this also fails to find historical substantiation. The US experienced a devastating civil war during the 1860s, but in spite of that the economy grew like never before. It grew rapidly during the conflict and immediately afterward. Of course, that case is exceptional and war often coincides with stagnation or even economic depression, or causes economic distortions that later lead to an economic downturn. Even so, it is seen that the traditional arguments do not necessarily square with the facts. [55]

Numerous authorities have also claimed that rampant crime hinders growth because it hampers business. This argument has been repeatedly used to explain why Sub-Saharan countries cannot leap out of poverty. But Botswana, which obtained its independence in 1966 and was as riddled by crime as any of its neighbors, managed to grow by 15% annually in the 1970s. Fast growth continued in the following decades and by the early 2000s it was a middle-income country and the second most developed in Africa. Equatorial Guinea, up to the 1980s, was plagued with crime and political violence as well as with corruption, nepotism and incompetence in government circles. In spite of that the economy averaged about 18% annually in the 1990s, which was the fastest in the world. Switzerland in this same decade had one of the lowest levels of crime in the world, lower even than that of other developed countries with low crime levels, such as Germany and Britain. In spite of that, it grew by just 0.5%. [56]

Crime has been a problem in every country of the world, for centuries; surely, this has hampered trade and business. However, for many nations there was a moment when the economy managed to burst out of stagnation and it happens to be precisely at that moment that crime began to fall. History shows that violence is an effect of the absence of growth and not its cause. That helps to

---

54. Aldcroft, Derek: *The British Economy* Vol. I, Wheatsheaf Books Ltd., London, 1986, p. 2, 166-170.
55. Krout, John: *The United States to 1877*, Barnes & Noble, New York, 1966, p. 137-146.
56. *Africa South of the Sahara 2002, Ibid.*, p. 332.

explain why developed countries have far lower levels of crime than developing nations.

It is when people endure hunger, homelessness and poverty that they resort to violence to improve their living conditions. Desperate people are driven towards violence as a means to acquire the resources they lack. Despite the arguments promoted by governments throughout history to explain why they go to war (whether in the name of religion, ethnic differences, cultural supremacy or something else), practically all wars have been wars of plunder, at some level.

The people recruited to fight in those conflicts may have been lured to defend their culture, their language, their religion, their ethnicity, but they were vulnerable to the lure because of economic hardship. When poverty and unemployment become unbearable, people tend to protest, and there is always a share of a population that will take up arms to make its protest heard. Religious, cultural or linguistic differences play only a marginal role and economic strain is actually the trigger mechanism of the violence. When the GDP is going up quickly, cultural, religious, linguistic and ideological differences become less important, and people are more likely to resolve their differences by non-violent means.

Even when nations have attained some growth and have achieved a relatively high level of development, the economy is always the determinant variable in causing or hindering wars as well as other forms of violence. By the early 20th century, for example, Europe had just experienced a century of unprecedented growth and living conditions had improved greatly. Relatively to the past, it was an impressive rate, but relative to what East Asia attained in the second half of the 20th century, it was nothing. In the 19th century Western Europe (the fastest growing portion of Europe) averaged GDP growth of about 2.5% per year. Such rates continued in the following years, and by 1914 the levels of wealth were still low. Life expectancy in the most developed countries was only about fifty years. The Europe of 1914 was poor. By 2000, even South Asia, despite being the second poorest region of the world, had a life expectancy of about sixty years. In Yugoslavia, where World War I started, life expectancy was barely forty years. Aggravating the situation was a recession that hit Germany and several of its neighbors in 1913, significantly increasing unemployment and poverty. This drove many German policy makers to conclude that a way out of the recession would be by conquering the natural resources they needed. [57]

---

57. Hardach: *Ibid.*, p. 246, 247.

Economic downturns also drive many people to embrace unscientific ideas. By 1914, European countries were experiencing a feverish nationalism as intellectuals and politicians advocated various chauvinistic views. The low education levels of the population made them susceptible to these nationalistic ideas. Even though Europe had the second highest level of education in the world, at that time, illiteracy was significantly higher than now and most of the population that was literate had barely finished primary school. By 1914, only some 2% of the college-age population was enrolled in post-secondary schools, while in 2000 it was about 50%.

High levels of ignorance reflect a low level of wealth. Education that encourages a scientific outlook tends to protect people from being swayed to action on the basis of emotional appeals and irrational causes like nationalism. Education has the capacity to encourage human beings to be tolerant of the ethnic, religious, linguistic, and cultural differences that separate them from other groups of people. [58]

Even when nations have established a relatively long-term record of respectable growth and attained relatively high levels of wealth, abrupt reverses or even a perceived threat to that growth can lead them towards war. After World War I, Germany recovered and grew relatively fast in the 1920s, its economy expanding by more than 4% annually. However, in late 1929 the economy collapsed and in the following three years it contracted by 10% per year. By 1932, the depression had subtracted so much wealth that about 30% of the German workforce was unemployed and about 900,000 had died of hunger and exposure. [59]

The traditional political parties systematically failed to bring recovery and the desperate Germans were attracted by the extremist approach of the Nazis. Without the economic crisis, the Nationalist Socialists would not have come to power. In the 1920s, the Nazis attracted no more than 2% of the vote. In 1932, they won 38% of the votes and became the largest party in parliament.[60] The economic squeeze made it easy to persuade the population that it was under some form of attack, and made it easy to motivate them to fight in the war that soon followed.

58. Gatrell, Peter: *The Tsarist Economy 1850-1917*, B.T. Batsford Ltd., London, 1986, p. 33, 34.
59. Bettelheim, Charles: *L'Economie Allemande sous le Nazisme* Vol. I, François Maspero, Paris, 1971, p. 18-21.
60. Berghahn, V.: *Modern Germany*, Cambridge University Press, Cambridge, 1985, p. 113-131.

There were many wars in the second half of the 20th century. A common denominator of many of them was the very low level of accumulated growth or a deterioration of the economy. Most of the conflicts were played out on the territory of countries with low living standards, and only occasionally in middle-income countries. The wars in the 1950s, 1960s and 1970s in Korea and Vietnam happened under conditions of extreme poverty in those East Asian nations.[61]

Africa and Asia saw the most violent conflicts in the second half of the 20th century and they were the continents with the lowest levels of wealth. Countries such as Zaire, Sierra Leone and Rwanda had accumulated very little wealth; from 1950-89 they grew by about 3% annually and before the 1950s they had stagnated. Then, in the 1990s, their economies actually contracted. Zaire, later was renamed Democratic Republic of Congo, "grew" by about -5% per year, Sierra Leone by -4% and Rwanda by -1%. Life was already miserable for most and when the economy fell into recession, the situation became desperate. Desperate people tend to turn to violence and Sub-Saharan Africans are no exception. The contraction was accompanied by civil war in the three countries.

In the 1970s, Angola's economy contracted by about 5% annually and civil war erupted. Since then, the country grew at a measly 2% and by the beginning of the twenty-first century the war was still raging. In Mozambique, the economy contracted by about 2% in the 1970s and in that decade a civil war also erupted. In the 1980s, the economy stagnated and the war continued. In the 1990s, however, the economy expanded by more than 5% and the civil war came to an end.[62]

Countries do not necessarily have to plunge into a recession in order to fall into war. It fundamentally depends on the level of accumulated growth at a given moment in time. Guatemala and El Salvador grew relatively fast in the 1950-79 period, averaging a rate of more than 4% annually. Prior to 1950 they had grown slowly, so that the progress made during the 1950s, 1960s and 1970s was not enough to extricate the population from poverty. Due to the relative fast growth of those decades, people began to develop positive expectations about the future. However, when in the 1980s the rates of growth decelerated to less than 1% and living conditions again deteriorated. The population lost patience and took the path of violence. Civil war erupted and thousands died.[63]

---

61. Harris, Seymour: *American Economic History*, McGraw Hill, New York, 1961, p. 46.
62. *Africa South of the Sahara 2002, Ibid.*
63. South America, *Central America and the Caribbean 2002, Ibid.*

If a country has already accumulated much wealth, like Japan by the 1980s, the deceleration of the economy to a rate of less than 2% per year (as in the 1990s) will not likely bring the country to war. By 1929, however, Japan had not accumulated much wealth and when the economy contracted the next year, policymakers and populace alike began to be restless. The next year they launched a major invasion over Manchuria and in 1937 they invaded the rest of China.[64]

Up to the 1950s the Indonesian economy was largely stagnant. Since the mid-1960s however, it began to grow on a sustained basis by about 5% per year. Living conditions improved in an unprecedented way, but due to the fast population growth, by 1997 the country was still poor. The improving living conditions generated a sense of tolerance among the numerous religious and cultural groups of the 13,000-island archipelago. However, when the economy contracted by about 13%, in 1998, life deteriorated rapidly and people revolted. Their rage and desperation took the form of ethnic cleansing, religious confrontation, and cannibalism. Thousands of people were murdered. [65]

History shows that only fast and sustained economic growth can liberate nations from war and violence.

Terrorism

Terrorism is a form of violence and as such it falls into the preceding category. However, as a result of the attacks on the US in the early 2000s, it attained a new dimension and commentators began to classify it in a separate category. Independent of how it was classified, analysts agreed that it acted as a hindrance on growth. For example, immediately after the attack, economists asserted that the US economy would weaken because of the increased security costs and a pessimistic climate among consumers. They thus forecast a recession. However, in the year after the attack, GDP grew by 3%. Thus, while such events may serve to dampen the economy, the situation is not that simple and various factors might be brought to bear to keep the economy moving, at least for some time.

Social scientists have claimed that the causes behind the surge of terrorist acts in the 2000s reside in the large cultural differences between Islam and the West. Rather, the fact that terrorism has systematically proliferated under cir-

---

64. Allen, G. C.: *A Short Economic History of Modern Japan*, George Allen & Unwin Ltd., London, 1972, p. 97-106.
65. Frederick, William (ed): *Indonesia — A Country Study*, Library of Congress, Washington D. C., 1992.

cumstances of high unemployment, underemployment and poverty suggests that it is triggered by (and not the trigger of) insufficient growth. During the second half of the 20th century the majority of terrorists worldwide came from some of the least developed countries. Middle-income countries produced fewer and developed nations almost none.

In the 1950s and 1960s, in the aftermath of the partition of Palestine and the wars of 1948 which dispossessed them, Palestinian terrorist groups regularly attacked Israel from their bases in Jordan, Egypt, Syria and Lebanon. However, parts of the Palestinian population were integrated within the Israel economic development: [66] at that time, Israel had a GDP growth rate of about 10% per year, and offered a large number of jobs for the Palestinian population. By the early 2000s, acts of terrorism were a constant event in Gaza and the West Bank. That coincided with an unemployment rate of about 40% and continuous economic stagnation due to the virtual economic blockade of Palestinian territory over the preceding decades and the fact that Israel, despite receiving substantially more aid from the U.S. government than any other country in the world, attained a GDP rate of just 3% during the 1980s, the slowest growth since the country was created in 1948.

History shows that terrorism does not prevent growth. Rather, the absence of growth and insufficient economic development contribute to fueling terrorism.

Education

Another variable that is sometimes presented as affecting economic growth is education. Most academics see education as very important and some see it as fundamental for prosperity, because a better-qualified workforce is considered essential for increasing production and efficiency. The problem is that this argument fails to establish a correlation between the two variables. [67]

In the late 1970s, China had a low level of education even by the standards of several developing Asian nations. On top of that, its educational system in the preceding three decades had concentrated on communist ideology and the workforce had not been trained to focus on such concepts as quality control and efficiency. Worse still, even though the government began to liberalize the economy in 1979, in the next two decades China remained one of the most

---

66. *Realites d'Israel*, Centre d'information d'Israel, Jerusalem, 1992, 26-46, 196-203.
67. How Asia's tigers Got their Stripes, *Businessweek International*, 25 December 1995, p. 6.

tightly regulated economies in the world. In spite of that, the country attained one of the fastest rates of growth in the world. Growth averaged almost 8% from 1980 to 2003 while Western Europe, which had a considerably better-educated workforce, averaged less than 3%. [68]

By the 1990s, the US had the highest share of the adult population with a college or university degree in the world and it also had the best universities in the world. In spite of that, it grew by less than 3% per year while Equatorial Guinea, which by 1989 had one of the lowest levels of education in the world, averaged a growth of 18% in the following decade. The situation of Equatorial Guinea was extremely unpromising; in the 1980s it had one of the worst educational systems in Africa and one of the lowest levels of literacy in the world. That, however, did not prevent a spectacular rate of growth in the 1990s. [69]

In the late 20th century the US had by far the highest educational levels in all of its history. About a fifth of the adult population completed college or university and four-fifths completed secondary school. Further, the information taught in the late 20th century had a far higher level of scientific value. In spite of that, growth was much faster in the late 19th century. Growth averaged about 8% annually in the 1880-99 years while the figure was of just 3% in the 1980-99 years. If education were the determining factor for growth or at least a very important one, the facts should have come out differently. [70]

By 1966 when the British granted independence to Botswana, the country was among the least developed in Africa and it had one of the lowest literacy levels. Due to its arid climate and lack of direct access to the sea, the British neglected the territory during colonial times. In spite of that, the economy grew by 13% during the 1970-89 years. [71]

Libya attained independence from Britain in 1951 and by 1959 it was one of the poorest and most illiterate countries in Africa. The Italians had not done much to develop it while they ruled the territory from 1911 to 1942; World War II brought destruction; and the British in the following years continued the pattern of neglect. At independence there were only ten university graduates and in the 1950s little progress had been made. In spite of that, the economy grew by 24% annually in the 1960s. [72]

68. Gray, J. & White, G.(ed): *China's New Development Strategy*, Academic Press Ltd., London, 1982, p. 93-131.
69. *World Development Report 2000: Ibid.*, p. 274-316.
70. History Lessons, *Newsweek*, 10 July 1995, p. 37.
71. Carter & O'Meara: *Ibid.*, p. 235-242.

History thus shows that education alone does not cause growth, but is generally an effect of it. Through the history of every country in the world, education always made the greatest advances when the economy grew rapidly. It frequently happened that governments allocated a very small share of available resources to education or even reduced the education budget, and in spite of that the economy accelerated and education progressed.

In the 1930s the US government reduced budgetary expenditures for defense and increased the budget for education, but the economy experienced a massive deceleration. After having grown by about 4% per year in the 1920s, it averaged less than 1% in the 1930s. In the 1940s, on the other hand, Washington cut expenditures in education and other civilian fields significantly, and transferred them to the military. The experts claimed that such a shift of resources would deliver economic ruin, but national security concerns left no other alternative. In fact, the US economy grew by about 5% annually. In this decade by far the fastest growth was attained during the war. As soon as the conflict ended, resources were again transferred to education and the economy contracted. [73]

The share of education in the budgets of Switzerland and Japan in the 1990s increased but the economy of both experienced a considerable deceleration and averaged about 1% per year. Overall expenditures in education (public and private) as a share of GDP in both countries were higher than ever before. In spite of that both attained their slowest growth figures during the second half of the 20th century. [74]

During the second half of the 20th century East Asia attained the fastest GDP rates in the world and that coincided with the fastest development of education. The progress was even more noticeable in the fastest growing countries. By the late 1990s Japanese, Korean, Taiwanese and Singaporean students attained the highest scores in international exams of mathematics and natural sciences, outperforming those of the West. By then South Korea had more people with a doctorate degree as a share of the total population than any other country in the world.

However, investments in education were not large. Hong Kong, which was the fastest growing economy in the region, was among those that invested the least in schools. During 1950-99, Latin American governments spent more on

72. Balta: *Ibid.*, p. 36.
73. Boulding, Kenneth: *The Structure of a Modern Economy*, Macmillan Press, London, 1993, p. 70-72.
74. *La Vie Economique*. Monthly editions of 1999-2001, Berne.

education than did East Asia. Expenditures on public education as a share of GDP in Latin America averaged about 4% while in East Asia it was 3%. However, economic growth in Latin America was of about 3.6% per year while in East Asia it was about 5.6%. [75]

During this period the United Arab Emirates, Qatar, Bahrain and Kuwait achieved the fastest economic growth in the Middle East and that coincided with the fastest development of education in that region. They also attained one of the fastest GDP rates in the world and they experienced one of the fastest developments of education in the world. The economy averaged a growth of about 8.7% annually. In 2003 Qatar inaugurated an Education City that included ultra modern teaching facilities and imported branches of top American universities. [76]

History shows that education is one of the many effects of economic growth. It is not, in itself, responsible for growth. Some other variable is responsible for growth and when that variable is strongly present, the economy expands rapidly. Once it starts to grow rapidly, every sector benefits from the expansion of resources. The greater resources therefore allow for more schools, training centers and universities.

Science and Technology

Another variable linked to education and which has been frequently classified as a growth factor is science. Science and technology have certainly contributed much to the development of civilization. This has led many economists to conclude that science plays a major role in economic growth. They posit that scientific discoveries, in particular those that deliver a major breakthrough, produce an accelerating effect on the economy. Thus, they frequently advise governments to spend more on research and development (R&D). This is a very seductive idea, but the historical evidence cannot substantiate it. [77]

In the 19th century one of the countries that made the most scientific discoveries was Great Britain; its economy grew by about 2.7% per year. Canada made practically no discoveries, but managed to grow at about the same pace (2.6%). During the 20th century the country that was responsible for the

75. Schools-No Tigers, *Businessweek International*, 9 June 1997, p. 48.
76. *The Middle East and North Africa 2002, Ibid.*
77. Needham, Joseph: *Clerks and Craftsmen in China and the West*, Cambridge University Press, Cambridge, 1970.

greatest number of scientific discoveries was the US, and its economy expanded by about 3.5% per year. Hong Kong, on the other hand, did not make a single scientific discovery and in spite of such a poor performance, it attained an economic growth of about 6.0%. [78]

During the second half of the 20th century the four fastest growing economies in the world were the United Arab Emirates, Qatar, Hong Kong and Kuwait. Such an achievement was attained while not making a single scientific discovery and spending practically nothing in R&D. Sweden and Switzerland had by the 1990s the highest number of scientists in per capita terms and the highest registration of patents per person in the world. In spite of that, they had one of the slowest rates of economic growth in the world, averaging 1.5% and 0.5% respectively. Japan spent very little in R&D during the 1950s because it imported most of the technology it used. However, in the following decades it rapidly increased its expenditures and by the 1990s it spent more in R&D as a share of GDP than ever before. In spite of that, growth was slower than in any other decade of the 20th century. While growth averaged about 9.1% in the 1950s, it was of only 1.5% in the 1990s. In the 1990s Japan spent more in R&D as a share of the total economy than most countries in Western Europe and North America. It still grew slower than the large majority of Western nations. [79]

Over a period of a decade the nations with the fastest GDP growth in history were Nauru, Qatar, Libya, United Arab Emirates, Equatorial Guinea and Botswana. The first two averaged about 30% in the 1970s, the third and fourth 24% in the 1960s and 1970s respectively. The fifth managed 18% in the 1990s and the sixth 15% in the 1970s. All of these nations did not have a single scientist and made no scientific discoveries in those decades. [80]

Science and technology are thus not sufficient in themselves to bring economic growth. History shows, rather, that advances in science and technology follow growth; and that is why a nation that has attained fast growth often shows fast development of technology. When underdeveloped nations grow rapidly (such as the six just mentioned), they import the technology from the rest of the world at a very fast pace. When a nation that is among the most developed enjoys strong GDP growth, scientific discoveries are made at a rapid pace. Western Europe and North America during the 1950-69 years attained a

78. *The US and Canada 1994*, Europa Publications, London, 1994, p. 395-425.
79. Mende, Tibor: *Soleils*, Editions du Soleil, Paris, 1975, p. 68.
80. Business in Asia, *The Economist*, 9 March 1996, p. 24.

GDP rate of about 5.4% per year, while during the 1980-99 years growth was of just 2.7%. That coincided with a rate of patent registration that was about twice as fast in the first period. [81]

Infrastructure

Most economists see infrastructure as a factor that affects the economy decisively. They argue that if a country does not possess adequate roads, highways, bridges, ports, railways, airports and telecommunication systems as well as an adequate supply of electricity, it will have difficulty producing goods and developing internal and external trade. The World Bank, the Inter-American Development Bank, the Asian Development Bank and the African Development Bank have concentrated on lending to infrastructure projects. The argument sounds consistent, but the empirical evidence does not corroborate it. [82]

Infrastructure development clearly contributes to long-term economic growth, but it can take years to pay off, and other countervailing factors can still drag the economy down. During the 1930s, for example, the US government invested more than ever before in infrastructure and allocated a larger share of total resources for the construction of highways, hydroelectric dams and ports. In spite of that the economy decelerated significantly and grew by less than 1% annually, recording the worst performance in the 19th and 20th century. In the 1990s the Japanese government invested more in infrastructure as a share of GDP than ever before. In spite of that it had the slowest economic growth in the 20th century. In 1959, the infrastructure of Libya was one of the worst in the world, but in the 1960s GDP expanded by 24% per year.

In the 1980s China's infrastructure was one of the least developed in Asia. There were no highways, the railroad system was antiquated, and electricity was in short supply. In spite of that the economy grew in real terms by more than 7%, while New Zealand, which had a far superior transportation, electrification and communication system, grew by less than 2%. In the 1990s Vietnam's infrastructure was even worse than China's in the preceding decade. In spite of that the economy expanded in real terms by about 6%, while Canada, which had one of the best infrastructures in the world, grew by just 2%. In 1989 the infrastructure of Equatorial Guinea was perhaps the worst in the world, but that did not keep the country from growing by 18% in the 1990s. Switzerland on the

---

81. How to Build a Really, Really, Really Big Plane, *Fortune*, 5 March 2001, p. 77-82.
82. Asia's New Bank for the Poor, *Asiaweek*, 19 November 1999, p. 169.

other hand had in the same decade one of the best infrastructures in the world and despite that advantage its economy grew by less than 1% per year. [83]

Even when longer periods of time and groups of countries are analyzed, the same lack of correlation is observed. During the second half of the 20th century, the infrastructure in East Asia was considerably inferior to that of North America. In spite of that, East Asia grew faster, averaging a rate of about 5.6% while North America's was 3.8%. [84]

Even when comparing a country against itself, and thus eliminating all arguments based on differences in economic systems, culture and other variables, it is still not possible to make the facts support the infrastructure argument. During the second half of the 20th century the US had the best infrastructure in the world, with the most extensive highway system, an extensive and efficient railroad system, a state of the art telecommunications system, modern airports, efficient ports, and ample electricity. The economy grew by about 3.4% annually. In 1850-99, there were no airports, telecommunications were almost non-existent, electricity was practically unavailable, highways did not exist, railroads were few and primitive, and ports were few. But, the economy grew much faster than it did a century later, averaging about 6.3%. [85]

An absence of a correlation indicates an absence of causality. The historical evidence shows that infrastructure improvements are also one of the many "luxuries" that become possible when there is economic growth. Countries do not grow fast by investing abundantly in infrastructure or by possessing a highly developed infrastructure. There is some other variable that causes growth and once the economy expands rapidly, more resources become available for the development of highways, airports and the like. That is why, in every country of the world where the economy has grown rapidly, there was always a rapid development of infrastructure.

The US, for example, had the fastest growing economy in the world in the 19th century and it also showed the fastest development of infrastructure. By 1900 the US had the most modern railroad system in the world and the highest per capita electricity consumption. The region with the fastest GDP figures in the second half of the 20th century was East Asia and it was also the region with

---

83. Fraser, J. & Gerstle, G.: *The Rise and Fall of the New Deal Order*, Princeton University Press, Princeton, 1989, p. 4-34.

84. Diminishing Returns, *The Economist*, 10 March 2001, p. 65.

85. Faulkner, Harold: *Histoire Economique des Etas Unis d'Amérique* vol. IV, Presses Universitaires de France, Paris, 1958, p. 370-390.

the fastest growth of infrastructure. By the early 2000s the most developed economies in that region were the only countries in the world with modern airports
created on artificial islands.

In this period the United Arab Emirates, Qatar, Kuwait and Bahrain
attained the fastest GDP figures in the Middle East and they experienced the
fastest development of infrastructure in that region. They also attained the
fastest rate of growth in the world and saw the fastest development of construction. By the early 2000s they had glamorous airports, impressive highways,
state of the art telecommunications, and dazzling skyscrapers. In Libya in the
1960s, Botswana in the 1970s and Equatorial Guinea in the 1990s, growth was
spectacular and infrastructure progressed impressively. [86]

Health

Some economists have argued that the health of a population plays an
important role in growth and in the 1990s the World Bank began to embrace this
idea. It thus began to advice governments in developing countries to invest more
in health-related matters in the belief that healthy people are more productive.
Although the idea seems sensible, the empirical evidence does not corroborate
it.[87]

During the second half of the 20th century the population in the US experienced the highest levels of health ever and life expectancy was unprecedented
averaging about 73 years. A century earlier, in the 1850-99 years, the quality of
health was much lower and life expectancy was just 38 years. In spite of that it
was in the second half of the 19th century when the US economy grew the
fastest, averaging a rate almost twice as fast as a century later. [88]

Western Europe attained its highest levels of health in the 1990s and life
expectancy was of about 77 years, which was an unprecedented figure. In the
1950s life expectancy was just 68 years and infant mortality was much higher
than four decades later. However, the economy grew by about 6.1% in the 1950s
and by only 2.6% in the 1990s. [89]

---

86. Davis, L., Hughes, J. & McDougall, D.: *American Economic History*, Richard Irwin Inc.,
   New York, 1969, p. 280-290.
87. Helping the Poorest, *The Economist*, 14 August 1999, p. 11.
88. Can We Stay Young? *Time*, 9 December 1996, p. 66.
89. *World Development Report 1981*, 1991 & 2000-Basic Indicators.

In Libya in 1951, about 90% of the population had trachoma and numerous other diseases were also rampant. Life expectancy was 45 years and infant mortality was among the highest in the world. In the following years health improved little, but in the 1960s the economy grew by about 24.4%. If good health is important for growth, Libya should have experienced stagnation or at best slow growth. [90]

India had very poor quality of health in the 1990s and life expectancy was almost twenty years lower than in Germany. In spite of that the Indian economy grew more than three times faster than that of Germany, averaging about 5.0%. In Japan life expectancy was even higher than in Germany, reaching 80 years, but the economy performed worse than in Germany and averaged only 1.5%. Sub-Saharan Africa was the region of the world suffering most from AIDS in the 1990s and Botswana was the country worst hit. In this decade about 30% of the population from Botswana was contaminated with the virus. Life expectancy fell dramatically and a large share of the working population died. Even so, the economy grew much faster than in many countries that had low levels of AIDS and had the highest levels of health in the world. While Botswana's economy grew annually by about 4.3%, that of Western Europe, where only 0.2% of the population was contaminated with the virus and which was free of any major health problem, grew by just 2.6%. [91]

History shows that health does not guarantee a country fast economic growth. There is no causal link. The empirical evidence shows, again, that health is one of the many effects of growth. Every country has witnessed a rapid improvement in health when the economy grew rapidly. In the second half of the 20th century the region with the fastest growth was East Asia and it was also the region with the fastest improvement of health conditions. By the early 2000s Japan, Hong Kong and Singapore had the highest life expectancy in the world and the lowest infant mortality. Sub-Saharan Africa attained unprecedented GDP figures in the 1950-99 years and health improved more than in any other half a century period. However, improvements in health were slower than in most other regions and that coincided with one of the slowest rates of economic growth in the world. Eastern Europe and the Soviet Union made health improvements from the 1950s to the 1980s, when the economy expanded by about 3%

90. Parker, Richard: *North Africa-Regional Tensions and Strategic Concerns*, Praeger, 1984, p. 66-77.
91. AIDS in the Third World, *The Economist*, 2 January 1999, p. 40.

annually. In the 1990s the economy of the region contracted by about 2% and the health of the population deteriorated significantly. In the Soviet Union, life expectancy fell from about seventy years in 1989 to sixty years a decade later. [92]

Throughout history, diseases and epidemics have claimed more lives than famine and war put together. However, many of the worst diseases such as tuberculosis and the plague, that over the centuries have killed millions, were closely linked to malnutrition and this was the result of a weak economy. Whenever the economy grew rapidly, agriculture did likewise and the per capita food supply increased. Through history the rate of food production has run in parallel with the GDP rate and malnutrition has fallen, in sync with the pace of economic growth. [93]

Typhus, cholera, malaria, schistosomiasis, guinea worm, sleeping disease, hepatitis, diphtheria, yellow fever and numerous others were by the early 2000s a major problem in developing countries. These diseases are fundamentally the result of contaminated water, an absence or a poor sewage system, and inadequate rubbish collection. In the course of history, this insalubrious situation was the norm. However, for countries such as those in Western Europe and North America, there came a moment in the 19th century when the situation began to improve and eventually these problems were eliminated. That moment always coincided with the time when the economy emerged from stagnation and began to grow rapidly. Only with fast growth is enough wealth created to finance an adequate sewage system, water supply and rubbish collection for the whole country. [94]

History demonstrates that it is the rate of economic growth that determines the health of a nation. How fast that rate grows over sustained periods of time determines how soon a country overcomes diseases and epidemics. By the early twenty-first century the world of medical technology had learned how to suppress numerous diseases, but a large share of the world population could not access the medicine because their purchasing capacity was too low. Only fast growth can increase the purchasing power of those populations.

Countries do not grow faster by investing more in health. It is some other variable that causes growth and when that variable is present, the increased

---

92. Keep, John: *Last of the Empires*, Oxford University Press, Oxford, 1995, p. 84-88, 233-244, 265.
93. Deane, Phyllis: *The First Industrial Revolution*, Cambridge University Press, Cambridge, 1979, p. 30-32.
94. Der Kampf ums Wasser, *Der Spiegel*, 22 Mai 2000, p. 151.

wealth allows for better nutrition, improved sanitation, more hospitals, and improved medical technology.

Income Distribution

Most economists and social scientists believe that income differentials affect growth. Although most are not fixated with the subject of redistribution, practically all agree that wide income differentials have a dampening effect on the economy. For liberal academics, the effect is slight; but even they agree that when income differentials become too great, the potential for violence and crime increases. Violence and crime have a cost on business that elevates costs of production. They also have social costs, which are hard to quantify because the physical and psychological injuries caused by violent acts are hard to erase from the life of the victims. Even liberal economists advise governments to spend a certain share of the budget on redistribution through programs such as public education.

History however cannot substantiate this position. Income disparities in Hong Kong in the late 19th century were extraordinarily high and in the 20th century the government undertook very minor redistribution efforts. By the 1990s there were considerable income disparities, with a significant number of US-dollar billionaires and millionaires, while a noticeable share of the population lived in very modest conditions. In spite of that, during the 20th century Hong Kong attained the fastest rate of economic growth in the world, averaging about 6.0% per year. Germany invented the welfare system in the late 19th century and in the 20th century German governments undertook among the largest redistribution measures in the world. Only some communist countries and a few other West European nations did more on this front. Income disparities were among the lowest in the world. Notwithstanding, this situation the economy grew by just 3.7%. [95]

Since the birth of Brazil in the 16th century, it has seen large income disparities, which tended to parallel ethnic differences. By the 1960s they had become more blatant and Brazil had one of the most uneven distributions of income in the world. In spite of that the economy grew by about 8.2% in the 1970s, even though budgetary resources for redistribution measures were

---

95. Jao, Hungdah Chiu & Wu, Yuan-li (ed): *The Future of Hong Kong*, Quorum Books, New York, 1987, p. 44-46.

reduced. In this decade the Brazilian military reduced allocations for welfare and used the capital to finance export-oriented manufacturing. [96]

During 1960-79, China had one of the lowest income disparities in the world, but the economy grew by just 2.6% annually. During 1980-99, income inequalities grew rapidly and fewer resources were allocated for redistribution. Beijing reduced allocations for welfare and agriculture and increased them for manufacturing. In spite of that, the economy accelerated greatly and averaged about 7.4%. In the 1990s Western Europe allocated a larger share of GDP for redistribution purposes than any other region in the world. In spite of that, six other regions grew faster. [97]

History shows that income disparities do not hinder growth and it also shows that by allocating more funds for redistribution does not decrease inequalities. Western Europe in the 1990s allocated a much larger share of its total resources for redistribution than in the 1950s. Nonetheless, in the 1950s income inequalities decreased while in the 1990s they increased. That coincided with fast growth in the first period and slow growth in the second.

In North America income disparities fell considerably during the late 19th century even though redistribution measures were non-existent. In the late 20th century inequalities increased, even though, by then, the US and Canada had the most developed welfare systems in their history. That coincided with fast GDP figures in the first period (about 8% annually in 1880-99) and much slower ones in the second (3% in the years 1980-99). [98]

In Japan inequalities diminished rapidly in the 1950s and 1960s, when the economy grew by 10% per year and diminished less quickly in the following two decades, when the GDP rate averaged about 5%. In the 1990s, on the other hand, the economy grew by less than 2% and the improving trend all of a sudden reversed. In this decade inequalities rose even though by then social welfare expenditures as a share of GDP were much higher than in the 1950s and 1960s.

History shows that the only effective way to decrease inequalities is through fast and sustained economic growth. The events of the past two centuries show that income differentials begin to decrease only when GDP rates are over 3% for developed countries and above 6% for developing nations. In 1980-99 in Western Europe and North America GDP rates averaged less than 3%. The

96. Abreu, Marcelo & Verner, Dorte: *Long-Term Brazilian Economic Growth 1930-94*, OECD, Paris, 1997, p. 18-25, 78-80.
97. Second Board — Second Thoughts, *The Economist*, 4 August 2001, p. 59.
98. Out of Sight — Out of Mind, *The Economist*, 20 May 2000, p. 27.

evidence shows that when the rates are slow, not even the most elaborate social welfare system can prevent an exacerbation of income disparities. [99]

In most countries, the people enduring unemployment and underemployment are those who have the lowest incomes. Since fast economic growth is the best means for reducing and eliminating joblessness, fast GDP figures deliver an immediate uplift of the incomes of the poor as they get supplied with jobs. This puts them at parity with the share of the population that is full-time employed.

Exogenous Factors

Another variable that economists have used to explain why at certain times the economy prospers and at others it underperforms are those exogenous factors that stem from the performance of a major economy to which another nation is strongly linked through trade and investment. This theory has had a certain following since the 19th century, when the countries of Western Europe and North America established a considerable level of interdependence.

In the second half of the 20th century trade and investment were liberalized, thus creating new kinds of ties between countries. During that period the US economy was by far the largest and economists constantly argued that the performance of the US was a major factor affecting GDP rates in the rest of the world. The link between Western Europe and the US economy was particularly strong and when GDP growth decelerated considerably in Western Europe in the 1970s, it was argued that this was largely the result of the deceleration of the US. The fact that Japan was also strongly tied to the US and it also experienced a major downturn seemed to further confirm this idea. [100]

However, Latin America was also strongly linked and it even had a relation of dependency with the US economy. In spite of that, GDP figures were almost identical in the 1970s as in the preceding decade, averaging about 4.6% in the 1960s and 4.4% in the following decade.

The case of Hong Kong, Taiwan, South Korea and Singapore or the Newly Industrialized Countries (NICs), also refutes the exogenous variable argument. These economies were extremely closely tied to the US as their main export market and their main source of foreign investment. On top of that their national security was dependent on US military protection. The NICs were actually more

---

99. Rich man — poor man, *The Economist*, 24 July 1993, p. 65.
100. *German Unification*, International Monetary Fund, Washington D.C., 1990, p. 130-133.

closely bound through trade and investment with the US than Germany and France, which conducted most of their trade with other European countries. In spite of that the NICs did not experience a downturn and actually accelerated their GDP figures. After growing by about 9.5% in the 1960s, they expanded by 9.7% in the following decade. [101]

Interesting to notice is that American economists used the exogenous argument to explain the deceleration of the US in the 1970s. After growing by more than 4% in the 1950s and 1960s the figure fell to 3% in the following decade. It was claimed that the main culprit was the exponential increase in the international price of oil, which increased costs of production. However, the NICs, which were even more dependent on foreign oil than the US, not only grew far faster, but even accelerated their growth rates a little. [102]

In the 1990s, Germany had the slowest GDP growth figures in the second half of the 20th century, averaging just 1.6% annually. German economists blamed the poor performance on the high costs of the unification of the former East Germany and West Germany. Western Europe grew slowly in that decade and countries such as France and Italy grew by about 1.7% and 1.2% respectively. Since Germany was the largest economy in Europe and the most important trading partner for most countries in the region, economists in most countries blamed the slow growth on the situation in Germany. However, Luxembourg was one of the countries whose economy was most closely tied to Germany's; since the early 19th century it had maintained free trade agreements with the German States. In the 1990s, Luxembourg was tied to Germany more than France and Italy were. In spite of that, Germany's poor performance did not affect it — it grew by about 5.4%. Luxembourg's economy even accelerated relative to the 1980s. [103]

The evidence shows that the reason why France, Italy and several other countries in the region grew slowly was not Germany's poor performance. This was further confirmed by the case of Ireland, which grew by 7.9%. History shows that exogenous variables do not have a determinant or even an important effect on the performance of the economy.

---

101. Wade, Robert: *Governing the Market*, Princeton University Press, Princeton, 1990, p. 45-53, 96.

102. Bruno, M. & Sachs, J.: *Economics of Worldwide Stagflation*, Harvard University Press, Cambridge, Mass., 1985.

103. Eastern German's Slow Revival, *The Economist*, 27 May 2000, p. 31.

Democracy

Many social scientists have claimed that the political system has a significant effect on growth. Many have asserted that democracy facilitates growth because the freedom enjoyed by the population helps economic agents allocate their resources more rationally. Others have argued that an autocratic system is more effective because it brings order to the chaotic behavior of people. The problem with these ideas is that both fail to present a long-term cross-country correlation.

Those in favor of democracy have a hard time finding historical evidence to bolster their theory. Germany was autocratically ruled in 1880-99, while a hundred years later, in 1980-99, it was a very advanced democracy. In spite of that the economy grew by about 5% annually in the first period and by only 2% a century later. The US experience was similar; in the late 19th century women could not vote, African-Americans had few rights and there were numerous irregularities in the electoral process. Nonetheless, the economy grew more than twice as fast as it had done a century later when a full-fledged democracy was in place. [104]

The Soviet Union had a totalitarian system during 1920-39, but the economy grew by about 7%. In the 1990s, when Russia for the first time in its history practiced democracy, the economy collapsed and endured a terrible depression, averaging about -3%. The US was an advanced democracy by the late 20th century while China had one of the most authoritarian systems; yet China grew more than twice as fast in 1980-99. Switzerland had the most developed system of direct democracy by the 1990s while Vietnam was a communist autocracy. Vietnam grew about twelve times faster: Switzerland averaged 0.5%, Vietnam, 6.0%. [105]

Even over a long period of time the argument is incapable of presenting a consistent correlation. During the whole 20th century Hong Kong was not ruled democratically; it was ruled as a colony by a British governor named by the crown. Hong Kong's economy grew almost twice as fast the US's.

The arguments in favor of autocracy have also failed to find confirmation in fact. Most countries in the course of history have been autocratically ruled, at

---

104. Bushnell, David & Macaulay, Neill: *The Emergence of Latin America in the 19th century*, Oxford University Press, Oxford, 1988, p. 224-234.
105. Dobb, Maurice: *Soviet Economic Development since 1917*, Routledge, London, 1960, p. 106-288.

least up to the 18th century; and their economies remained perennially stagnant. Even in more recent times autocratic regimes were unable to attain fast growth on a sustained basis. Communist dictatorships grew rapidly at times, and at times they did not. The Soviet Union experienced a continuous deceleration since the 1960s, and in the 1980s it fell into stagnation. China grew slowly in the 1960s and 1970s, and Vietnam did likewise in the 1970s and 1980s. Non-communist dictatorships such as that of Khadafi in Libya during the 1970-99 period performed miserably, averaging negative GDP growth (-1.0%). Iraq also endured negative growth (-0.5%) in 1980-99 during the totalitarian rule of Saddam Hussein. Iran did only slightly better under the religious dictatorship of the mullahs during 1980-99, averaging about 2.2%. Strongman rule in numerous Sub-Saharan countries also coincided with dismal figures. In Zaire during 1970-99, the economy averaged negative growth (-1.0%) and Equatorial Guinea in 1970-89 contracted at about 0.5% per annum. [106]

In the 1990s, some sixteen studies were conducted to measure the link between political systems and economic growth. Three showed that the practice of democracy was marginally helpful for growth; three others favored autocracy; and ten found no conclusive results. These studies analyzed mostly the second half of the 20th century or parts of it, but their results matched what the preceding history of the world had shown. The type of political system is not a decisive factor in growth. [107]

History actually shows that the practice of a political system like democracy is an effect more than a cause of fast and sustained economic growth. For democracy to function adequately, the situation has to be reasonably stable and the population of a given nation must have a high level of tolerance for other people within the same nation with different views of the world. Tolerance on a sustained basis, however, is unlikely if levels of economic development are low. If a population or a large share of it must struggle for survival on a daily basis, the level of pain will be too high and people will instinctively search for scapegoats, and aggression between groups may arise. This will drive the government to acts of violent repression, inimical to democracy.

As the history of the 19th and above all the 20th century in Latin America, Asia, and Africa demonstrate, democratically-elected governments in countries where living conditions are poor have been unstable and vulnerable to over-

---

106. *The Middle East and North Africa 2002: Ibid.*
107. Measuring the Prince of Politics, *The Economist*, 27 January 1996, p. 78.

throw. The military and other groups that have overthrown civilian governments argue that they are motivated by the inability of the government to take the country out of poverty. Most coups have taken place where the economy had contracted, stagnated or grown slowly during the preceding years.

Argentina, for example, attained its independence in 1816 and immediately sought to establish a democratic system. However, stagnation had prevailed during colonial rule and in the decades after independence the economy only accelerated marginally. Coups, civil war, power struggles and autocratic governments characterized the first half of the 19th century. In the 1850s, the economy finally emerged out of stagnation and continuously accelerated its pace in the following decades. In the second half of the 19th century, Argentina had one of the fastest GDP growth rates in the world averaging about 4.3% annually. Germany, which had the fastest growth among the large nations of Europe, grew by just 3.9%. The exponential acceleration of the Argentinean economy since the 1850s coincided with the end of dictatorial government and in the following decades elections were regularly held. Although women were excluded from politics, voting among men was largely restricted to the wealthiest, and manipulations were frequent, the cause of democracy gained considerable ground in the second half of the 19th century. From 1900-29, economic growth averaged about 4% and democracy continued to strengthen as electoral fraud rapidly diminished. In the 1930s, however, Argentina was hit by the world crisis and GDP grew by just 1%. Unemployment and poverty rapidly increased, followed by urban violence and a military coup. In the decades that followed, the economy never regained the dynamism of the past. From the 1930s to the 1980s, the economy averaged only 1.5% growth and during that time the military were continuously involved in politics. Almost every time an elected government stumbled in the economic arena, urban revolts occurred, and the military overthrew the government. [108]

History also shows that even when circumstances call for autocratic rule, fast and sustained economic growth goes hand-in-hand with increased stability in the country, which allows the autocrat to progressively allow greater freedoms.

China saw its first democratically-elected government take office in the 1910s; but it failed in just a few years. The decades-long economic crisis and the international turmoil called for strong leadership. Chiang Kaishek ruled China

---

108. Ferns, H. S.: *Argentina*, Ernest Benn Ltd., London, 1969, p. 94-97.

autocratically during the 1930s and 1940s. The population was restless and violent. The leaders constantly had to confront a communist insurgency. After defeat and retreat to Taiwan, Chiang continued to rule autocratically. Even though he was never legitimized by an election, he became increasingly accepted and respected by the population in Taiwan during his quarter-century rule, which is credited with creating an average GDP growth rate of about 9% annually. As the situation in Taiwan stabilized, Chiang progressively liberalized the political system. When he died in 1975, his son endorsed a more enthusiastic political liberalization. In the meantime the economy continued to grow rapidly. When he died, in the late 1980s, the ruling party allowed democratic elections and other parties competed for a share of power. Since the early 1990s, democracy has been firmly established in Taiwan and has rapidly gained in strength. Mainland China, meanwhile, was far from endorsing a democratic system in the early 1980s, but China's rapid economic growth and stronger global position since then have allowed for a rapid easing of authoritarian rule.[109]

Corruption

Corruption has always been classified as affecting the economy negatively. Social scientists and economists agree that corruption is a hindrance for economic growth. Since the 1990s, the subject of corruption began to be touted as an important factor affecting development and the World Bank began to demand that governments reduce corruption if they wanted to receive loans and aid.

The argument might sound very reasonable, but the facts again do not substantiate the idea. In Libya during the 1960s for example, King Idris was an absolute ruler. His family and the most important members of his government indulged in one of the highest levels of corruption the world has ever seen, regularly negotiating bribes with foreign oil companies. In spite of that, the economy grew by 24% per year. It was largely the excessive corruption what drove Colonel Khadafi to overthrow the government in a coup in 1969. Contrary to most other military governments in Africa and in the rest of the world, Khadafi's rule from the 1970s to the 1990s was characterized by an absence of corruption.

---

109. Rawski, Thomas: *Economic Growth in Pre-War China*, University of California Press, US, 1989.

However, the economy in the 1970s averaged only 2% growth per year and in the following two decades the performance was even worse. [110]

Transparency International is a Berlin-based international organization that specializes in measuring levels of corruption worldwide, and it has systematically rated China as one of the most corrupt. Corruption during the 1980s was one of the reasons why students protested in Beijing at Tiananmen Square in 1989. Even so, the country attained one of the fastest GDP growth rates in the world, averaging in real terms more than 7% per year. During this same period the US was one of the least corrupt nations. It had a vast array of laws to regulate the conduct of public officials, supervised by a very strong and independent judicial system. Still, economic growth averaged less than 3%.

In the 1990s, Transparency International rated Ireland as one of the most corrupt nations in Western Europe. In spite of that, Ireland had by far the fastest GDP growth in the region, averaging about 8%. [111]

General Obiang seized power through a coup in Equatorial Guinea in 1979 and he has ruled autocratically since then. In the 1990s he and his family, his friends and high government officials had a monopoly over most of the economy. Corruption in this decade was perhaps the highest in the world. Several international organizations suspended their aid programs in protest. Even China compared favorably to Equatorial Guinea. Despite the abuses, Equatorial Guinea's GDP grew fastest in the world, averaging 18% annually. Switzerland, on the other hand, which is considered to have one of the most trustworthy and law-abiding bureaucracies in the world, did not average even 1%. [112]

In Japan, corruption was high in the 1950s but during the following decades it progressively declined. However, as it declined the economic growth lost speed. By the 1990s, at a time when Japan was experiencing the lowest level of corruption in perhaps all of its history, economic growth was at its slowest in the 20th century: growth averaged more than 9% in the 1950s and less than 2% in the 1990s. In Western Europe, corruption in the 1950s was not high by world standards, but it was much higher than in the 1990s. Corruption in this region progressively declined during the course of the second half of the 20th century, and during the same time period economic growth also declined. [113]

---

110. Cooley, John: *Libyan Sandstorm*, Holt-Rinehart and Winston, New York, 1982, 43-59.
111. To good to be true? *Time*, 20 May 2002, 31.
112. *The CIA Fact Book* — 2002, US.
113. Allen: *Ibid.*, p. 170-245.

In the late 19th century corruption in the US was rampant, while a century later it was far less prevalent. Even so, economic growth was more than twice as fast in the late 19th century. In Argentina corruption was much higher in the years 1880-99 than it was a century later, but in the late 19th century the economy grew about three times faster. [114]

Corruption is obviously not beneficial for a country, but the historical evidence conclusively demonstrates that economic growth is not determined by the presence or absence of corruption. The evidence also shows that it is growth that affects corruption. When there is fast growth, wages rise. As the wages in a country increase, those of government officials also rise and when they reach a relatively high level, public officials stop demanding bribes. That is one reason why developed countries have lower levels of petty corruption than developing nations, and why they all show a decrease in corruption as they emerge from poverty. History shows that some forms of corruption goes hand in hand with insufficient development and the best mechanism to eradicate it is fast and sustained economic growth.

Foreign Investment

Foreign investment has long been considered capable of affecting the performance of the economy. Economists and in particular those from the World Bank, the International Monetary Fund and the World Trade Organization believe that foreign investment considerably helps nations attain faster economic growth. Any inflow of foreign capital, even when it flows into real estate or the stock exchange, traditionally has been seen as positive. However, most of these experts say that the most useful form of foreign investment is when foreign companies invest their capital in long-term operations such as a hotel, a factory, a plantation, or a shopping mall. This type of investment, foreign direct investment (FDI), is said to be more helpful for developing nations because the foreign companies bring superior technology and better management practices as well as capital.

However, not all inflows of capital have proven useful. When large inflows of foreign capital are used to speculate in real estate, the exchange rate, or securities, they have repeatedly proved to have highly detrimental effects on the economy. In the 1990s, this became particularly noticeable as countries opened up their financial systems like never before. In very short periods of time large

114. Davis, Hughes & McDougall: *Ibid.*, p. 132-134.

amounts of capital flowed into the countries that liberalized, and this was followed by rampant speculation, financial crises and recession. Numerous developed, middle income and developing countries suffered. [115]

Even if only FDI is taken in consideration (although it has never been responsible for speculation and financial crises), it is still not possible to find a consistent correlation that can substantiate the economists' claims. China, for example, received on average about $2 billion annually in FDI during the 1980s, and the economy grew by about 7% in real terms. Many economists trying to make sense of that fact, given that China was one of the most regulated economies in the world, argued that the fast growth was largely the result of FDI. However, in the 1990s FDI increased massively — the country received about $20 billion per year; but the economy only accelerated a little to a rate of about 8%. The absence of a correlation was even more clearly observed in 2000-03, because FDI went up still more, averaging about $50 billion annually, and in this period the economy actually decelerated a little. It was evident that some other variable, yet to be identified, was responsible for China's fast growth. [116]

A more useful way of measuring the effect of FDI on growth is to consider the amount of foreign capital in proportion to the size of the population. In per capita terms China actually received very little FDI in the 1990s in comparison to Hong Kong, Mexico and many other countries. China, however, had a faster GDP growth. Hong Kong grew by 4% annually, Mexico by 3% and most developed countries, which were the largest recipients of FDI, grew by even less[117]

Also worth mentioning is the fact that the Soviet Union during the 1920s and 1930s had the fastest GDP rates in the world even though it received no FDI. In the 1990s, on the other hand, when Russia and the other fourteen nations that formed the USSR received more FDI than ever before, the economy of the fifteen republics went into recession and experienced the worst contraction of the country's history. [118]

The evidence clearly suggests that notwithstanding the numerous benefits of FDI, it is not the answer to economic growth.

---

115. Missing Pieces, *Far Eastern Economic Review*, 25 February 1999, p. 10.

116. Major, J. & Kane: *China Briefing 1987*, Westview Press, US, 1987.

117. Investing Abroad, *The Economist*, 26 October 1996, p. 140.

118. Nove, *An Economic History of the USSR*, Penguin Press, London, 1969, p. 18-50.

Female Emancipation

Since the beginning of recorded history women in all regions of the world have been relegated to a secondary status in society. For thousands of years, women were primarily expected to bear and rear children; their only other task was to cater to the needs of men, and their liberty was considerably restricted. Throughout most of history, as well, the world as a whole experienced relative economic stagnation. By the late 20th century, this situation still prevailed in many developing countries. Social scientists have claimed that by limiting women to household work, the economy is unable to maximize its resources and is thus hindered in its growth. Since the 1990s, the World Bank has increasingly endorsed this idea. [119]

The problem is that no correlation can be documented between female emancipation and fast economic growth. The fastest growing economies during the years 1950-99 were the United Arab Emirates and Qatar, even though women there were largely restricted to household activities. During this period those countries progressively granted more liberties to women, but even by the 1990s they still had fewer liberties than women in North America had in the early 20th century.

During the latter half of the 20th century the women who enjoyed the greatest liberty in the world and who were most engaged in non-household work were those of North America and Western Europe. Economic growth, however, averaged 3.8% and 4.0% respectively, while in the United Arab Emirates, Qatar, Kuwait and Bahrain the average was 8.7%. Women in Japan during this period operated under more constraints than those in the West; nevertheless, the Japanese economy grew by about 6.2%. Also worth mentioning, in the years 1950-99, the share of women in the workforce in Western Europe and Japan grew and liberties increased. However, the economy of both, instead of improving, progressively decelerated. [120]

History shows that female emancipation is not vital to economic growth. The evidence suggests that emancipation is an effect of growth. Nations where emancipation had gone the furthest by the early 2000s had enjoyed the fastest GDP rates in the world over the last two centuries. Even the Muslim countries

---

119. Wolpert, Stanley: *A New History of India*, Oxford University Press, New York, 1982, p. 153.
120. Yapp M. E.: *The Near East since the First World War — A History to 1995*, Longman, London, 1996.

mentioned above experienced dramatic progress relative to their situation in the mid 20th century. By the early 2000s, these were the wealthiest Middle East countries and they were also the Muslim countries that granted women the most liberties. Culture surely plays a role in the speed by which emancipation takes place, but the evidence suggests that the GDP growth rate is by far the most important variable. [121]

Worldwide, women began to enjoy more rights in the 19th century — just around the same time that the world economy experienced unusual growth. In the 18th century, the world economy is understood to have averaged about 0.2% per year while in the 19th century the rate was of about 1.2%. However, female emancipation saw considerable progress in just a few nations, and those happen to be the countries that had the fastest economic growth (West European and North American countries as well as Japan, Australia, Argentina, New Zealand and a few others). In the 20th century the situation of women worldwide improved more than in any previous century, progressing in step with an unprecedented GDP growth rate. The world economy expanded at an average of about 3.0%. [122]

The record shows that the situation of women does not improve with the enactment of laws that guarantee them a quota of jobs or political posts. Nor does it improve with education campaigns that preach new values to men. The facts show that fast and sustained economic growth is the only effective mechanism for improving the living conditions of the female population of a nation.[123]

The faster the GDP grows, the sooner a population attains comfortable living conditions. People are less desperate and more liberal. In the opposite case, when men suffer poverty and unemployment, they often take it out on women. Studies show that in developed and developing nations, the women who are married or related to the men with the lowest incomes endure the most physical abuse. As a rule, unemployed men tend to beat and even murder their women much more often than their full-time employed counterparts. [124]

Economic growth tends to be accompanied by technological development. The faster the GDP goes up, the faster the growth of technology and the spread of science. The higher a nation's level of economic development, the higher the

---

121. Looking Bold and Talking Big, *The Economist*, 10 November 2001, p. 45.

122. Berghahn: *Ibid.*, p. 14-27.

123. Frankfurter Allgemeine, *Bundesregierung will Frauen vor Gewalt schützen*, 17 März 2000, p. 1.

124. The Battle of the Belly-Button, *The Economist*, 24 September 1994, p. 69.

level of education. If we accept the notion that ideology is every idea that is not scientifically substantiated, and education is the learning of science, when a population attains a high level of education, ideology loses its grip. Many ideas that through history were used to justify the second-class status of women had no scientific basis; therefore, as a nation increases its level of development, the traditions and religious strictures that were used to limit women's roles are weakened and challenged by new perspectives. [125]

Business Performance

The business psychology prevailing at any given moment is also thought to have an impact on the economy. Experts have claimed that when the majority of the businessmen in a country are "in the mood" to invest and expand, growth is the result. When they are less optimistic, stagnation or recession takes place. This manic-depressive idea has mostly been used to explain short-term fluctuations of the economy, but it has also been used to explain the long-term performance of the economy and has been linked to cultural variables such as entrepreneurial drive. It is thus argued that the businessmen from certain countries have as a permanent characteristic a higher propensity for saving and investment as well as for risk-taking.

Such an argument is easily refuted because, if the businessmen of a country characteristically possessed entrepreneurial drive, such enterprising and investment-prone energy would deliver regular behavior and the GDP figures would reflect that. From the 16th to the 18th centuries, for example, it was claimed that the British were more entrepreneurial than their counterparts in the rest of Europe and the world. However, by the late 19th century a growing number of thinkers began to claim that the commercial class in North America, several countries of continental Europe, and Oceania showed higher levels of business energy. In the 20th century this idea gained even more sympathizers. If entrepreneurialism were so closely bound to the nature of a nation, it is unlikely that it could be present one year and gone the next. [126]

Similar situations are observed in other regions. Up to the early 19th century, German intellectuals and foreigners as well had claimed that German businessmen lacked entrepreneurial drive and were risk-averse. However, since

125. America's New Growth Economy, *Businessweek International*, 16 May 1994, 45.
126. Bagwell, Philip & Mingay, G.: *Britain and America 1850-1939*, Routledge Kegan Paul Ltd., London, 1970, p. 1-40, 249, 257.

the latter part of that century the argument was overturned and it was asserted that Germans were more driven to business and invention than the populace of most countries in Europe and the world. For most of the 20th century, most people continued to see Germans in that light, but in the last decades of the century and in the early 2000s that view was revised, and it was even asserted that the Germans had become "lazy." [127]

Up to the early 19th century nobody spoke of Americans as creative and innovative in business and science. However, since the middle of the century, the country began to enjoy a reputation for men who could develop better business ideas and who were rational risk-takers. In the 1930s, all of a sudden, economists claimed that Americans had lost their entrepreneurialism; then, from the 1940s to the 1960s, it was back. In the 1970s and in particular the 1980s, the hard-driven and imaginative businessmen once again disappeared and analysts claimed that Americans had somehow lost their edge. [128]

Up to the late 19th century Western thinkers thought that East Asians lacked drive, inventiveness and creativity. Since then, however, the Japanese are no longer seen as lacking drive; but that opinion still touched businessmen from the rest of the region. Since the 1950s, there was an impressive burst of business activity in economies such as Hong Kong and Taiwan. In the decades that followed, a growing number of countries in the region saw a massive multiplication of business activity. Academics began to claim that the region was endowed with highly motivated businessmen and such high business energy was the result of culture. Interestingly enough, in the 1990s, it was claimed that the Japanese had lost their drive. [129]

How can erratic performance on a national scale be squared with the fact that people who possess mental energy and a propensity for work maintain those qualities throughout their whole life? The abrupt changes observed through history suggest that this variable has not been a telling factor in growth.

In the cases mentioned, the periods when scholars claimed that a population was endowed with entrepreneurial drive tended to coincide with fast economic growth or with faster growth than in all or most other nations. Then,

---

127. Bramsted: *Ibid.*, p. 122-124.
128. Bogart Ernest & Kemmerer, Donald: *Economic History of the American People*, Longmans Green & Co., New York, 1947, p. 474.
129. Hopkins, Keith (ed): *Hong Kong — The Industrial Colony*, Oxford University Press, London, 1971, p. 2-13.

during a period of stagnation or lower GDP growth, they asserted that the population no longer excelled in those qualities.

Britain, for example, grew faster than other nations from the 16th to the
18th century. In the 19th century its rate of growth accelerated, but several countries grew faster and by the later part of the century the growth gap had become
very large. In the 20th century, Britain grew at an unprecedented pace, but more
countries grew even faster.

In the US a parallel is also observed. The economy grew faster than any
other in the 19th century. In the 1930s, it stagnated and grew slower than many
others. From the 1940s to the 1960s, the economy once again grew rapidly, but in
the following decades it considerably decelerated. Worse still, in this last period
US growth rates were much slower than those of many of its competitors. [130]

In Germany the economy grew slower than most nations in Western
Europe up to the early 19th century, but after the Napoleonic Wars German governments began to enthusiastically promote railroads and manufacturing. The
economy accelerated considerably and it progressively gained in speed, eventually growing faster than the majority of European countries. GDP growth rates
remained higher than most of its neighbors until the 1950s, and in the following
decade they began to decelerate. By the late 20th century and early 2000s, GDP
rates were not only weak, they were slower than many others. [131]

The Japanese economy began to grow faster than most Western nations' in
the late 19th century, and during practically the whole 20th century GDP rates
retained their faster pace. In the 1990s, however, not only were its rates the
slowest in the 20th century, they were also lower than those of the majority of
developed countries and much lower than several of its Asian neighbors.

East Asia as a region also presents a parallel between growth and entrepreneurialism. The region was largely stagnant until the 1940s, but since the 1950s it
began to grow faster than any other region in the world. [132]

History suggests that the superior business qualities of a population have
been an effect, more than a cause, of growth. When a nation has attained fast
growth and in particular the fastest in the world, it soon tends to possess the
largest enterprises and the most advanced technology. Since these firms tend to
have the best technology, they outperform all others. This drives the rest of the

130. Kolko: *Ibid.*, p. 311-314.
131. Kitchen, Martin: *The Political Economy of Germany 1815-1914*, McGill-Queen's University
    Press, Montreal, 1978, p. 45-184.
132. Vogel, Erza: *Japan as No. 1*, Harvard University Press, Cambridge, Mass., 1979.

world to admire those businesses and to believe that the men managing them are responsible for the success. Thus, when the economy deteriorates and other countries achieve faster growth rates, the quality of the country's goods deteriorates and they are less capable of competing. Slower GDP growth figures translate into a slower pace of technological development, and all of a sudden those companies and those businessmen lose their luster even though their abilities have not changed.

History substantiates such a thesis. The empirical evidence shows that the faster the rate of economic growth, the larger the profit margins of companies and the faster the growth of sales. Over the centuries, the sales and profit possibilities of enterprises all over the world have correlated with the rate of economic growth. During periods of fast growth, bankruptcies are rare but during periods of slow growth, stagnation or recession, they multiplied.

In the late 19th century, companies, entrepreneurs and multimillionaires mushroomed in the future OECD countries and that correlated with unprecedented rates of economic growth. In the US, big new enterprises appeared on the scene and millionaires such as Morgan, Rockefeller, Vanderbilt and Carnegie cropped up; and the US attained the fastest GDP growth in the world. The US economy during the years 1870-99 grew on average by more than 7% annually. Yet, in the 1930s, American firms went bankrupt in larger numbers during an almost stagnant economy that averaged less than 1% growth. In Japan in that same decade business flourished, coalescing with an economic growth of more than 5%. [133]

During 1950-69, OECD countries attained an average rate of growth of about 5.4%. Profit margins as a share of GDP for the enterprises from these countries were about 10%. In 1980-99, the economy of these countries grew by half that, about 2.7%, and profit margins accounted only for about 4% of GDP. Sales grew much faster in the first period.

By 2000 there were more US$ billionaires in Hong Kong as a share of the total population than anywhere else in the world; this followed fifty years of unprecedented business activity. During 1950-99, companies in Hong Kong had flourished and grown faster than anywhere else in East Asia, coincidental with the fastest rates of economic growth in the region. Many economists argued that this resulted from the very liberal market policies endorsed by the colonial authorities and by the entrepreneurial bent of the population. However, a

---

133. Boulding: *Ibid.*, p. 207-209.

century earlier Hong Kong was also under British colonial rule and the same free trade and free market policies applied. The culture was also the same; but at that time business activity was stagnant. Economic growth was about 1% annually during the years 1850-99 and 9% a century later. [134]

It is interesting to note that in the 1990s and early 2000s, sales and profit margins were more attractive in China than in Hong Kong, even though China was a communist-ruled country and had one of the most regulated economies, while Hong Kong had one of the most market-driven and business-friendly economies in the world. China's GDP growth rate was more than twice that of Hong Kong. Increasingly, Hong Kong entrepreneurs preferred China as an investment destination.

Among OECD countries, the US was the most market-driven and business-friendly in the 1990s and early 2000s. In spite of that, American firms performed better in China than in the US. It was easier to make a profit in China than in the US. In this decade the bankruptcy rate in the US was dramatically higher than in China; and the GDP rate in the US was a fraction of that in China.[135]

No doubt knowledge of product development, marketing, financing, accounting, human resources, business law and good instincts are useful tools for the management of an enterprise, but history shows that the most important factor in business success is a fast rate of economic growth. That is why reputed and well-established companies in North America and Western Europe witnessed a constant loss of market share to the new comers from East Asia during the second half of the 20th century. First it was the Japanese; then it was the businessmen from the NICs; and finally it was the Chinese that outperformed Europeans and Americans. The businessmen in these Asian countries little understood how world markets functioned when they first decided to fight for market share. Japan, for example, was a militaristic inward-looking economy up to the 1940s. Hong Kong and Singapore were mostly trading posts, while Korea and Taiwan were largely agricultural. China was in an even worse situation because it had a centrally-planned economy, where market forces were not considered, even up to the 1970s. Regardless — they all systematically defeated the best from the West and grabbed market share throughout the world. Worse

---

134. *Trade Policy Review — Hong Kong* Vol. I, GATT, Geneva, 1994.
135. A Survey of China, *The Economist*, 15 June 2002.

still, they even took market share in the home markets of IBM, General Motors, Siemens, General Electric, Renault, Phillips and Volkswagen. [136]

The common denominator in all of these cases is that these East Asian economies grew much faster than those of the West. While North America and Western Europe grew on average by about 4% during the second half of the 20th century, the East Asian nations cited expanded at twice that pace. China for example grew rapidly since the 1980s and exported at such an impressive speed that practically every developed and developing country complained that Chinese firms were making their domestic producers lose market share or go bankrupt. The case of China made clear the impressive causal relationship between fast growth and good business performance, because during the late 20th century most Chinese firms were in state hands. Communist-trained bureaucrats managed these enterprises and they knew hardly anything about Western professional management techniques. Nevertheless, they basically out-performed the whole world. [137]

Japan had by far the fastest rate of economic growth among developed nations during 1950-89, and Japanese companies systematically outperformed their Western competitors. American and European businessmen by the 1980s were convinced that Japanese businessmen were superior and actually invin-cible. In the 1990s, however, Japan had a slower rate of growth than most of the nations in North America and Western Europe and all of a sudden Toyota, Sony, Mitsubishi and Matsushita were no longer so impressive. Japan averaged a growth of 1.5% per year while the US grew by 2.9% and Western Europe by 2.6%. Japanese companies were no longer gaining market share and were actually losing it, even in their home market. Up to the 1980s, Japanese firms had been acquiring Western companies, but in the 1990s Western companies were buying up ailing Japanese firms. [138]

Bank Performance

Different economists accord different weight to the impact of the financial system on economic growth, but they generally believe it has considerable importance, for they believe capital plays a fundamental role in the economy. That is why they have regularly advised governments to stimulate the devel-

---

136. Private Sector Makes Jobs, *Far Eastern Economic Review*, 16 May 2002, p. 24.
137. Stealing the Land, *Far Eastern Economic Review*, 7 February 2002, p. 56.
138. Nafziger, Wayne: *Learning from the Japanese*, M.E. Sharpe Inc., New York, 1995.

opment of banks. They maintain that an efficient and developed financial system is more capable of providing companies with funds.

This idea, however, is as flawed as the others. By the 1970s, for example, China had one of the most inefficient and primitive financial systems in the world. That did not change much, in the following two decades, because all the banks remained in state hands, foreign banks were not allowed in the country, and there was very little competition among Chinese banks. Also, by 1980 China's banks had little in the way of assets. In spite of that China, attained one of the fastest GDP growth rates in the world in 1980-99. China grew almost three times as fast as North America and Western Europe — even though the countries in these regions had the most efficient and developed financial systems in the world. [139]

Western Europe and Japan experienced a progressive development of their financial systems during the course of the second half of the 20th century because banks and other financial institutions progressively became larger and were exposed to more competition. However, instead of accelerating, the economy of these countries progressively lost ground.

In the US and in Argentina, the financial systems in the second half of the 19th century were extremely underdeveloped and inefficient compared to those of a century later. Still, their economies grew twice as fast in 1850-99 as in 1950-99. In the US, growth was about 6.3% in the second half of the 19th century and 3.4% a century later, while in Argentina the respective figures were 4.3% and 2.0%. [140]

In Russia, all the banks and other financial institutions were nationalized in the early 1920s and from then on operated under a centrally-planned system. They became terribly inefficient and all financial linkages with the rest of the world were cut. Yet, the economy grew spectacularly in the years 1920-39. During this period the Soviet economy grew faster than any other nation in the world, even though so many of them had more efficient financial systems. In real terms, the Soviet Union grew about three times faster than the US. [141]

In the 1950s, Libya had one of the most underdeveloped banking systems in the world, but that was not a hindrance to the vast investments that were made in the following decade, which delivered an economic growth of about

139. Building a Wall or a Bridge? *Far Eastern Economic Review*, 7 February 2002, p. 30.
140. San Martino, Ma. Laura: *Argentina Contemporànea — de Peron a Menem*, Ediciones Ciudad Argentina, Buenos Aires, 1996, p. 876-1333.
141. Campbell, Robert: *Soviet Economic Power*, Macmillan & Co., London, 1967, p. 112-123.

24% per year. The US, which had the largest gold reserves in the world, grew by just 4% in that decade. In the 1960s, Botswana had one of the least developed financial systems in Africa and lacked any serious capital. In spite of that the economy grew by about 15% in the following decade. The US, which had the largest amount of capital and the most efficient banks, grew by just 3% in the 1970s. By the 1980s the banks in Equatorial Guinea were among the least efficient and the poorest in Africa. In spite of that, gigantic investments were made in the following decade and the economy grew by 18%. Japan, which had the largest foreign exchange reserves in the world in the 1990s, grew by less than 2%.[142]

History shows that an efficient financial system or banks with an abundance of capital are not essential to rapid growth. Growth is not determined by the financial system; GDP growth determines the performance of banks. That helps explain why, in countries that have experienced fast economic growth, banks have generally attained positive results and when stagnation prevails, bank failures have multiplied. Under a weak economy, bank customers may go bankrupt or become unemployed; banks inevitably experience a deterioration of their balance sheets, as these cannot repay their debts. Insurance companies undergo a similar situation in a weak economy as businesses and consumers buy fewer insurance policies. History shows that competition helps keep a financial system efficient, but that alone is not what brings prosperity.

Banks and other financial institutions are sometimes seen as a world apart from the rest of the economy because they have numerous characteristics and practices that distinguish them from the standard behavior of other enterprises. However, on matters relating to growth they react in exactly the same way as service companies, construction ventures, primary sector enterprises or manufacturing firms. It is fundamentally the rate of economic growth that determines the performance of banks.

In the US, banks increased their assets and their profits tremendously from 1870 to 1910. This was a time of stunning economic growth, which averaged about 7% per year. In the following two decades the economy slowed to a rate half as fast and the share of non-performing loans increased, assets grew at a slower pace, and profits were smaller. In the 1930s, the economy stagnated, with a rate of less than 1% growth, and non-performing loans increased considerably. Bank failures did likewise and more banks went bankrupt than in all of the pre-

---

142. Carter & O'Meara: *Ibid.*, p. 242.

ceding history of the country. During 1940-69, the US economy recovered and averaged a growth rate of almost 5% annually. Banks improved their balance sheets. Then, during the period 1970-99, the economy decelerated to a rate of less than 3% growth and non-performing loans went up again, while profits were lower than in the previous three decades. In the 1980s, more banks failed than in any other decade since the 1940s, and the 1980s saw the slowest GDP figures since the 1940s. [143]

In the 1990s, Eastern and Central Europe returned to a capitalist mode of production. State banks were privatized *en masse* and numerous private banks were founded. However, almost as fast as they were created, they also collapsed. Thousands of banks in Russia, in the former Soviet republics, and in central Europe went bankrupt — coinciding with the worst recession in the region's history. [144]

Most economists argued that this situation resulted from the inexperience of the new bankers, who had no knowledge of competitive financial markets. That argument, however, could not explain why the banks in China and Vietnam did not experience similar problems. Bank assets actually grew very rapidly in these communist countries. Yet, those East Asian bankers were even more ignorant concerning competitive financial markets because banks were only modestly liberalized and none was privatized. But this was a time of rapid economic growth in China and Vietnam, which in the 1990s averaged about 8% and 6% respectively. [145]

Another illustration is Japan. Japanese bank assets grew relentlessly after World War II. In the four decades since the end of the war, assets of Japanese banks grew so fast that by the late 1980s they were larger than those of the US, even though Japan had a population half as large. That was matched by a GDP that grew more than twice as fast as in the US. In the 1990s, that fast growth came to an end and the Japanese economy slowed to a rate of 1.5%. Suddenly, bank assets began to shrink relative to those of the US (which grew at double that speed). Problems multiplied. In the 1980s, when the economy had averaged a rate of 4.0%, non-performing loans in Japan accounted for about 2% of GDP, but in the 1990s, they accounted for about 8%. [146]

---

143. Kolko: *Ibid.*, p. 2-35.

144. Another Russian Shortage, *Businessweek International*, 27 February 1995, p. 19.

145. The New Spendthrifts, *The Economist*, 20 April 2002, p. 73.

146. Tsuru, Shigeto: *Japan's Capitalism*, Cambridge University Press, Cambridge, 1993, p. 104-129.

Environmental Protection

The protection of the environment is a new concept, which gained a following only in the second half of the 20th century. Since its birth, however, politicians have pondered its cost and economists have lucubrated over its effect on growth. Most have associated the high costs of reducing pollution and protecting ecosystems as a variable that delivers a limiting effect on growth as it reduces capital available for investment in productive activities.

The main reason why the environmental movement has achieved only a fraction of its goals during the last decades is that governments see such investments as growth-hindering. Most governments are convinced that the measures demanded by the "Green" lobby will hurt the performance of the economy and jobs will be lost. Since unemployment and underemployment in OECD countries increased in the late 20th century, governments have become increasingly fearful of anything that might aggravate the situation. The Conference on Global Warming in the Netherlands in the early 2000s failed because the Bush Administration refused to sign onto an agreement that might jeopardize the fast economic growth enjoyed in the preceding years in the US. [147]

However, the empirical evidence suggests the fear is misplaced. Singapore, for example, made impressive progress during the 1990s with a major river clean up and other projects relating to the protection of the environment. Regulations in the island multiplied, approaching levels similar to those in Western Europe, but Singapore achieved impressive rates of economic growth. GDP averaged about 8% annually, about three times the rate of Western Europe. The evidence suggests that growing environmental regulations were not the reason why the West grew slowly and unemployment increased since the 1970s. [148]

This was further confirmed by Ireland, which also implemented new environmental protecting regulations in the 1990s, but went on to grow by about 8% per year. The case of Ireland also debunked the argument claiming that because of differences in culture and geographic location, Singapore was less affected by environmental regulations. [149]

The business community has tended to associate efforts to halt environmental degradation as having a negative effect on their profit margins. Studies nonetheless show that, in the long term, enterprises that significantly invest in

---

147. State of the Planet, *National Geographic,* September 2002, 108.
148. Winds of Change, *Fortune,* 19 March 2001, p. 30-40.
149. Irish Eyes are Smiling, *Time,* 29 November 1999, p. 46.

making environmentally-friendly goods achieve greater sales due to consumer awareness of their ecologically-correct efforts. However, the large majority of enterprises in developed countries in the early 2000s remained unconvinced by such arguments; they are under constant short-term pressures from stock markets and other forces, and the long-term benefits to their balance sheets from environmentally-correct efforts were small and far from guaranteed.

The facts show that the most effective way to improve the profitability of the enterprises of a country is through fast economic growth. Environmental protection does not hinder growth; that means that countries with a clear understanding of the causes growth can attain high profits for their firms while simultaneously endorsing a very enthusiastic environmental protection policy.

Effective protection of the environment is largely dependent on advanced technology to reduce pollution and restore ecosystems. History shows that the rate of technological development is not fixed; it fluctuates. And, it runs in parallel with the rate of economic growth. During the 20th century the world as a whole made more technological progress than during the preceding 100,000 years of human history. At the same time, the economic growth was significantly faster than ever before. That means that with a clear understanding of the causes of growth, countries could considerably accelerate their GDP rates and thus accelerate the rate of technological development, which would increase the pace by which environmental protection technology appears.

Environmental Sustainability in the Developing World

In the 2000s, about four-fifths of the world population live in countries that are not developed, and which have the fastest rates of population growth. The vast bulk of the pollution worldwide was caused by countries that are already developed. Since developing countries all want to attain the levels of development of OECD countries, it is feared that they will cause irreparable damage to the environment. The fast population growth in those countries only makes matters worse, it is thought. Many see the demographic pressure as the largest long-term threat to the environment. [150]

Events of the 20th century show that the higher a nation's level of economic development, the lower its birthrate tends to be. That means that fast economic growth is the best mechanism for reducing the rate of population growth

---

150. The Next Bottom Line, *Businessweek*, 3 May 1999.

in developing countries; and thus is the most effective way to reduce the demographic pressure on the environment.

Developing countries, in particular those situated in warm climate zones, are hosts to the tropical forests of the world. These forests are particularly important for maintaining the stability of the world climate, as well as providing a home for the largest diversity of plants and animals. At present most governments in emerging economies believe they are better endowed for producing primary sector goods, and they therefore concentrate their production efforts on this sector. Rapid deforestation due to intensive wood production and the clearing of land for agriculture is the result. In Sub-Saharan Africa, for example, during 1970-99, about a quarter of the region's forests disappeared, but the rate of economic growth was slow and averaged just 2% per year. Since the population grew faster (almost 3%), per capita incomes fell. Major ecological damage was sustained and poverty actually increased (the worst of possible worlds). [151]

By the early 2000s, the variables that cause economic growth were still unknown but it was evident that agriculture and forestry were not among them. The vast majority of countries that attained fast growth during the 1800-2000 period did so while shifting investment priority from agriculture to other sectors. That suggests that fast economic growth in Sub-Saharan Africa, Latin America, Southeast Asia and South Asia, which contain the tropical forests of the world, might be attained by shifting their policies from the exploitation of agriculture and forestry to other endeavors, perhaps including the establishment of national parks in those areas, freeing them from depredation.

The rate of economic growth is fundamentally responsible for determining the rate of rural-urban migration. The faster the economic growth, the faster is the flow of peasants to the cities. Nations do not need to keep a large share of their populations in rural areas. By 2000, in nations like the US, Luxembourg and even Taiwan only 1% of their respective populations lived in rural areas and the national living standards were among the highest in the world. Fast economic growth would rapidly transfer the populations in developing countries to the cities, creating the possibility of halting the destruction of forests by poor rural dwellers who clear land for agriculture. [152]

---

151. What if the Forests were Silent, *Businessweek*, 30 August 1999, p. 102.
152. Condition Critical — How to save the earth, *Time* (special edition), April-May 2000, p. 20.

The World Economic Forum (WEF) introduced the Environmental Sustainability Index in the early 2000s; and it was the countries that were most advanced that were listed as taking better care of the environment. When nations are poor, protecting ecosystems or endangered species cannot be a priority. The environment can only be cared for when the population is secure from disease and hunger, when nations have overcome poverty and the general population is no longer fighting for survival. Fast economic growth is the only means to reach a developed stage. [153]

It has been argued that if India or other large but less-developed nations were to attain the level of development of the US, world pollution would increase to intolerable levels. The idea of putting one billion new cars on the road certainly gives one pause. However, when we consider the technological possibilities that emerged in the last decades, it becomes evident that technology can generate new ways to reduce pollution. During the second half of the last century, inventions such as scrubbers, electrostatic precipitators, incinerators, catalytic converters, recycling plants, solar energy generating-machines, wind energy generating-equipment and chlorofluorocarbon substitutes reduced the rate of environmental degradation and in several cases they even reversed the damage. OECD countries were as a matter of fact considerably less polluted in the 1990s than they were in the 1950s. A variety of non-polluting automobiles have been developed, and if concern over pollution outweighs other priorities, the way will be found to bring them to market. [154]

Fast economic growth in developing countries and, more particularly, faster growth than that of developed countries, such as in China since the 1980s, would eventually transform these countries into technology producers. History shows that when nations that are lagging technologically grow faster than the most developed countries, over sustained periods, they eventually catch up with the most advanced. The US, for example, lagged behind Western Europe up to the 18th century but in the 19th century it grew faster than any European country. In the early 19th century, it was still almost completely dependent on imported technology but due to fast growth, it imported technology at a fast pace and rapidly increased the educational level of the population. Eventually, a significant share of the population had some scientific knowledge, and they

---

153. Green and Growing, *The Economist*, 27 January 2001, p. 86.
154. Garbage Gap Alert, *Newsweek*, 28 October 1996, p. 17.

began to create their own technology. By the end of the 19th century, the US was creating technology at a faster pace than any European country.

Japan did the same; it was almost totally dependent on technology imports in the 1950s. However, since it grew much faster than North America and Western Europe in the post-war decades, by the 1970s it had caught up and in the following decade it surpassed them. In the 1980s, patents were registered in Japan at a faster pace than elsewhere. As a result, by the late 20th century Japan began to develop environmental protecting technology. Japanese companies were the first to introduce electric automobiles that are competitive in price and features with oil-powered vehicles. [155]

Very fast economic growth in developing countries would soon convert these nations into creators of technology, and thus they would contribute to developing new technology to reverse pollution and climate change.

SCHOOLS OF ECONOMIC THOUGHT

Economic growth is a pre-requisite for better protection of the environment, profitable business performance, decreasing corruption, for progress in the treatment of women, better income distribution, the development of democracy, the reduction of violence, amelioration of unemployment and the elimination of poverty. Figuring out what are the variables that determine economic growth must be the top priority of society. That is why numerous scholars have devoted themselves to analyzing the causes of growth. They have developed ideas and presented variables, such as those mentioned above, as fundamental or important factors for growth. Those ideas that were more systematically developed and which attracted the most sympathizers evolved into schools of thought.

Throughout history, a number of schools have claimed to hold the key to fast growth. Mercantilism, physiocratism, liberalism, Marxism, Keynesianism, import-substitution, neo-mercantilism, and mainstream economics have all claimed to have a solution to the fundamental problems of society. In the following pages the most relevant schools will be analyzed.

---

155. Fertilizing the Sea, *Scientific American*, April 1998, p. 24.

Mercantilism

The mercantilist school of thought made its appearance in the 16th century in Western Europe. It was largely driven by the discovery of the American continents and the vast amounts of precious metals that were extracted, which mostly accrued to Spain. For thousands of years precious metals, especially gold and silver, had represented wealth. [156]

The Treaty of Tordesillas in 1494 barred European nations (with the exception of Spain and Portugal) from the Americas. Some West European nations began to think about ways to capture the precious metals of those continents. In an era when extreme poverty was common, violence was, too. Several governments promoted piracy in order to steal the silver from Spanish ships. England excelled in it. [157]

That, however, allowed for the acquisition of only a minor share of the precious metals and some nations, such as the Netherlands, were not large enough to confront the power of Spain. Dutch strategists therefore devised a mechanism that would allow the Netherlands to acquire more bullion without resorting to violence. They realized that by exporting to Spain substantially more goods than Spain sold to the Netherlands, the Dutch would end up with a large trade surplus and the surplus would have to be covered with gold and silver. The Dutch government began to promote exports and, indeed, it soon succeeded in developing a large trade surplus with Spain and thus it acquired a large cache of precious metals. [158]

Mercantilism was the policy of attaining the largest possible trade surplus; governments that practiced it tried to promote exports while blocking imports. Inspired by the success of the Netherlands (not only in accumulating precious metals but also in attaining faster economic growth than anyone else), many Western European nations began to endorse similar policies. In the mid 17th century, the English government promoted a similar policy and immediately achieved much faster economic growth and brought in more precious metals. This incited other countries to follow. Mercantilism remained one of London's principal macroeconomic policies until the mid 19th century. Most of continental Europe promoted similar policies until the early 20th century. [159]

---

156. Blaug, Mark: *La Pensée économique, Economica*, Paris, 1996, p. 13-31.
157. Hudson, Rex (ed): *Brazil — A Country Study*, Library of Congress, Washington D. C., 1998, p. xxvii.
158. Furtado, Celso: *La Formation Economique du Bresil*, Publisud, France, 1998, p. 12-23.

In most other regions of the world mercantilism was practiced in a less methodical way but it was endorsed at the top. In China, for example, there were some mercantilist efforts during the Song dynasty in the eleventh and twelfth centuries, during the Ming dynasty in the 15th and 16th centuries, and under the Manchu dynasty in the 18th and 19th centuries. During most of the time that mercantilism was practiced in Europe or elsewhere, rates of economic growth were stagnant or quasi-stagnant. Only occasionally did such a policy coincide with fast economic growth. The historical evidence suggests that creating trade surpluses and accumulating precious metals are not fundamental or even important for the well being of a nation. Mercantilism was certainly not the worst of possible macroeconomic policies; but it was incapable of providing nations with what they wanted.

Physiocratism

The physiocratic school was born as a reaction to mercantilism and in particular to France's mercantilist policies in the 17th century. The goal of mercantilism was to export as much as possible, but primary goods such as agricultural goods, minerals, wood and fish were hard to export. For one thing, the small ships of those days could only transport small amounts of goods with a high weight and volume, and primary goods tend to be heavy and bulky. And further, many of these goods were highly perishable; they would decompose in a relatively short period of time. Since sea vessels traveled slowly, perishable goods were difficult to transport. The goods that were easier to export were manufactured products, like textiles, which were relatively low in weight and had a very long life span. Such "value-added" goods could also command higher prices than primary goods. As a result, mercantilism drove governments to promote manufacturing and to de-emphasize support for agriculture and other primary activities. [160]

This was a major change in policy. Since the beginning of recorded history, some 5,000 years ago, most of the world had constantly struggled with a scarcity of food. Food production in per capita terms was low and famines, hunger, and malnutrition regularly ravaged populations in different regions. Leaders thus focused on increasing the food supply and practically all the food came from agriculture. The economic advisors of the time concluded that the fundamental

---

159. Blaug: *Ibid.*
160. *Ibid.*, p. 32-40.

source of wealth was agriculture, and they classified it as the only real productive activity. For thousands of years, the promotion of agriculture was most governments' only real growth strategy. The fact that the economy basically remained stagnant, and famines continued to prevail demonstrates that the policy of investing in agriculture alone was a fiasco. [161]

When West European governments in the 16th and 17th centuries began to shift resources from agriculture to manufacturing, for the promotion of exports, the economy accelerated its pace considerably and the incidence of famines decreased. This success is what drove an ever-larger amount of nations to endorse mercantilism. However, it was a relatively small improvement because famines and malnutrition continued to beset Western Europe until the 19th century.

The shift in resources to the detriment of agriculture was not large, but it marked a clear change in policies. Since living conditions only improved by a small amount and were not clearly perceptible, many French thinkers in the 17th century concluded that the neglect of agriculture was a terrible mistake. The neglect of agriculture was more pronounced during the reign of Louis XIV, and it galvanized the theoreticians to formalize in a structured way the policies that for millennia had given priority to agriculture. [162]

The idea that agriculture was fundamental or at least very important for the well being of a nation continued to be popular with economists and policy-makers until the early 20th century in the future OECD countries. In most other nations of the world, it was still prevalent in the 2000s. [163]

Throughout history, the endorsement of physiocratism coincided with stagnation. At times, when it was only partially endorsed and not all resources were allocated to agriculture, it coincided with rates that were not stagnant, but never did such a policy give rise to or even coincide with fast and sustained economic growth. Worse still, whenever governments increased budgetary allocations for agriculture and reduced taxes on farming, the economy usually deteriorated.

---

161. Clough, S. B.: *Grandeur et Décadence des Civilisations*, Payot, Paris, 1954.
162. Keller, Henry: *Labour, Science and Technology in France 1500-1620*, Cambridge University Press, Cambridge, 1996, p. 64-90.
163. Cameron, Rondo (ed): *Essays in French Economic History*, Richard D. Irwin, Homewood-Illinois, 1970, p. 130-178.

Liberalism

The Scottish economist Adam Smith invented Liberalism in the late 18th century. He claimed that the best economic performance was attained when governments allowed market forces to operate undisturbed. According to him market distortions, such as the trade barriers and the export subsidies that supported mercantilism, hampered efficiency and translated into a lower rate of economic growth. Government subsidies to agriculture in support of physiocratic ideas were also policy errors that hampered progress. The best policy for governments was simply to do nothing, he said, for all government intervention disturbed the forces of supply and demand. For him, markets were much better at allocating resources than government officials, and appropriate allocation of resources was essential for increasing efficiency, which was essential for economic growth. [164]

Smith's ideas ultimately carried the day, and its proponents significantly influenced macroeconomic policies in the 19th and 20th century. The economy in the vast majority of countries of the world accelerated considerably in the 19th century and in the following century GDP figures accelerated even more. However, there is little confirmation that it was the policies that emanated from Smith's ideas that delivered the faster rates of growth.

Export subsidies actually increased in the 19th century in many countries. Manufacturing subsidies increased even more, and reached unprecedented levels as a share of GDP. Many governments also supplied significant subsidies to construction and services. All this amounted to a pervasive distortion of market forces. To finance these subsidies, governments increased public expenditure. The larger expenditures were accompanied by increased regulations on trade, prices, finance, and labor, which distorted market forces even more.

In the 20th century, governments increased taxation in per capita terms, still more, while they simultaneously borrowed in larger amounts. Government expenditure as a share of GDP increased dramatically. The state directed more and more resources to manufacturing, mining, infrastructure, housing, education, social services and other activities. The level of subsidization worldwide increased —and regulations did likewise. Market forces were thus distorted more than ever, and in spite of that the world economy accelerated in an unprec-

---

164. Blaug: *Ibid.*, p. 43-80.

edented way. [165] It is hard to support the argument that the progressive acceleration of the world economy in the last centuries was the result of liberal policies.

Comparative Advantage

The comparative advantage school was actually a complement to liberalism; Smith had talked about the same subjects but had not gone very deeply into them. Its creator was another British economist, David Ricardo, who published his most important ideas in the early 19th century and put the accent on foreign trade and specialization.

He asserted that foreign trade was fundamental for the attainment of fast economic growth and in order to promote it most effectively, governments had to practice free trade. He also claimed that by specializing in what each country did best, and trading with other nations for what they did better, the best possible performance would be attained for all nations. He called this specialization "comparative" advantage because it was not an absolute one. Countries did not have to concentrate exclusively on the goods they could produce more efficiently, but they ought to emphasize them. [166]

His assertion that foreign trade was a positive proved right, but the historical record does not substantiate the claim that it was fundamental and neither can it corroborate the claim that free trade policies most promoted economic growth. In the 19th century a few nations started to experience dramatic rates of economic growth, but that happened under policies that distorted trade considerably. Most of the future OECD countries applied high tariffs, in particular during the second half of the 19th century. Canada, Australia and New Zealand actually moved from a system of free trade in the first half of the 19th century to one of high tariffs in the second half, and the economy went from stagnation to approximately 4% growth per year in the second period. Most others, like the US and those in continental Europe, increased tariffs or maintained them at high levels. That coincided with much faster rates of growth in the period 1850-99. Only a few governments did what Ricardo recommended. One of them was his home country; Britain renounced protectionism in the mid 19th century. Interestingly enough, Britain was the only future OECD country that experienced a deceleration in its GDP figures in the second half of the 19th

---

165. *German Unification: Ibid.*, p. 28.
166. Blaug: *Ibid.*, p. 109-180.

century. After having grown by about 2.9% per year in the period 1800-49, GDP growth averaged 2.4% in the following fifty years. [167]

Ricardo's claim that foreign trade was fundamental for the attainment of fast growth also proved problematic. In the 20th century, several nations adopted a communist system and closed themselves off completely from foreign trade. If his claim had been valid, these nations should have experienced a sharp contraction in GDP, but the fact is that they grew and at times very rapidly. The Soviet Union during the 1920s and 1930s was closed to foreign trade and even so it grew faster (in real terms) than any other country in the world. And like Smith, Ricardo believed that in order to achieve the best results market forces should not be disturbed in other aspects of the economy, either. However, policymakers in Moscow during the 1920s and 1930s distorted market forces in every single aspect of the economy, yet the USSR grew faster than anybody else. Growth was about 7% annually, in real terms. [168]

After World War II, several countries decided to close their borders to foreign trade and to "manage" market forces; many of them did not experience recession or even stagnation. They grew, and at times even rapidly. When most of these nations decided in the early 1990s to abandon the centrally planned system and endorsed policies such as the ones Ricardo recommended, their economies collapsed and contracted. In the 1990s, the Soviet Union dismembered into fifteen independent countries and all of them experienced a catastrophic recession. The countries of Eastern Europe also endured recession, stagnation or slow growth. Only Poland averaged a respectable rate of growth, at about 4% per year. [169]

The historical evidence demonstrates that foreign trade and free trade are useful, for they improve efficiency and quality, but Ricardo's ideas on foreign trade alone are not the full answer.

His other basic tenet, which asserted that countries would grow faster if they specialized in what they did best, must be taken with a grain of salt. He said that not all countries were endowed with the ability to produce all types of goods. Some were better suited to produce primary goods such as agricultural goods, minerals, wood or fish, while others were better at producing manufactured goods such as textiles, metals, sea vessels and machinery. The division of

---

167. Cain, P. J.: *Economic Foundations of British Overseas Expansion 1815-1914*, The Macmillan Press Ltd., London, 1980, p. 11-20.

168. Westwood, J.: *Endurance and Endeavor*, Oxford University Press, Oxford, 1993, 300-411.

169. On the sidelines but in the game, *Businessweek European Edition*, 27 April 1998, p. 46.

labor among countries, as Ricardo saw it, would not be strictly in terms of economic sectors; different countries might specialize in different types of manufactured goods, or different raw materials and agricultural goods. Although the central idea was that specialization increased efficiency and efficiency generated faster growth, most analysts understood it as specialization by sectors. In the late 20th century the World Bank and numerous academics were still advising the least developed countries to concentrate in primary activities. Not only did they claim that such a policy would deliver fast growth, but they asserted that it was useless to try to produce factory goods because they were not endowed for such activities. Investment in non-primary activities would be wasteful because these countries lacked a comparative advantage in them. [170] While it is true that, at any given point in time, certain countries will be better positioned to produce certain kinds of goods and services than others, some of those capabilities can be acquired (or lost) over time, and under-developed countries must do something more than export raw materials if they are ever to become "developed."

Since the early 19th century, the countries that followed Ricardo's advice and specialized in the production of primary goods systematically failed to generate fast growth. Ricardo considerably influenced the policies that Britain applied to its South Asian colonies in the 19th century. London decided that India would be exclusively utilized for the production of primary goods. Agricultural goods that could not be produced in Britain due to the climatic and soil conditions were particularly promoted. On top of that, the British practiced a policy of free trade in India and allowed market forces to operate freely. The end result was total stagnation. The South Asian economy in the 19th century averaged a yearly growth rate of about 0.3%. As a result life expectancy was just twenty years by 1900. [171]

In the 17th and 18th centuries, the British held the opinion that it would not be advantageous to equip their North American colonies to produce manufactured goods efficiently. Since the territory was endowed with vast natural resources, they concluded that it would be most advantageous to concentrate on the production of primary goods. Economic stagnation prevailed. Once the United States became independent, the country took another course. With national security at stake, there was a need to produce weapons as well as the

170. Friend of the poor or evil Capitalist, *Businessweek European Edition*, 9 October 2000, p. 17.
171. Brown, Judith: *Modern India—The origins of an Asian Democracy*, Oxford University Press, Oxford, 1985, p. 70-98.

metals and machinery that weapon production required. It was also necessary to attain some degree of self-sufficiency in the production of civilian factory goods because, in times of war, blockades and embargoes blocked imports. Further, the building of an extensive railroad system was seen as a means to bond the territory and create more sense of unity; it also fostered the rapid development of the West. The US thus promoted the railroad industry, and the production of manufactured goods on a large scale. In the 19th century the US was churning out factory goods faster than any other country in the world, even though it had so little previous experience producing them. That coincided with the fastest rates of economic growth in the world (about 4.5% annually). [172]

In recent decades century numerous countries in Africa, above all, but also in Latin America, Eastern Europe and Asia continued to follow the advice of the World Bank and other economists, who counseled them to concentrate in areas where they had a comparative advantage. That meant specializing in the production of primary goods or in a service activity such as tourism. In those countries where such a policy was fully endorsed, it has coincided with recession, stagnation or slow growth. [173]

In the early 1960s the recently installed military government in South Korea presented a plan of accelerated development to the World Bank, which consisted in shifting investment priority from primary activities to export-oriented manufacturing. The World Bank asserted that the effort would fail because the country had never produced textiles, footwear, electrical goods and metals. Pressured by strong national security concerns, Seoul refused to give in to the pressure from Western economists and pushed forward with its plan. In the following four decades South Korea became one of the most competitive producers in the world, for all sorts of manufactured goods. It also had one of the fastest GDP and export growth rates in the world. The economy grew by about 9% annually and exports by 20%. [174]

History, and in particular recent history, is full of similar examples, in which academics asserted that a country should avoid producing manufactured goods if it had no previous experience making them. Economists have tended to interpret the failures of the past as a proof that countries lacking a comparative advantage could not establish one. For them, if a nation had never produced a

---

172. Niemi, Albert: *U. S. Economic History*, Rand McNally College Publishing Co., US, 1975, p. 96-100.

173. Death of a continent, *Fortune*, 13 November 2000, p. 115.

174. *Trade Policy Review — Republic of Korea* Vol. I, GATT, 1992, p. 12-165.

good, it was condemned to forever fail and so, to remain dependent on other nations. Those forecasts regularly proved false. [175]

China is the latest and most prominent example. When China began its Open Door Policy in 1979, few economists believed that China would soon be able to produce large quantities of factory goods in a competitive way. If the experts had not believed it possible for South Korea, which had long had a capitalist economy, how much less credence would they have in a centrally planned economy that knew nothing about cost-efficiency and quality control? Indeed, China was still an agrarian economy where three-fourths of the population worked the land. [176]

However, notwithstanding such supposedly commonsense considerations, by the 1990s China had become the developing country that exported factory goods in the largest amounts. It also became the fourth largest producer of manufactured goods in the world. In just a few years, Chinese goods became competitive in cost and quality. They became so competitive that by the 1990s China possessed a bilateral trade surplus with most of its trading partners. [177]

Economists said that China's effort to produce and export manufactures would be inefficient and noncompetitive, and they claimed that the only chance for success lay in thoroughly privatizing and liberalizing the economy. By the early 2000s, the bulk of the economy was still in state hands and privatizations had only barely begun. There had been considerable liberalization, but the economy was still more regulated than in most other countries. Even so, China had become competitive in the production of even high technology factory goods. [178]

Comparative advantage proved to be one more theory that has misled nations.

Marxism

Marxism appeared in the mid 19th century as the brainchild of the German economist Karl Marx, in opposition to the ideas of Smith and Ricardo. Marx believed that in a system where market forces operated freely, most of the popu-

---

175. *A Case of Successful Adjustment — Korea's Experience during 1980-84*, International Monetary Fund, Washington D.C., August 1985, p. 1-5.
176. Gray & White: *Ibid.*
177. The wait for free trade just got longer, *Businessweek European Edition*, 11 March 2002, p. 35.
178. India's China Challenge, *Businessweek European Edition*, 11 March 2002, p. 33.

lation was condemned to poverty because the strong would inevitably exploit the weak. Marx called for a system in which people would be less vulnerable to exploitation. He wrote long volumes in which he criticized capitalism, but he never gave clear indications of how communism (as his system came to be known) would function.

Marx's biggest problem, however, was not that he was long on criticism but short on alternatives; rather, it was that his basic tenet was faulty. He placed his focus on how a nation should redistribute wealth, rather than on the creation of wealth. He barely touched on the matter of growth, emphasizing instead that resources should be taken from the rich in order to provide better living conditions for the poor. Unfortunately, in the 19th century there was little real wealth to go around, and if anyone had decided to follow his advice and redistribute the wealth on equal terms, then every European would have ended in poverty — even if they each had one more slice of bread. The level of wealth was low overall, due to the history of slow or nonexistent economic growth. What Europe needed most was to achieve the fastest possible rates of growth, and on that matter Marx knew nothing. At least, most other prominent economic thinkers understood the pre-eminence of growth. [179]

Since Marx did not elaborate on how an anti-capitalist system would function, those people inspired by his ideas who eventually did come to power had to improvise on all counts. In 1917, communists gained control of the Russian government and rapidly set about forming a centrally-planned system in which private property was eliminated, foreign trade was obliterated, and all other market forces were suppressed. [180]

Liberal economists predicted that such a system would be terribly inefficient, and they were immediately proven right — for the quality of the goods produced was very low. They also predicted that the economy would collapse, but on that score they were dead wrong. The economy of the Soviet Union grew faster in the 1920s and 1930s than any capitalist nation in the world. In the decades that followed, up to the 1980s, it continued to grow despite the abundant inefficiencies of the system. Still, while liberal economists proved wrong in their forecasts, they were right in claiming that the system was incapable of providing what society wanted. The Soviet economy continued to

---

179. Blaug: *Ibid.*, p. 275-350.
180. Supple, Barry (ed): *The Experience of Economic Growth*, Random House, New York, 1963, p. 93-100.

expand during the 1950-89 period, but only at an average rate of 2.7%. To make matters worse growth progressively slowed, and in the 1980s it was almost stagnant. The weak performance of the last decades appears to be what drove Soviet leaders to abandon the system in the early 1990s and adopt a form of capitalism in its place. [181]

Other countries that practiced the same system, including Mongolia, North Korea, China, Vietnam, Cambodia, Laos, Burma, Cuba, Nicaragua, Angola, Mozambique, and those in Eastern Europe, saw uninspiring results. Most of these countries did have economic growth under communist rule, but none attained the fast and sustained GDP growth figures that nations aspire to, and several experienced recession.

The record of the 20th century shows that Marxism did not deliver fast, sustained growth and that in the end it hindered efficiency. The debate between liberals and Marxists was sterile and fruitless. They argued over ideas that turned out not to address the fundamental problem of society. What society has always wanted from economists is to identify the key to economic growth and to spell out clear policies to deliver it. On that count, both schools failed. Marxism failed faster.

Keynesianism

The Keynesian school had its origins in the early 20th century under another British economist, John M. Keynes. He was sympathetic to liberalism, but was disappointed with the performance of this school in the aftermath of the financial crisis that exploded in 1929 and the global depression that followed.

In the 1920s liberalism reigned in the US and in many other nations. Governments allowed capitalists to do whatever they thought best, and bankers worldwide and in particular in the US indulged in a frenzy of speculative activity. Eventually, the New York Stock Exchange collapsed and pulled other sectors of the economy down with it. The crisis immediately spread to other financial centers, where stock exchanges also collapsed and the economy contracted. Governments, following the advice of economists, did nothing, apparently convinced that the market would spontaneously find a rapid way to recovery. The economy contracted even more. By 1932, there was a massive rise

---

181. Aslund, Anders: *Gorbachev's Struggle for Economic Reform*, Pinter Publishers, London, 1991, p. 17-21.

in unemployment worldwide, accompanied by an increase in poverty, and a wider gap in income distribution. [182]

Keynes concluded that market forces were incapable of countering the effects of such a recession, so he propounded a plan of government intervention. By increasing government expenditure and/or by increasing the disposable income of consumers, he believed the economy could be reactivated.

Government expenditure could be increased by raising taxes, or by increasing borrowing. That would entail running large budget deficits. Liberal economists had, up until then, considered budget deficits to represent a major market distortion and a policy error. To promote government expenditure as a large share of GDP was seen as a terrible distortion; to create large expenditures while simultaneously running budget deficits was outright taboo. Keynes broke with this orthodox view and theorized that increasing expenditure and allowing budget deficits were a necessary evil in times of recession.

Keynes, however, did not believe that governments should increase expenditure in all economic activities. He recommended that policymakers concentrate on investing in infrastructure, education and job training, areas that were thought to be pivotal for growth. He also recommended increased expenditure for unemployment benefits, to keep consumption rates from falling through the floor as families lost their incomes. [183]

American governments and in particular the Roosevelt administrations in the 1930s applied Keynesian policies most decisively, and the results were at best mediocre. In 1930-32, there were timid efforts at public investment in infrastructure and education, and the economy contracted noticeably. From 1933-39, the US invested heavily in all the fields Keynes had indicated and the economy improved, but only barely. To fund such large investments, Washington broke with tradition and increased government expenditure while running large budget deficits. The average economic growth for the whole decade was just 0.6% per year. [184]

After World War II, Keynesian policies caught on in many countries that fell into stagnation or recession. However, only rarely did the economy react positively. In the early 1990s for example, Japan experienced a significant deceler-

---

182. Fite, Gilbert & Reese, Jim: *An Economic History of the United States*, Houghton Mifflin Co., Boston, 1965, p. 534-536.

183. Blaug: *Ibid.*, p. 823-880.

184. Adams, D.: *America in the 20th Century*, Cambridge University Press, London, 1967, p. 76-93.

ation and in an effort to return to the rates of the previous decades, Tokyo decreed thirteen reactivation programs that increasingly enlarged expenditure in infrastructure, construction, education, job training and unemployment benefits. To finance those programs the government ran growing budget deficits. The economy, however, never recovered. After having grown by 4.0% in the 1980s, it averaged only 1.5% in the 1990s, and in 2000-03 growth was just 0.8%.

In Switzerland, the experience was similar. In the 1980s, the economy grew by 2.1% per year and in the early 1990s it began to stagnate. Fifteen reactivation programs that gave priority to infrastructure, education, job training, and unemployment benefit were implemented, but the economy remained stagnant. During the 1990s, Switzerland's GDP averaged a yearly rate of just 0.5% and in 2000-03 it grew by 1.1%.

Keynesianism never pretended to know what it is that causes economic growth; it generally accepted the basic tenets of liberalism. Its fundamental claim was that it had an antidote to recessions. The historical evidence, however, shows that it was incapable of delivering even that.

Import Substitution

Proponents of import substitution also thought they had the solution to financial crises like that of 1929 and the terrible recession that followed. Up to the 1920s, the trading system worldwide had operated relatively smoothly and Latin America had been exporting quantities of primary goods to North America and Western Europe. After the crash of 1929, thousands of enterprises in developed countries went bankrupt, and governments raised trade barriers to protect those that remained. The high tariffs were a bar to imports so that Latin American nations ended with far lower foreign exchange earnings, which in turn prevented them from buying the manufactured goods they normally imported. Latin America was paralyzed and the economy contracted. [185]

An Argentinean economist, Raul Prebisch, concluded that the structure of production of Latin American countries had to be changed in order to reactivate the economies of the region and in order to avoid similar situations in the future. He called for Latin countries to stop producing primary goods alone, and recommended governments to promote the development of manufacturing. Given the trade barriers in the developed nations and the relatively low quality that could

---

185. Rock, David: *Argentina 1516-1987*, University of California Press, Berkeley, 1987, p. 165-223.

be expected in the early years of South American manufacturing, exporting factory goods to the most developed countries was unlikely to succeed; but Latin American countries could produce for their own domestic market. To secure the domestic market, he proposed to erect high trade barriers of their own. [186]

Most Latin American governments followed his advice from the 1930s onward, and they soon began to have faster rates of economic growth. During the 1940s, 1950s, 1960s and 1970s Latin governments continued endorsing those policies and the region experienced the fastest GDP growth rates in all of its history. [187]

The system, however, proved to be unsustainable. Since little in the way of manufactured goods could be exported and the exportation of primary goods continued to be insufficient to cover the cost of all that Latin American countries wanted to buy from the rest of the world, trade deficits grew larger and larger. At first, they could be covered by borrowing from developed countries; but as interest rates went up, this became a trap. By the early 1980s, Latin countries could not pay their debts. The banks from developed countries cut financing and GDP growth experienced a massive deceleration. After averaging about 4.2% per year from the 1940s to the 1970s, Latin America grew by just 1.6% in the 1980s. [188]

Not only was the economy practically stagnant in the 1980s, the growth rate of the period 1940-79 was already far from impressive. There was evidently something about import substitution that delivered positive effects, but even during its best moments it was insufficient to extricate the Latin countries from a cycle of poverty and unemployment. Worse still, it was unsustainable due to the ever-widening gap in the balance of payments that it generated.

Other nations in other continents had also endorsed import substitution policies in the decades after World War II. South Asian countries, and in particular India, opted immediately after independence (1947) to promote the development of manufacturing for domestic consumption and to erect high trade barriers to protect it. South Asian countries during that period had numerous balance of payments crises, even though none proved as serious as the Latin debt crisis of the early 1980s. The chronic trade deficits, however, were not the biggest problem. The real problem was that rates of growth were never adequate.

---

186. Prebisch, Raul: *Change and Development: Latin America's Great Task*, Praeger, New York, 1971.

187. Bulmer, Victor: *The Economic History of Latin America since Independence*, Cambridge University Press, Cambridge, 1994, p. 38, 63-69, 309.

188. Merrill & Miro: *Ibid.*, p. 148-150.

On average during the second half of the 20th century South Asia grew by about 3.1% per year, far from enough to pull the region out of poverty and unemployment. Worse still, the slowest rates during this period came during the years 1950-79, when the import-substitution policies were more enthusiastically endorsed. [189]

South Asia did not attain fast growth while it practiced import substitution; but it did grow faster during this period than ever before. Before independence, liberal policies had prevailed and the economy remained stagnant.

South Asia raised trade barriers to a higher level than Latin America and the end result was higher levels of inefficiency. A larger share of production was of very low quality and, despite extremely low labor costs, the costs of production tended to be relatively high. Since the 1980s, South Asian governments as well as those in Latin America started to abandon import substitution and began to reduce trade barriers. Quality and cost efficiency immediately improved. [190]

Many countries in Sub-Saharan Africa, the Middle East, and Southeast Asia also endorsed import substitution in the post World War II decades and progressively began to abandon the system since the 1980s. The level of trade barriers and the degree of subsidization for manufacturing varied from region to region, from country to country, and from one decade to the next. In all of these countries, rates of economic growth accelerated considerably with the adoption of import substitution policies and continued for a few decades.

However, in the vast majority of these cases, growth rates never became fast enough or sustained enough to overcome the fundamental problems. Sub-Saharan Africa averaged a yearly rate of growth of 2.8% in the second half of the 20th century while South East Asia managed 4.4% and the Middle East 5.1%. The rates in these last two regions were fairly respectable, but the countries that grew fastest were not those who practiced significant import substitution.

Import substitution also failed, in the long run, to answer society's needs.

---

189. Brass, Paul: *The Politics of India since Independence*, The New Cambridge History of India, Cambridge University Press, Cambridge, 1990, p. 245-254.
190. Stern, Robert: *Changing India*, Cambridge University Press, Cambridge, 1993, p. 181, 208-219.

Neo-Mercantilism

Neo-mercantilist policies came into being as a result of the pressing balance of payments constraints that some nations in East Asia experienced in the aftermath of World War II. Japan emerged from the war without foreign exchange reserves and with large war reparations to pay. To reactivate its devastated economy, it borrowed considerably from the West (in particular the US) to import vast amounts of machinery and equipment. Since it had to repay those loans in dollars, and since Tokyo did not want to take on a heavy burden of debt, it promoted exports as much as possible to earn more hard currency. [191]

In 1949, Taiwan broke off from China. Up to that date, the economy of China and Taiwan had been fairly stagnant, poverty was widespread and foreign exchange reserves were very low. The government in Taipei needed to quickly establish a military and economic basis strong enough to fend off communist China, which threatened to invade. To achieve that, it needed to import vast amounts of machinery, equipment and weapons. It promoted foreign direct investment, but that was not enough; so it also promoted massive exports to earn the foreign exchange needed to step up its imports. [192]

South Korea emerged after the end of the civil war with North Korea in 1953 with practically no foreign exchange reserves. Much of the economic base had been destroyed, and earlier rates of growth had been modest or stagnant. After the armistice, North Korea continued to threaten the South; Seoul urgently needed to attain military and economic strength. After several failed efforts, a new plan was endorsed by the military in 1961. To finance the vast imports of machinery, equipment and weapons the new regime needed, it decided to promote exports as much as possible. [193]

In 1979, Beijing decided to radically change economic policies in China in a bid to attain economic and technological parity with developed countries. To achieve that goal, it needed to import vast amounts of machinery and equipment from developed nations. Its foreign exchange reserves were very low due to the slow growth China had experienced during much of its history, exacerbated by its isolationism of the previous decades. China moved decisively to promote exports.

---

191. Takenaka Heizo: *Contemporary Japanese Economy and Economic Policy*, The University of Michigan Press, US, 1991, 5-30.
192. Wade: *Ibid.*, p. 40-96.
193. *Trade Policy Review — Republic of Korea: Ibid.*

In Japan, Taiwan, South Korea and China the governments supplied abundant export subsidies and erected high trade barriers to protect their fledgling industries. In all four cases, exports grew at an impressive pace and their original trade deficits rapidly transformed into surpluses. Their foreign exchange earnings grew and eventually became the largest in the world. [194]

Other nations in Southeast Asia such as Thailand, Indonesia and Malaysia began in the 1980s to partially implement neo-mercantilist policies; they considerably increased export subsidies and left trade barriers in place or reduced them just a little. These countries saw an increase in exports and an improvement of their balance of payments. [195]

For most of the time that Japan, South Korea, Taiwan and China practiced these policies, their economies enjoyed impressive rates of growth. However, there were moments in which export promotion continued to deliver trade surpluses and abundant foreign exchange reserves, but the economy did not grow quickly. Japan during the 1990s, for example, maintained constant trade surpluses and the largest foreign exchange reserves in the world, but the economy only barely grew — achieving a rate of 1.5% annually. In 2000-03, trade surpluses and foreign exchange reserves continued to grow, but the economy continued to stagnate, growing by just 0.8%. [196]

The neo-mercantilist system has performed better than any other in history, but cases like Japan in the 1990s suggest that economic growth cannot be guaranteed by export promotion, trade surpluses, and large foreign exchange reserves. Even though South Korea and Taiwan retained high growth rates up to the 1990s, they significantly decelerated since the 1980s. In the 1970s, both averaged a GDP rate of about 10% per year but by the 1990s the figure was just 6%. Six percent was fast for countries that by 1989 had attained a relatively developed status; but think what might have been possible if the rates of the 1970s had been maintained! On top of that, in 2000-03 trade surpluses and foreign exchange reserves continued to increase in both countries, but the economy experienced a further deceleration and averaged only 4%. [197]

It is also worth noting that nations that did not endorse the full neo-mercantilist program attained similar fast rates of growth. Hong Kong and Sin-

194. A Crackup for World Trade? *Newsweek*, 25 August 2003, p. 33.

195. Kulick, Elliot & Wilson, Dick: *Thailand's Turn — Profile of a New Dragon*, Macmillan, London, 1992, p. 107-141.

196. Diminishing Returns: *Ibid.*

197. The Burden on the Banks, *The Economist*, 23 September 2000, p. 115.

gapore did not erect trade barriers. During the years 1950-99, these two practiced free trade and nonetheless attained a faster growth GDP rate than Japan, which practiced neo-mercantilism the whole time. The situation in Thailand, Indonesia and Malaysia also showed inconsistencies because the GDP figures in the years 1980-99, under neo-mercantilism, were the same as in the preceding two decades, under a program of import substitution. In both periods growth was not particularly impressive, averaging about 5.7 in the 1960-79 years and 5.3% in the following two decades. [198]

There is much evidence to suggest that neo-mercantilist policies have delivered fast growth, but not because of the goals they pursued. By chance, some of those policies inadvertently pressed the button that is fundamentally responsible for the creation of wealth. In fact, neo-mercantilism was first implemented under the pressure of circumstances and only afterwards the experts elaborated a theoretical framework to support it.

Mainstream Economics

Liberalism experienced a serious setback during the depression of the 1930s, for most politicians thought it had been responsible for leading the world into that crisis. Some countries made a bit of a recovery as Keynesian policies were applied in refutation to several aspects of liberalism. Even more damaging to the liberal line, in the few countries that fully recovered in the 1930s, such as Germany and Japan, the policies in place turned back the basic tenets of liberalism even more. During World War II, liberalism received a further blow as large-scale government intervention in countries with liberal traditions such as the US, Canada and Britain coincided with unprecedented economic growth. Then there was the case of the Soviet Union in the 1920s, 1930s and 1940s, mentioned above, when the government's complete intervention in the economy went hand-in-hand with dramatic economic growth. [199]

These facts shook the belief in liberal economics and the Smithian idea of "no state intervention" was found untenable. Most policymakers concluded that some intervention and regulation was necessary for the adequate functioning of the economy. Areas such as infrastructure, education, health, social security and

---

198. Let the Good Times Role, *The Economist*, 15 April 2000, p. 82.
199. *The Cambridge History of Japan Vol. 6*, Cambridge University Press, Cambridge, 1988, p. 471-481.

the environment were classified as domains in which market forces alone could not resolve problems adequately.

In the 1950s and 1960s, most OECD countries achieved their fastest rates of economic growth ever. At the same time, there was a considerable increase in state intervention in the fields mentioned. There was also greater state subsidization of manufacturing, mining and other industries. This situation seemed to corroborate the position of those who had always mistrusted the basic tenet of liberalism. It seemed more and more that state intervention could have some positive effects. [200]

In the 1970s, however, growth rates decelerated considerably in most developed countries and unemployment began to rise. Even in middle income and developing nations, a similar phenomenon took place. Liberal economists claimed that the slowdown was the result of too much state intervention and reverted to their basic principle that market forces should be distorted as little as possible. In the following decade, rates of growth slowed further and liberal economists went more on the offensive. In the early 1990s, with the collapse of central planning in the former USSR, they felt particularly reassured in their beliefs and increasingly demanded that governments endorse liberalization, privatization, the elimination of budget deficits, and a reduction of government expenditure. [201]

Despite their renewed self-assurance, they never fully reverted to the Smithian idea of a government that would limit its activity to providing national defense. By the early 2000s, most economists in developed countries were advocating a middle-of-the-road position in which trade liberalization, privatization, deregulation, fiscal restraint and sound monetary policy were seen as keys for growth. They nonetheless also endorsed a certain level of government intervention in several areas of the economy where it was thought that the market could not solve problems. This refurbished version of liberalism, in which policies are basically oriented to let market forces operate freely but several exceptions are made, has come to be known as mainstream economics. Since the 1970s, this school of thought has been gaining new adherents among the worldwide community of economists and as of the 1990s it had seduced most them, particu-

---

200. Cipolla, Carlo (ed): *The Fontana Economic History of Europe—Contemporary Economies Part I*, William Collins Sons & Co., Glasgow, 1976, p. 95-98.

201. Hayward, Jack: *The State and the Market Economy*, Wheatsheaf Books, United Kingdom, 1986, p. 21-25, 191-212.

larly in OECD countries, but also in developing nations (which had long rejected or mistrusted those ideas). [202]

Due to its rising acceptance among the economists of the world, governments gradually adopted the policies that emanated from mainstream economics. The application of these policies nonetheless coincided with a gradual slowdown in the rates of growth for the great majority of countries. In the 1960s the world economy was expanding by about 4.8% annually; in the 1970s the rate fell to 4.1%; in the 1980s it fell further to 3.2%; and in the 1990s it was just 2.5%.

In the 1990s these economists became more assertive than at any point in the post-World War II period, mostly as a result of the collapse of communism. The world at first was impressed, and honored them in numerous ways. The most liberal economists of this group were always those of the University of Chicago, and they received by far the most Nobel prizes. [203]

However, due to the lack of results, by the early 2000s the world had become increasingly disillusioned. These economists had claimed that the application of their policies would deliver faster rates of growth and as rates slowed down since the 1970s, they excused themselves by blaming the failure on an incomplete application of their policies. In the 1980s, governments implemented the liberal policies even more completely, but the world economy still decelerated; the economists again blamed it on the failure to implement several aspects of the policy that had not been fully adopted. The collapse of communism gave a major boost to liberalization worldwide and governments went even further with "mainstream" policies. But, by then, even though economists continued to look for scapegoats, the world increasingly had come to the conclusion that its fundamental problems could not be solved by these policies. [204]

The Lesser of Evils

Why, despite so many failures, did these ideas seduce so many of the best economists? Because this was the only school that made useful discoveries. This school succeeded in deciphering which are the policies that increase efficiency and quality. It is useful to improve efficiency and quality, but that is only a small part of what it takes to eliminate poverty and unemployment. The mainstream school also discovered how to control inflation and keep it low. This is also

---

202. Get Real — and win a Nobel Prize, *Businessweek*, 27 October 1997, p. 39.
203. Lucas the Keynes — killer, *Newsweek*, 23 October 1995, p. 31.
204. Stiglitz, Joseph: *Where Global Markets are Going Wrong*, W.W. Norton, 2002.

useful to society, but of marginal importance because low inflation does not assure fast economic growth.[205]

Identifying such a small part of what it takes to build a healthy economy is not a great accomplishment, but it is better than nothing at all — and that is what the other schools of economic thought had done. In consequence, the best brains in the economics profession are now inclined to side with mainstream economics. Governments in their turn have no alternative but to listen to what the best brains in the economics profession advise. [206]

The actual record of history can be read in the following charts and tables. With the powerful tool of standardized statistics that allow for comparisons across centuries and continents, the achievements and failures of different economic approaches and the effects of different environments can now be assessed. They should lead to new conclusions and new questions that can occupy economists for the next generation.

205. The Future of Economics, *The Economist*, 4 March 2000, p. 90.
206. Krugman, Paul: *Peddling Prosperity — Economic Sense and Nonsense in the Age of Diminished Expectations*, W.W. Norton, 1994.

PART II

CHAPTER 1. WORLD AND REGIONAL STATISTICS

THE WORLD

	GDP	Average Life Expectancy
16th Century	0.1	19
17th Century	0.1	19
18th Century	0.2	20
19th Century	1.2	26
20th Century	3.0	49
1800-49	0.6	23
1850-99	1.8	28
1900-49	2.1	38
1950-99	3.8	59
1950s	4.5	50
1960s	4.8	56
1970s	4.1	61
1980s	3.2	64
1990s	2.5	66

The following charts display the economic figures of the world as a whole and of all its regions. Gross Domestic Product (GDP) figures as well as those of Manufacturing (Man), Agriculture (Agri), Services (Ser), Inflation (Inf), Population (Pop), Unemployment (Unem), Exports (Ex), and Construction (Const) are presented on an average annual rate basis.

WORLD ECONOMY

	Man	GDP	Agri	Serv	Const	Inf	Pop
16th Century	0.1	0.1	0.0			0.1	0.1
17th Century	0.2	0.1	0.1			0.0	0.1
18th Century	0.3	0.2	0.2			0.0	0.2
19th Century	1.5	1.2	0.7			0.2	0.5
20th Century	3.8	3.0	1.9	3.5		3.4	1.4
1800-49	0.8	0.6	0.4			0.0	0.3
1850-99	2.2	1.8	1.0			0.4	0.6
1900-49	2.6	2.1	1.3	2.4		1.7	0.9
1950-99	5.0	3.8	2.5	4.6	4.0	5.1	1.8
1950s	6.0	4.5	2.7	5.2	4.1	3.0	2.0
1960s	6.3	4.8	3.0	6.0	5.2	3.4	2.1
1970s	5.6	4.1	2.3	5.4	4.6	9.0	2.0
1980s	4.0	3.2	2.7	3.8	3.3	5.8	1.8
1990s	3.0	2.5	1.6	2.5	2.3	4.1	1.0

EAST ASIA

	Man	GDP	Agri	Serv
16th Century	0.1	0.1	0.1	
17th Century	0.3	0.2	0.2	
18th Century	0.4	0.3	0.2	
19th Century	0.7	0.5	0.3	
20th Century	6.4	3.9	2.2	
1800-49	0.3	0.2	0.1	
1850-99	1.1	0.8	0.5	
1900-49	2.8	2.1	1.0	
1950-99	9.9	5.6	3.3	8.4
1950s	10.7	5.8	3.9	9.4
1960s	12.9	6.9	3.5	10.1
1970s	11.5	6.2	3.5	9.2
1980s	9.5	5.7	3.2	8.4
1990s	5.0	3.6	2.4	5.1

China, Hong Kong, Japan, Korea, Mongolia, Taiwan

EASTERN EUROPE AND THE EX-SOVIET UNION

	Man	GDP	Agri	Serv
16th Century	0.2	0.1	0.1	
17th Century	0.3	0.2	0.1	
18th Century	0.5	0.3	0.3	
19th Century	2.2	1.7	1.2	
20th Century	4.4	2.3	1.9	
1800-49	1.1	0.8	0.6	
1850-99	3.3	2.6	1.8	
1900-49	4.1	2.6	2.0	
1950-99	4.7	1.9	1.7	4.7
1950s	10.0	3.9	4.2	7.9
1960s	6.8	2.8	3.0	5.8
1970s	7.6	3.3	3.3	6.8
1980s	2.5	1.0	0.5	2.4
1990s	-3.5	-1.7	-2.7	0.5

Albania, Armenia, Azerbaijan, Belarus, Bosnia, Bulgaria, Croatia, Czech Republic, Estonia, Georgia, Hungary, Kazakhstan, Kyrgyz Republic, Latvia, Lithuania, Macedonia, Moldova, Poland, Romania, Russia, Slovak Republic, Slovenia, Tajikistan, Turkmenistan, Ukraine, Uzbekistan, Yugoslavia

LATIN AMERICA AND CARIBBEAN

	Man	GDP	Agri	Serv
16th Century	0.1	0.1	0.0	
17th Century	0.1	0.1	0.1	
18th Century	0.3	0.2	0.2	
19th Century	1.2	0.9	0.7	
20th Century	3.8	2.8	2.1	
1800-49	0.5	0.4	0.3	
1850-99	1.8	1.4	1.1	
1900-49	2.6	2.0	1.4	
1950-99	5.0	3.6	2.7	4.3
1950s	5.9	4.2	3.1	5.8
1960s	6.5	4.6	3.4	5.7
1970s	6.5	4.4	3.1	5.1
1980s	2.3	1.6	1.8	1.3
1990s	3.8	3.2	1.9	3.7

Argentina, Bahamas, Bolivia, Brazil, Chile, Colombia, Costa Rica, Cuba, Dominican Republic, Ecuador, El Salvador, Guatemala, Haiti, Honduras, Jamaica, Mexico, Nicaragua, Panama, Paraguay, Peru, Puerto Rico, Uruguay, Venezuela

MIDDLE EAST AND NORTH AFRICA

	Man	GDP	Agri	Serv
16th Century	0.1	0.1	0.0	
17th Century	0.2	0.1	0.1	
18th Century	0.2	0.2	0.1	
19th Century	0.7	0.6	0.4	
20th Century	4.4	3.3	2.1	
1800-49	0.5	0.4	0.3	
1850-99	0.9	0.8	0.5	
1900-49	1.9	1.5	1.1	
1950-99	6.9	5.1	3.1	6.2
1950s	7.1	5.3	3.0	8.1
1960s	8.8	6.5	3.7	6.3
1970s	10.8	7.9	3.2	7.9
1980s	3.7	2.6	4.0	3.4
1990s	4.1	3.2	1.5	5.5

Algeria, Bahrain, Egypt, Iran, Iraq, Israel, Jordan, Kuwait, Lebanon, Libya, Morocco, Oman, Qatar, Saudi Arabia, Syria, Tunisia, Turkey, United Arab Emirates, Yemen

NORTH AMERICA

	Man	GDP	Agri	Serv
16th Century	0.0	0.0	0.0	
17th Century	0.1	0.1	0.1	
18th Century	0.4	0.3	0.2	
19th Century	4.2	3.6	2.1	
20th Century	4.3	3.7	1.9	4.0
1800-49	2.0	1.7	1.0	
1850-99	6.4	5.5	3.2	
1900-49	4.1	3.5	1.8	3.9
1950-99	4.4	3.8	1.9	4.0
1950s	5.7	4.9	3.1	5.6
1960s	6.2	5.0	1.4	4.9
1970s	3.9	3.6	1.6	4.1
1980s	3.3	2.9	2.2	3.5
1990s	2.9	2.6	1.1	2.0

Canada, United States of America

OCEANIA

	Man	GDP	Agri	Serv
16th Century	0.0	0.0	0.0	
17th Century	0.0	0.0	0.0	
18th Century	0.0	0.0	0.0	
19th Century	1.9	1.6	1.0	
20th Century	3.7	3.2	2.0	
1800-49	0.4	0.4	0.2	
1850-99	3.4	2.8	1.8	
1900-49	2.9	2.5	1.4	
1950-99	4.5	3.8	2.5	4.0
1950s	6.1	5.0	3.1	5.7
1960s	5.9	5.3	2.9	5.0
1970s	3.1	2.6	1.6	3.1
1980s	2.7	2.4	2.9	2.5
1990s	4.5	3.6	2.0	3.5

Australia, New Zealand, Papua New Guinea

SOUTH ASIA

	Man	GDP	Agri	Serv
16th Century	0.2	0.1	0.1	
17th Century	0.3	0.2	0.2	
18th Century	0.0	0.0	0.0	
19th Century	0.5	0.3	0.2	
20th Century	3.3	2.1	1.6	
1800-49	0.2	0.1	0.1	
1850-99	0.7	0.5	0.3	
1900-49	1.3	1.0	0.7	
1950-99	5.3	3.1	2.4	4.7
1950s	3.8	2.0	1.8	3.4
1960s	5.3	2.7	2.7	4.6
1970s	4.1	2.1	1.9	4.4
1980s	6.4	3.9	3.1	5.4
1990s	6.8	4.3	2.6	5.8

Bangladesh, Bhutan, India, Nepal, Pakistan, Sri Lanka

SOUTHEAST ASIA

	Man	GDP	Agri	Serv
16th Century	0.0	0.0	0.0	
17th Century	0.0	0.0	0.0	
18th Century	0.1	0.1	0.1	
19th Century	0.6	0.5	0.4	
20th Century	4.3	2.9	1.8	
1800-49	0.3	0.2	0.2	
1850-99	0.9	0.7	0.6	
1900-49	1.8	1.4	0.9	
1950-99	6.7	4.4	2.6	7.1
1950s	5.9	4.1	2.7	6.0
1960s	7.3	4.8	3.3	9.9
1970s	7.8	5.3	2.8	8.3
1980s	5.2	3.2	1.6	5.0
1990s	7.4	4.8	2.7	6.5

Brunei, Cambodia, Indonesia, Laos, Malaysia, Myanmar (Burma), Philippines, Singapore, Thailand, Vietnam

SUB-SAHARAN AFRICA

	Man	GDP	Agri	Serv
16th Century	0.0	0.0	0.0	
17th Century	0.0	0.0	0.0	
18th Century	0.0	0.0	0.0	
19th Century	0.1	0.1	0.1	
20th Century	2.5	1.7	1.4	
1800-49	0.0	0.0	0.0	
1850-99	0.2	0.1	0.1	
1900-49	0.8	0.6	0.4	
1950-99	4.1	2.8	2.3	
1950s	4.7	3.6	2.7	
1960s	5.8	3.7	2.6	4.5
1970s	3.5	2.2	1.7	3.8
1980s	3.0	1.9	2.1	2.2
1990s	3.4	2.4	2.6	2.7

Angola, Benin, Botswana, Burkina Faso, Burundi, Cameroon, Central African Republic, Chad, Congo, Democratic Republic of Congo, Equatorial Guinea, Ethiopia, Ghana, Guinea, Ivory Coast, Kenya, Liberia, Madagascar, Mali, Mauritania, Mozambique, Namibia, Niger, Nigeria, Rwanda, Senegal, Sierra Leone, Somalia, South Africa, Sudan, Tanzania, Togo, Uganda, Zambia, Zimbabwe

WESTERN EUROPE

	Man	GDP	Agri	Serv
16th Century	0.3	0.2	0.2	
17th Century	0.3	0.2	0.1	
18th Century	0.7	0.5	0.4	
19th Century	3.0	2.5	1.5	
20th Century	4.4	3.6	1.9	4.0
1800-49	1.7	1.4	1.1	
1850-99	4.3	3.6	1.9	
1900-49	3.9	3.2	2.0	3.6
1950-99	4.8	4.0	1.7	4.3
1950s	7.4	6.1	3.9	7.1
1960s	6.6	5.2	1.5	5.1
1970s	4.2	3.6	0.9	4.1
1980s	2.8	2.5	0.8	2.9
1990s	2.9	2.6	1.3	2.2

Austria, Belgium, Denmark, Finland, France, Germany, Greece, Iceland, Ireland, Italy, Luxembourg, Malta, Netherlands, Norway, Portugal, Spain, Sweden, Switzerland, United Kingdom

CHAPTER 2. EAST ASIA

CHINA

	Man	GDP	Agri	Serv	Pop	Inf	Ex
16th Century	0.2	0.1	0.1		0.1		
17th Century	0.2	0.1	0.1		0.1		
18th Century	0.6	0.4	0.3		0.8		
19th Century	0.2	0.1	0.1		0.3		
20th Century	7.4	2.7	2.2		1.0		
1800-49	0.3	0.2	0.2		0.6		
1850-99	0.0	0.0	0.0		0.0		
1900-49	0.6	0.5	0.4		0.3		
1950-99	14.2	4.9 (9)	4.0	10.1	1.7		9.1
1900s	0.4	0.3	0.2		0.2		
1910s	0.7	0.5	0.3		0.3		
1920s	1.2	0.9	0.6		0.4		
1930s	2.9	2.1	1.4		0.6		
1940s	-2.3	-1.4	-0.5		0.0		
1950s	17.0	4.6 (13)	5.0	12.0	2.3		7.9
1960s	10.1	2.2 (5)	1.5	7.1	1.9		3.1
1970s	10.8	3.0 (6)	3.2	8.7	1.9		7.0
1980s	16.2	7.1 (10)	6.3	13.5	1.4	5.8	12.2
1990s	17.0	7.7 (11)	4.2	9.2	1.2	7.0	16.1

Notes: Two considerably different sets of GDP figures for the period 1950-99 are presented. The ones in parenthesis are the official statistics. The ones to their left are calculated to express the rate by which "real wealth" was created; they are much lower because inefficiency was high during this period. The same applies for North Korea and Mongolia. In several other regions of the world there are numerous countries in the same situation and in those cases figures are presented in a similar way.

HONG KONG

	Man	GDP	Agri	Serv	Pop	Inf	Ex	Unem
18th Century	0.0	0.0						
19th Century	0.5	0.4						
20th Century	7.4	6.0						
1800-49	0.0	0.0						
1850-99	1.0	0.8						
1900-49	4.0	3.3						
1950-99	10.7	8.7		10.5	2.2	5.6	13.3	
1900s	2.4	2.0						
1910s	4.0	3.2						
1920s	3.3	2.8						
1930s	4.7	4.0						
1940s	5.5	4.5						
1950s	15.8	12.3		14.2	2.8	4.0	14.0	
1960s	14.4	10.2		13.8	2.5	2.4	12.7	
1970s	10.6	9.4	-11.0	11.0	2.6	7.9	8.3	
1980s	8.1	7.4		8.4	1.2	7.1	16.1	2.7
1990s	4.8	4.1		5.0	2.1	6.4	15.0	3.1

JAPAN

	Man	GDP	Agri	Serv	Pop	Inf	Ex	Unem
16th Century	0.2	0.1	0.1		0.1			
17th Century	0.3	0.2	0.2		0.2			
18th Century	0.2	0.1	0.1		0.0			
19th Century	1.7	1.3	0.7		0.5			
20th Century	7.0	5.4	1.8	6.1	1.1			
1800-49	0.3	0.2	0.1		0.2			
1850-99	3.0	2.4	1.3		0.8			
1900-49	6.3	4.5	1.7	5.7	1.3			
1950-99	7.6	6.2	1.9	6.6	0.9	3.7	10.3	2.3
1850s	1.2	0.9	0.6					
1860s	1.7	1.4	0.8					
1870s	2.5	2.0	1.1					

1880s	3.6	3.0	1.7					
1890s	6.0	4.7	2.1					
1900s	7.0	5.2	2.6	6.6				
1910s	8.4	6.3	2.9	8.2				
1920s	3.1	2.4	1.8	3.0				
1930s	8.5	5.4	2.5	8.0				
1940s	4.5	3.0	-1.7	2.6				
1950s	11.1	9.1	3.8	10.0	1.3	3.1	14.2	3.6
1960s	13.4	11.3	4.0	11.7	1.0	4.9	17.0	0.9
1970s	6.2	5.2	1.1	4.9	1.1	8.2	9.1	1.7
1980s	5.3	4.0	0.4	3.9	0.6	1.3	7.4	2.2
1990s	1.9	1.5	0.3	2.3	0.5	1.2	3.8	3.1

KOREA (SOUTH KOREA)

	Man	GDP	Agri	Serv	Pop	Inf	Ex	Unem
18th Century	0.3	0.2	0.1		0.1			
19th Century	0.6	0.4	0.3		0.3			
20th Century	6.5	4.3	2.0		1.2			
1800-49	0.3	0.2	0.1		0.2			
1850-99	0.9	0.6	0.4		0.4			
1900-49	2.0	1.5	1.1		0.9			
1950-99	11.0	7.1	2.9	7.7	1.5	16.3		
1900s	0.9	0.7	0.3		0.4			
1910s	2.1	1.6	1.3		1.0			
1920s	2.6	2.0	1.7		1.4			
1930s	4.0	3.1	2.5		1.8			
1940s	0.2	0.1	0.3		0.0			
1950s	1.1	0.7	0.5	1.3	0.7	36.3		
1960s	15.0	8.4	4.2	10.8	2.5	15.1	34.1	
1970s	17.8	10.3	4.8	11.6	1.9	18.2	25.7	
1980s	13.6	9.7	3.3	9.2	1.2	5.0	14.2	
1990s	7.5	6.4	1.5	5.8	1.0	7.0	7.0	3.1

The figures from 1700 to 1949 are for the whole Korean peninsula (from then on just for South Korea)

MONGOLIA

	Man	GDP	Agri	Serv	Pop	Inf	Ex
18th Century							
19th Century	0.1	0.1	0.1				
20th Century	3.8	1.8	1.9				
1900-49	2.0	1.3	1.0				
1950-99	5.6	2.3 (3.8)	2.8	5.3	2.7		
1950s	10.0	4.0 (8.0)	5.0	9.0	3.0		
1960s	3.7	1.4 (2.8)	1.7	4.0	2.9		
1970s	7.0	3.0 (6.0)	3.1	6.8	2.9		
1980s	6.6	2.8 (5.4)	1.4	5.9	2.7		
1990s	0.7	0.5 (0.7)	2.9	0.8	1.9	60.0	

NORTH KOREA

	Man	GDP	Agri	Serv	Pop	Inf	Ex
1950-99	8.7	1.9 (5.8)					
1950s	8.0	2.0 (5.0)					
1960s	20.0	5.0 (15.0)					
1970s	15.0	3.0 (9.0)					
1980s	5.6	1.0 (3.0)					
1990s	-5.0	-1.4 (-3.2)					

TAIWAN

	Man	GDP	Agri	Serv	Pop	Inf	Ex	Unem
18th Century	0.2	0.1	0.1		3.5			
19th Century	0.3	0.2	0.2		3.0			
20th Century	6.8	4.9	2.9		1.6			
1800-49	0.2	0.1	0.1		3.6			
1850-99	0.4	0.3	0.2		2.4			
1900-49	1.9	1.4	1.0		0.9			
1950-99	11.7	8.4	4.8	10.5	2.3	8.2	16.4	

1900s	1.0	0.7	0.5					
1910s	2.6	1.8	1.4					
1920s	3.3	2.3	2.0					
1930s	4.4	3.4	2.2					
1940s	-1.8	-1.0	-0.9					
1950s	12.2	7.8	5.0	10.1	3.5	20.3	6.1	
1960s	14.0	10.1	6.1	13.0	3.0	2.4	25.3	
1970s	13.2	9.6	5.2	12.3	2.1	10.2	30.2	
1980s	11.1	8.1	4.6	9.2	1.6	5.1	13.4	
1990s	7.8	6.3	3.3	7.7	1.1	3.2	7.1	2.6

CHAPTER 3.EASTERN EUROPE AND THE EX-SOVIET UNION

ALBANIA

	Man	GDP	Agri	Serv	Pop	Inf	Ex
18th Century	0.3	0.2					
19th Century	1.6	1.2	0.9				
20th Century	3.6	1.9	2.1				
1900-49	2.2	1.8	1.1				
1950-99	5.0	1.9 (4.0)	3.0				
1950s	11.0	4.0 (9.0)	4.0				
1960s	5.5	2.0 (4.3)	2.6	4.2	2.8		
1970s	5.2	1.8 (4.0)	2.3	4.0	2.5		
1980s	2.0	0.7 (1.5)	2.0	-0.4	2.1		
1990s	1.3	1.0 (1.3)	4.2	4.0	0.3	35.0	

BULGARIA

	Man	GDP	Agri	Serv	Pop	Inf	Ex
18th Century		0.3	0.2				
19th Century	2.1	1.5	1.2				
20th Century	4.4	2.2	2.0				
1900-49	3.3	2.4	2.1				
1950-99	5.5	2.0 (3.9)	1.9	4.8	0.3		
1950s	9.3	3.3 (6.6)	4.4	8.0	1.0		
1960s	8.5	3.0 (5.9)	3.0	7.2	0.8		14.4
1970s	9.0	3.1 (6.2)	4.0	8.0	0.6		11.2
1980s	5.2	1.8 (3.4)	-2.1	3.3	0.0	1.4	-3.5
1990s	-4.4	-1.0 (-2.7)	0.3	-2.3	-0.7	108.5	0.3

Czech Republic

	Man	GDP	Agri	Serv	Pop	Inf	Ex
18th Century	0.5	0.4	0.3				
19th Century	2.5	2.1	1.5				
20th Century	4.8	2.8	2.7				
1900-49	4.6	3.4	2.7				
1950-99	5.0	2.2 (4.1)	2.6	4.0			
1950s	12.2	5.4 (10.0)	4.7	9.0			
1960s	4.0	1.6 (3.1)	3.0	3.5	0.5		6.7
1970s	6.0	2.5 (4.8)	2.4	5.0	0.7		6.6
1980s	2.0	0.9 (1.7)	0.4	1.4	0.2	1.6	
1990s	0.9	0.7 (0.9)	2.6	1.1	0.0	19.1	

The figures up to the 1980s are for Czechoslovakia

Hungary

	Man	GDP	Agri	Serv	Pop	Inf	Ex
18th Century	0.5	0.4	0.3				
19th Century	2.6	2.1	1.5				
20th Century	5.0	2.7	2.1				
1900-49	4.4	3.2	2.3				
1950-99	5.6	2.2 (4.1)	1.8	4.8			
1950s	11.0	4.0 (8.0)	5.0	9.4			
1960s	5.0	2.0 (3.8)	2.4	4.0	0.4		9.7
1970s	8.6	3.5 (6.4)	3.0	8.0	0.4		8.6
1980s	1.6	0.8 (1.3)	1.7	2.1	-0.2	7.5	3.6
1990s	2.0	0.8 (1.0)	-3.2	0.6	-0.3	16.7	4.0

POLAND

	Man	GDP	Agri	Serv	Pop	Inf	Ex
18th Century	0.4	0.3	0.2				
19th Century	2.4	2.0	1.1		0.9		
20th Century	4.2	2.6	1.5		0.6		
1800-49	0.6	0.4	0.3				
1850-99	4.2	3.6	1.9				
1900-49	2.7	2.1	1.4		0.4		
1950-99	5.7	3.0 (4.5)	1.5	4.0	0.8		
1900s	4.1	3.4					
1910s	-3.0	-2.6					
1920s	2.5	2.0					
1930s	2.0	1.6					
1940s	7.8	6.0					
1950s	6.6	2.9 (5.0)	2.8	4.5	1.4		
1960s	6.1	2.7 (4.3)	2.0	4.0	1.0		-0.3
1970s	7.5	3.8 (6.1)	3.2	5.1	0.9	4.5	7.3
1980s	2.2	1.3 (2.2)	-0.4	2.8	0.7	38.1	6.1
1990s	6.3	4.4 (4.7)	0.0	3.8	0.2	30.8	9.0

ROMANIA

	Man	GDP	Agri	Serv	Pop	Inf	Ex
18th Century		0.2					
19th Century	2.2	1.5	1.2				
20th Century	4.5	2.5	2.3				
1900-49	3.3	2.4	1.9				
1950-99	5.7	2.5 (4.9)	2.7	4.8			
1950s	8.0	3.0 (6.0)	3.4	7.0			
1960s	10.0	4.4 (8.6)	4.0	8.4	1.0	-0.2	9.4
1970s	11.2	5.6 (10.6)	6.2	9.0	0.9	0.8	4.7
1980s	0.7	0.3 (0.5)	0.3	0.8	0.4		
1990s	-1.6	-0.8 (-1.2)	-0.5	-1.0	-0.4	110.0	

119

RUSSIA

	Man	GDP	Agri	Serv	Pop	Inf	Ex
16th Century	0.2	0.1	0.1		0.1		
17th Century	0.3	0.2	0.1		0.2		
18th Century	0.7	0.5	0.3		1.1		
19th Century	2.3	1.7	0.9		1.2		
20th Century	6.9	2.4 (4.9)	1.9		0.9		
1800-49	0.5	0.3	0.2		0.2		
1850-99	4.0	3.0	1.6		2.2		
1900-49	9.0	3.1 (6.4)	2.0		0.8		
1950-99	4.7	1.7 (3.4)	1.6	3.3	1.0		
1800-39	0.3	0.2	0.2				
1840s	0.5	0.4	0.3				
1850s	0.8	0.6	0.4				
1860s	2.8	2.0	1.2				
1870s	3.2	2.5	1.7				
1880s	5.0	3.9	2.0				
1890s	8.0	6.1	2.8				
1900s	3.0	2.2	2.0				
1910s	-3.5	-2.6	-3.0				
1920s	21.1	8.0 (16)	5.9				
1930s	17.2	5.8 (14)	0.1				
1940s	7.1	2.2 (5)	5.1				
1950s	12.2	4.1 (9)	4.8	4.6			
1960s	9.1	3.0 (7)	2.9	5.7			
1970s	6.2	2.3 (4)	2.0	4.0			
1980s	4.3	1.4 (2)	1.1	3.8	0.6		
1990s	-9.0	-3.0 (-6)	-2.6	-1.8	-0.1	413.8	

YUGOSLAVIA

	Man	GDP	Agri	Serv	Pop	Inf	Ex
18th Century	0.4	0.3	0.2				
19th Century	2.0	1.6	1.0				
20th Century	3.6	2.3	1.9				
1900-49	3.3	2.4	1.8				
1950-99	3.9	2.2 (3.4)	2.0				
1950s	10.0	4.7 (8.0)	4.8	8.0			
1960s	6.3	3.3 (5.8)	3.3	6.9	1.0	12.6	7.7
1970s	7.0	4.0 (5.9)	3.0	5.7	0.9	17.8	4.7
1980s	1.7	0.8 (1.3)	1.0	1.2	0.7	96.9	0.4
1990s	-5.4	-2.0 (-4.0)	-2.0		-0.7	11,600,000.0	

The statistics for the 1990s comprise all the territories that were part of Yugoslavia up to the 1980s.

CHAPTER 4. LATIN AMERICA AND THE CARIBBEAN

ARGENTINA

	Man	GDP	Agri	Serv	Pop	Inf	Ex
16th Century	0.0	0.0	0.0				
17th Century	0.0	0.0	0.0				
18th Century	0.1	0.1	0.1				
19th Century	3.0	2.4	1.7		1.8		
20th Century	3.6	2.5 (3.1)	1.9	3.7	2.0	77.0	4.5
1800-49	0.6	0.4	0.4		0.6		
1850-99	5.3	4.3	3.0		2.9		5.7
1900-49	4.4	3.0 (3.7)	2.0	4.4	2.6	4.3	4.8
1950-99	2.8	2.0 (2.5)	1.8	2.9	1.4	149.7	4.2
1800s	0.3	0.2	0.2		0.6		
1810s	0.3	0.2	0.1		0.5		
1820s	0.6	0.4	0.3		0.5		
1830s	0.8	0.6	0.5		0.7		
1840s	1.1	0.8	0.7		0.8		
1850s	2.5	2.0	1.4		1.6		2.6
1860s	4.8	3.6	2.7		2.5		5.1
1870s	5.6	4.6	3.0		2.9		6.0
1880s	6.6	5.5	3.8		3.6		7.0
1890s	7.1	6.0	4.0		4.0		7.7
1900s	6.5	5.0	4.0	6.6	4.1	1.2	7.5
1910s	3.0	2.1	1.3	3.5	2.0	5.7	1.8
1920s	6.8	5.0	3.0	6.0	3.7	0.1	8.1
1930s	1.5	0.9 (1.1)	1.2	1.7	1.6	2.1	0.4
1940s	4.0	2.2 (3.0)	0.4	4.1	1.6	12.4	6.0
1950s	3.1	1.9 (2.3)	1.4	3.3	1.4	27.0	1.4
1960s	4.6	2.7 (3.5)	1.7	3.8	1.4	23.4	2.8
1970s	2.4	1.5 (2.0)	2.5	2.5	1.6	128.2	10.1
1980s	-0.9	-0.5 (-0.7)	0.4	0.0	1.5	334.8	0.6
1990s	5.0	4.6 (4.9)	3.1	4.8	1.3	235.1	6.0

BAHAMAS

	Man	GDP	Agri	Serv	Pop	Inf	Ex
18th Century							
19th Century	0.8	0.6					
20th Century	5.2	4.2					
1900-49	2.4	2.0					
1950-99	7.9	6.4					
1950s	8.5	7.0					
1960s	9.6	8.0					
1970s	10.0	8.0					
1980s	5.0	4.0					
1990s	6.3	5.0					

BOLIVIA

	Man	GDP	Agri	Serv	Pop	Inf	Ex
18th Century		0.2					
19th Century	0.7	0.5	0.4				
20th Century	3.0	2.1	1.7				
1900-49	1.5	1.1	0.8				
1950-99	4.4	3.1 (3.6)	2.6	3.9			
1950s	4.5	3.0 (3.5)	2.4	4.0			
1960s	6.0	4.4 (5.2)	3.0	5.4	2.3	3.5	9.8
1970s	6.7	4.5 (5.2)	3.1	6.0	2.5	32.4	2.0
1980s	-0.4	-0.2	1.9	-0.5	2.0	391.9	1.0
1990s	5.0	4.0 (4.2)	2.5	4.5	2.4	12.2	4.9

BRAZIL

	Man	GDP	Agri	Serv	Pop	Inf	Ex
16th Century	0.1	0.1	0.1				
17th Century	0.1	0.1	0.1				
18th Century	0.1	0.1	0.1		2.4		
19th Century	1.0	0.8	0.6		1.1		
20th Century	5.3	3.6 (4.2)	2.9	5.1	2.3	118.5	4.6
1800-49	0.5	0.4	0.3		0.4		
1850-99	1.5	1.1	0.9		1.8		2.2
1900-49	4.1	2.6 (3.1)	2.0	4.2	2.2		3.5
1950-99	6.4	4.6 (5.3)	3.8	5.9	2.4	230.4	5.7
1800s	0.2	0.1	0.1				
1810s	0.4	0.3	0.2				
1820s	0.5	0.4	0.3				
1830s	0.6	0.4	0.3				
1840s	0.9	0.7	0.5				
1850s	1.0	0.8	0.6				
1860s	1.1	0.8	0.6				
1870s	1.4	0.9	1.0				
1880s	1.6	1.2	1.0				
1890s	2.4	2.0	1.3				
1900s	3.0	2.3	1.4	3.0	2.3		2.0
1910s	4.2	3.3	2.0	3.6	2.2		0.9
1920s	1.4	1.0	1.0	3.0	2.0	8.3	2.3
1930s	5.4	3.0 (4.0)	2.5	5.5	2.1	9.0	0.4
1940s	6.3	3.6 (4.7)	3.0	6.0	2.5	10.1	12.1
1950s	8.6	5.6 (7.0)	4.0	7.0	3.3	18.2	5.6
1960s	6.0	4.0 (5.0)	4.0	8.0	2.9	48.0	5.1
1970s	10.9	8.2 (8.8)	5.0	8.7	2.2	31.7	7.0
1980s	3.4	2.6 (2.9)	2.9	3.2	2.0	328.2	5.6
1990s	3.1	2.7 (2.9)	3.0	2.7	1.4	726.1	5.1

CHILE

	Man	GDP	Agri	Serv	Pop	Inf	Ex
18th Century	0.1	0.1					
19th Century	2.3	1.8	1.4				
20th Century	3.4	2.8	2.1	3.2			
1900-49	2.3	1.8	1.3	2.2			
1950-99	4.5	3.8 (4.1)	2.9	4.2	1.8	67.8	6.1
1950s	3.7	2.5 (3.0)	1.9	3.6	1.9	36.0	3.4
1960s	5.2	4.0 (4.5)	2.6	4.5	2.1	29.0	0.6
1970s	2.0	1.6 (1.9)	3.5	2.8	1.7	242.6	10.0
1980s	4.0	3.6 (3.8)	5.0	2.8	1.6	20.5	6.6
1990s	7.5	7.2	1.3	7.5	1.5	11.1	9.7

COLOMBIA

	Man	GDP	Agri	Serv	Pop	Inf	Ex
18th Century	0.1	0.1	0.1				
19th Century	1.1	0.8	0.6				
20th Century	4.0	3.1	1.9				
1900-49	2.6	2.0	1.4				
1950-99	5.4	4.2 (4.5)	2.4	5.7	2.4		3.7
1950s	6.3	4.4 (4.8)	3.6	6.2	2.8		2.6
1960s	5.8	4.6 (5.1)	3.5	5.7	3.0	11.9	2.2
1970s	6.6	5.3 (6.0)	4.8	7.2	2.3	21.5	0.9
1980s	4.6	3.3 (3.5)	2.8	3.1	2.0	24.3	7.5
1990s	3.8	3.3	-2.6	6.3	1.9	20.0	5.2

COSTA RICA

	Man	GDP	Agri	Serv	Pop	Inf	Ex
18th Century		0.1	0.1				
19th Century	1.0	0.8	0.6				
20th Century	4.4	3.2	2.4				
1900-49	2.6	2.1	1.5				
1950-99	6.1	4.2 (4.7)	3.3	4.9			
1950s	5.0	3.4 (4.0)	2.8	4.8			
1960s	9.0	5.5 (6.5)	5.7	5.7	3.4	1.9	9.6
1970s	8.2	5.3 (6.0)	2.6	6.0	2.5	15.4	4.4
1980s	3.6	2.8 (3.0)	3.1	3.1	2.6	24.8	6.1
1990s	4.7	4.0 (4.1)	2.5	4.9	2.0	20.0	9.7

CUBA

	Man	GDP	Agri	Serv	Pop	Inf	Ex
18th Century	0.2	0.2	0.1				
19th Century	0.8	0.6	0.4				
20th Century	4.8	2.7	2.1				
1900-49	2.5	2.0	1.5				
1950-99	7.1	3.4 (5.8)	2.6				
1950s	5.0	4.0	3.0				
1960s	5.0	2.1 (3.9)	2.2				
1970s	15.0	6.0 (12.0)	5.0				
1980s	13.3	6.1 (11.0)	4.0				
1990s	-3.0	-1.2 (-2.0)	-1.3				

DOMINICAN REPUBLIC

	Man	GDP	Agri	Serv	Pop	Inf	Ex
18th Century		0.1					
19th Century	0.8	0.6	0.4				
20th Century	4.4	3.0	1.9				
1900-49	2.6	1.9	1.3				
1950-99	6.1	4.1 (4.9)	2.5				
1950s	3.7	2.4 (3.0)	2.0				
1960s	6.0	4.0 (4.6)	2.1	5.0	2.9	2.1	-2.3
1970s	10.0	6.3 (8.0)	4.0	7.7	2.9	8.4	5.6
1980s	3.6	2.5 (3.0)	0.4	3.5	2.3	19.1	3.0
1990s	7.0	5.2 (5.7)	3.8	5.7	1.9	8.0	7.0

ECUADOR

	Man	GDP	Agri	Serv	Pop	Inf	Ex
18th Century	0.1	0.1	0.1				
19th Century	0.6	0.5	0.3				
20th Century	3.5	2.3	1.9				
1900-49	0.9	0.7	0.5				
1950-99	6.0	3.9 (4.7)	3.3	5.1	2.7		
1950s	6.6	4.0 (5.0)	3.3	6.6	2.6		
1960s	8.1	4.8 (6.0)	3.4	6.8	3.1	3.3	2.9
1970s	10.5	7.0 (8.3)	3.4	8.6	3.1	14.7	8.2
1980s	2.2	1.6 (1.9)	4.3	1.7	2.5	34.4	4.2
1990s	2.7	2.0 (2.2)	2.0	1.9	2.1	30.0	4.4

EL SALVADOR

	Man	GDP	Agri	Serv	Pop	Inf	Ex
18th Century		0.1	0.1				
19th Century	1.0	0.8	0.6				
20th Century	3.9	2.8	1.5				
1900-49	2.5	2.0	1.3				
1950-99	5.2	3.6 (4.1)	1.7	4.6			
1950s	5.0	3.5 (4.0)	2.6	5.0			
1960s	8.5	5.0 (5.7)	3.0	6.5	2.9	0.5	5.4
1970s	6.0	4.0 (5.0)	3.2	5.1	2.9	10.8	4.2
1980s	0.7	0.5 (0.7)	-1.1	0.7	1.1	16.8	-3.0
1990s	5.6	4.9 (5.3)	0.9	5.6	2.1	7.0	11.0

GUATEMALA

	Man	GDP	Agri	Serv	Pop	Inf	Ex
18th Century	0.1	0.1					
19th Century	0.9	0.7	0.5				
20th Century	3.8	2.7	2.4				
1900-49	2.3	1.9	1.5				
1950-99	5.3	3.5 (4.1)	3.3	4.8			
1950s	5.0	3.3 (4.0)	3.0	7.0			
1960s	7.8	4.7 (5.6)	4.3	5.5	2.8	0.1	9.1
1970s	8.0	5.0 (5.9)	5.1	5.5	2.9	10.6	4.5
1980s	1.0	0.7 (0.9)	1.2	0.9	2.5	13.4	-1.8
1990s	4.5	4.0 (4.3)	2.7	4.9	2.6	7.0	6.4

HAITI

	Man	GDP	Agri	Serv	Pop	Inf	Ex
18th Century		0.1					
19th Century	0.7	0.5	0.3				
20th Century	1.7	1.1	0.4				
1900-49	1.1	0.8	0.5				
1950-99	2.2	1.4 (1.7)	0.3				
1950s	7.0	5.0 (6.0)	4.0				
1960s	-0.3	-0.2 (-0.3)	-0.6	0.9	1.5	4.1	0.0
1970s	7.1	4.0 (5.0)	2.6	3.7	1.7	10.9	7.0
1980s	-0.6	-0.2 (-0.4)	-0.1	0.9	1.9	6.8	1.2
1990s	-2.0	-1.7 (-2.0)	-4.3	-0.3	2.1	17.0	2.4

HONDURAS

	Man	GDP	Agri	Serv	Pop	Inf	Ex
18th Century	0.1	0.1	0.1				
19th Century	0.6	0.4	0.3				
20th Century	3.0	2.2	1.8				
1900-49	1.3	1.0	0.7				
1950-99	4.6	3.4 (3.9)	2.9	4.6	3.0		5.3
1950s	5.0	3.6 (4.1)	3.0	5.0	2.8		8.0
1960s	5.8	4.8 (5.3)	5.7	4.8	3.1	2.9	11.1
1970s	5.5	3.3 (4.0)	1.3	7.0	3.3	8.4	4.3
1980s	3.3	2.3 (2.7)	2.7	2.5	3.1	4.7	1.1
1990s	3.6	3.0 (3.2)	1.8	3.7	2.9	20.0	2.0

130

JAMAICA

	Man	GDP	Agri	Serv	Pop	Inf	Ex
18th Century	0.1	0.1	0.1				
19th Century	0.9	0.7	0.5				
20th Century	2.8	2.3	1.7				
1900-49	2.4	1.9	1.5				
1950-99	3.2	2.7	1.9	2.8			
1950s	8.0	6.0	4.0	7.0			
1960s	7.0	6.0	1.5	4.7	1.4	3.9	4.7
1970s	-1.3	-0.5 (-0.9)	0.9	0.2	1.6	17.4	-6.8
1980s	2.4	2.0 (2.3)	0.6	1.8	1.2	18.5	2.0
1990s	0.1	0.1	2.3	0.3	0.9	26.0	0.1

MEXICO

	Man	GDP	Agri	Serv	Pop	Inf	Ex
16th Century	0.1	0.1	0.1				
17th Century	0.1	0.1	0.1				
18th Century	0.3	0.2	0.2		0.6		
19th Century	1.3	0.9	0.7				
20th Century	4.5	3.2 (3.7)	2.3		2.2		4.2
1800-49	0.4	0.3	0.2				
1850-99	2.2	1.5 (1.7)	1.1				2.5
1900-49	3.5	2.3 (2.8)	2.2		1.6		2.8
1950-99	5.5	4.1 (4.6)	2.4	4.6	2.7	23.3	5.6
1800s	0.5	0.4	0.3				
1810s	0.0	0.0	0.0				
1820s	0.1	0.1	0.1				
1830s	0.7	0.5	0.3				
1840s	0.9	0.7	0.4				
1850s	1.3	0.9	0.5				
1860s	1.2	0.8	0.6				
1870s	1.7	1.2	0.9				
1880s	3.0	2.1	1.6				1.1
1890s	4.0	2.7	2.1				1.3
1900s	4.2	2.8 (3.2)	2.1		1.9		2.9
1910s	0.4	0.3 (0.4)	0.4		0.0		0.3

1920s	1.8	1.1 (1.4)	1.0		1.0		1.3
1930s	4.3	2.5 (3.4)	2.0		2.4		2.7
1940s	7.0	5.0 (5.7)	3.8		2.6	2.0	6.8
1950s	7.4	5.6 (6.2)	4.4	8.1	3.1	3.0	4.0
1960s	8.7	6.5 (7.3)	3.4	6.9	3.5	3.8	4.4
1970s	6.7	5.0 (5.9)	2.1	4.7	3.1	16.7	10.9
1980s	0.9	0.6 (0.7)	0.8	0.9	2.1	72.7	3.7
1990s	3.6	2.6 (2.7)	1.3	2.4	1.8	20.1	4.8

NICARAGUA

	Man	GDP	Agri	Serv	Pop	Inf	Ex
18th Century		0.1	0.1				
19th Century	0.7	0.5	0.4				
20th Century	3.2	2.1	2.0				
1900-49	1.9	1.3	1.0				
1950-99	4.5	2.9 (3.4)	3.0	2.5			
1950s	7.0	5.0 (6.0)	4.0	6.0			
1960s	9.6	6.0 (7.2)	6.0	5.7	2.9	1.9	9.7
1970s	3.3	2.0 (2.6)	2.0	1.3	3.3	12.2	2.0
1980s	-2.3	-1.3 (-1.9)	-2.2	-1.5	2.7	3,600.0	-3.9
1990s	5.0	2.8 (3.2)	5.4	1.1	2.8	36.0	10.3

PANAMA

	GDP		Agri	Serv	Pop	Inf	Ex
18th Century			0.1				
19th Century	0.8	0.6	0.5				
20th Century	3.7	3.1	2.2				
1900-49	2.5	2.1	1.5				
1950-99	4.9	4.0	2.9	4.4			
1950s	5.0	4.0	2.5	4.8			
1960s	9.4	7.8	5.7	7.6	2.9	1.6	10.5
1970s	3.8	3.4	2.2	4.9	2.3	7.4	0.6
1980s	0.6	0.5	2.5	0.7	2.1	2.5	-0.9
1990s	5.5	4.2	1.7	4.2	1.8	2.0	0.0

PARAGUAY

	Man	GDP	Agri	Serv	Pop	Inf	Ex
18th Century		0.1					
19th Century	0.9	0.7	0.5				
20th Century	3.5	2.6	2.4				
1900-49	2.5	1.9	1.4				
1950-99	4.4	3.2 (3.8)	3.4	4.5			
1950s	2.3	1.2 (1.6)	1.0	2.3			
1960s	4.2	3.5 (4.2)	3.0	6.5	2.6	3.1	5.4
1970s	9.9	7.0 (8.3)	6.8	8.6	2.9	9.3	8.4
1980s	2.9	2.1 (2.5)	3.6	3.1	3.0	23.2	7.0
1990s	2.8	2.2 (2.4)	2.8	2.0	2.7	10.0	3.1

PERU

	Man	GDP	Agri	Serv	Pop	Inf	Ex
18th Century	0.3	0.2	0.2				
19th Century	1.8	1.3	0.9				
20th Century	3.2	2.4	2.2				
1900-49	2.2	1.8	1.4				
1950-99	4.1	3.0	3.0	3.4	2.4		2.9
1950s	5.1	3.5 (4.0)	2.6	5.0	2.5		1.8
1960s	5.7	4.0 (4.9)	3.7	5.3	2.8	10.4	2.0
1970s	3.7	2.5 (3.1)	0.1	3.6	2.7	26.8	1.7
1980s	-0.7	-0.2 (-0.3)	2.7	-0.7	2.2	160.3	0.0
1990s	6.7	5.0 (5.4)	5.8	4.0	1.7	30.0	9.0

Puerto Rico

	Man	GDP	Agri	Serv	Pop	Inf	Ex
18th Century		0.1					
19th Century	1.1	0.8					
20th Century	4.8	4.0					
1900-49	3.0	2.5					
1950-99	6.5	5.5					
1950s	9.4	8.0					
1960s	10.0	8.4					
1970s	4.7	4.0					
1980s	4.0	3.3					
1990s	4.4	3.7					

Uruguay

	Man	GDP	Agri	Serv	Pop	Inf	Ex
18th Century	0.1	0.1					
19th Century	2.5	2.0	1.6				
20th Century	3.3	2.5	2.1				
1900-49	3.4	2.5	2.1				
1950-99	3.2	2.4 (2.7)	2.0	2.7			
1950s	6.0	4.0 (4.4)	3.0	5.0			
1960s	1.7	1.2 (1.5)	1.9	1.0	1.1	51.1	2.2
1970s	3.9	2.5 (3.0)	0.8	2.0	0.3	64.0	4.3
1980s	0.5	0.4 (0.5)	0.0	0.8	0.6	59.2	4.0
1990s	3.7	3.7 (4.0)	4.3	4.5	0.7	36.0	6.0

VENEZUELA

	Man	GDP	Agri	Serv	Pop	Inf	Ex
18th Century	0.1	0.1	0.1				
19th Century	0.8	0.6	0.5				
20th Century	4.3	3.1	2.8	4.0			
1900-49	3.1	2.6	1.6	3.0			
1950-99	5.5	3.5 (4.5)	3.9	5.0	3.0		
1950s	11.0	6.5 (8.5)	6.0	9.4	3.6		
1960s	6.4	4.3 (6.0)	5.8	7.3	3.4	1.3	1.6
1970s	5.7	4.2 (5.5)	3.8	7.2	3.3	10.4	
1980s	1.6	0.8 (1.0)	3.0	0.5	2.7	16.0	2.8
1990s	2.6	1.5 (1.7)	0.7	0.8	2.2	50.0	5.6

CHAPTER 5. MIDDLE EAST AND NORTH AFRICA

AFGHANISTAN

	Man	GDP	Agri	Serv	Pop	Inf	Ex
18th Century							
19th Century		0.3					
20th Century	1.3	0.9	0.6				
1900-49	0.8	0.6	0.4				
1950-99	1.7	1.2	0.8				
1950s	3.4	2.2	1.5				
1960s	3.1	2.0	1.4		2.3	11.9	2.5
1970s	5.8	4.2	2.3		2.6	4.4	3.0
1980s	-1.0	-0.4	0.0				
1990s	-3.0	-2.0	-1.0				

ALGERIA

	Man	GDP	Agri	Serv	Pop	Inf	Ex
18th Century	0.1	0.1					
19th Century	1.1	0.8	0.5				
20th Century	4.2	2.9	1.9				
1900-49	3.1	2.5	1.4				
1950-99	5.3	3.2	2.4	3.2			
1950s	6.5	5.3	3.3	6.3			
1960s	7.0	3.5 (4.6)	0.4	-3.0	2.8	2.3	4.5
1970s	8.0	4.0 (5.8)	0.6	6.1	3.3	13.3	0.0
1980s	3.4	2.0 (2.7)	4.6	3.6	3.0	5.2	4.1
1990s	1.6	1.3 (1.6)	3.0	3.1	2.2	20.0	2.2

BAHRAIN

	Man	GDP	Agri	Serv	Pop	Inf	Ex
18th Century							
19th Century	0.5	0.4					
20th Century	6.0	4.8					
1900-49	2.4	2.0					
1950-99	9.6	7.6					
1950s	11.0	9.0					
1960s	12.0	10.0					
1970s	17.0	13.0					
1980s	2.5	2.0					
1990s	5.3	4.0			2.6	-0.4	

EGYPT

	Man	GDP	Agri	Serv	Pop	Inf	Ex
16th Century	0.1	0.1	0.1		0.1		
17th Century	0.2	0.1	0.1		0.1		
18th Century	0.1	0.1	0.1		0.1		
19th Century	0.8	0.6	0.4		0.6		
20th Century	3.8	2.5 (3.0)	1.8		1.9		
1800-49	0.8	0.6	0.4		0.5		
1850-99	0.8	0.6	0.4		0.7		
1900-49	1.6	1.2	0.7		1.3		
1950-99	5.9	3.8 (4.7)	2.8	6.1	2.4		
1900s	1.0	0.8	0.7		0.9		
1910s	1.1	0.8	0.6		1.2		
1920s	1.3	1.0	0.8		1.3		
1930s	1.7	1.3	0.9		1.4		
1940s	2.7	1.9	0.7		1.7		
1950s	4.8	2.6 (3.3)	3.0	4.0	1.9		
1960s	5.4	2.6 (4.0)	2.8	4.7	2.6	2.8	3.2
1970s	8.2	5.3 (6.6)	2.2	10.6	2.5	8.0	3.0
1980s	5.8	4.6 (5.2)	2.7	6.9	2.7	11.1	6.2
1990s	5.1	4.1 (4.4)	3.1	4.3	2.1	9.0	3.1

IRAN

	Man	GDP	Agri	Serv	Pop	Inf	Ex
16th Century	0.2	0.1					
17th Century	0.1	0.1					
18th Century	0.1	0.1	0.1				
19th Century	0.7	0.5	0.4				
20th Century	4.8	3.3	2.7				
1800-49	0.3	0.2	0.2				
1850-99	1.0	0.7	0.6				
1900-49	2.5	1.8	1.1				
1950-99	7.1	4.7 (5.7)	4.2	6.3		13.8	
1900s	1.0	0.8			0.7		
1910s	1.8	1.4					
1920s	2.7	2.0					
1930s	3.5	2.5					
1940s	3.6	2.5					
1950s	10.0	7.0 (8.0)	4.0	11.1		6.0	
1960s	13.4	9.0 (11.3)	4.6	10.0	2.7	-0.5	12.6
1970s	5.5	3.2 (4.0)	4.4	5.5	2.7	20.0	
1980s	2.7	1.4 (1.8)	4.3	-1.0	3.3	13.5	6.9
1990s	4.0	3.0 (3.4)	3.8	5.8	1.6	30.0	0.2

IRAQ

	Man	GDP	Agri	Serv	Pop	Inf	Ex
18th Century	0.2	0.2					
19th Century	0.8	0.6	0.4				
20th Century	3.8	2.8	1.8				
1900-49	2.1	1.6	1.0				
1950-99	5.5	3.9 (4.5)	2.5		3.0		
1950s	8.0	6.0 (6.4)	4.0		2.9		
1960s	6.6	5.6 (6.1)	5.7	8.3	3.1	1.7	
1970s	13.4	9.0 (10.5)	0.8	10.4	3.3	14.1	
1980s	6.3	4.0 (5.0)	3.0	6.0	3.6		
1990s	-7.0	-5.0 (-5.5)	-1.0		2.2		

ISRAEL

	Man	GDP	Agri	Serv	Pop	Inf	Ex
18th Century		0.2	0.1				
19th Century	1.2	0.9	0.6				
20th Century	6.1	5.0	3.2				
1900-49	3.9	3.3	2.0				
1950-99	8.2	6.6	4.4	7.9		35.4	11.3
1950s	13.3	10.7	7.4	12.0		9.0	19.6
1960s	11.0	9.3	6.0	11.0	3.4	5.2	11.0
1970s	6.0	4.6	3.5	5.5	2.7	34.3	9.8
1980s	4.1	3.4	2.3	4.3	1.7	117.1	7.7
1990s	6.5	5.1	3.0	6.6	3.0	10.3	8.5

JORDAN

	Man	GDP	Agri	Serv	Pop	Inf	Ex
18th Century	0.3	0.2					
19th Century	0.6	0.4	0.3				
20th Century	3.7	2.7	1.7				
1900-49	1.8	1.4	0.9				
1950-99	5.6	3.9 (4.6)	2.4	5.1			
1950s	5.3	3.3 (4.0)	2.7	5.0			
1960s	6.0	4.1 (4.8)	3.3	6.2	4.0		10.1
1970s	8.0	5.0 (6.1)	4.1	7.0	4.2		13.3
1980s	2.7	2.2 (2.5)	6.0	2.0	3.8		5.9
1990s	6.2	5.0 (5.4)	-4.0	5.5	4.0	3.3	7.4

KUWAIT

	Man	GDP	Agri	Serv	Pop	Inf	Ex
18th Century		0.3					
19th Century	1.0	0.8					
20th Century	5.9	4.8					
1900-49	1.7	1.4					
1950-99	10.0	8.2		8.4			
1950s	23.0	20.0		19.3			
1960s	6.9	5.7		6.2	9.8	0.6	
1970s	2.4	2.0		2.6	6.0	17.7	
1980s	1.8	1.3		0.9	4.4	-2.7	
1990s	16.0	12.1		13.0	-1.1	3.4	

LEBANON

	Man	GDP	Agri	Serv	Pop	Inf	Ex
18th Century		0.2					
19th Century	0.9	0.7	0.5				
20th Century	3.1	2.6	2.2				
1900-49	2.3	1.8	1.5				
1950-99	3.9	3.4	2.9				
1950s	6.5	5.3	4.0	6.0			
1960s	5.0	4.9	6.3	4.8	2.8	1.4	14.2
1970s	2.5	2.0	1.4	2.0	0.8	12.0	2.3
1980s	1.5	1.0	0.7		1.9		
1990s	4.0	4.0	2.0	4.3	1.8	17.8	15.6

LIBYA

	Man	GDP	Agri	Serv	Pop	Inf	Ex
18th Century		0.1					
19th Century	0.6	0.4					
20th Century	3.5	2.7					
1900-49	1.0	0.7					
1950-99	6.0	4.7			2.8		
1950s	2.7	2.1	1.0		0.8		3.7
1960s	30.3	24.4	6.6	22.2	3.8	5.0	68.0
1970s	3.2	1.9	11.8	3.0	4.1	18.7	-6.5
1980s	-7.6	-6.0			3.1	0.2	
1990s	1.4	1.0			2.2		

MOROCCO

	Man	GDP	Agri	Serv	Pop	Inf	Ex
18th Century	0.2	0.1	0.1				
19th Century	0.5	0.4	0.3				
20th Century	3.7	2.8 (3.1)	2.0				
1900-49	2.4	1.9	1.3				
1950-99	4.9	3.7 (4.2)	2.7				
1950s	5.0	4.0 (4.3)	2.5				
1960s	4.5	3.5 (4.2)	4.7	4.0	2.5	2.0	2.5
1970s	7.3	5.2 (6.1)	-0.3	7.4	2.9	7.3	1.3
1980s	4.5	3.7 (4.2)	6.7	4.2	2.2	7.4	5.7
1990s	3.1	2.0 (2.3)	0.0	2.5	1.8	2.0	3.0

OMAN

	Man	GDP	Agri	Serv	Pop	Inf	Ex
18th Century							
19th Century	0.4	0.3	0.2				
20th Century	5.6	4.3	2.5				
1900-49	1.4	1.1	0.6				
1950-99	9.7	7.5	4.4	7.5			
1950s	1.9	1.4	0.8	2.0			
1960s	7.8	6.1	3.4	7.0	2.5	3.5	
1970s	17.0	13.0	6.8	13.0	4.0	25.0	
1980s	16.0	12.0	7.0	10.5	4.7	-6.0	
1990s	6.0	4.8	4.0	5.0	3.5	0.5	

QATAR

	Man	GDP	Agri	Serv	Pop	Inf	Ex
18th Century							
19th Century		0.5					
20th Century	6.1	5.1					
1900-49	1.2	1.0					
1950-99	11.0	9.1					
1950s	6.0	5.0					
1960s	12.2	10.0					
1970s	36.0	30.0					
1980s	-3.0	-2.3					
1990s	3.7	3.0					

SAUDI ARABIA

	Man	GDP	Agri	Serv	Pop	Inf	Ex
18th Century		0.1					
19th Century	0.5	0.4	0.2				
20th Century	4.7	4.0	3.0				
1900-49	1.3	1.0	0.5				
1950-99	8.1	7.0	5.5	7.5	3.9		
1950s	14.4	12.3	3.8	12.1	3.0		
1960s	12.0	10.0	4.0	10.0	3.4	11.0	10.9
1970s	12.6	11.1	4.2	11.9	4.5	25.2	5.6
1980s	-0.3	0.0	14.6	1.3	5.2	-4.4	-11.3
1990s	1.8	1.6	0.7	2.0	3.4	2.1	

SYRIA

	Man	GDP	Agri	Serv	Pop	Inf	Ex
18th Century		0.2	0.2				
19th Century	0.8	0.6	0.4				
20th Century	3.9	2.4	2.0				
1900-49	1.9	1.3	1.0				
1950-99	5.9	3.5 (4.5)	3.0	4.8			
1950s	1.8	0.9 (1.3)	1.0	1.8			
1960s	6.3	3.5 (5.0)	4.4	6.2	3.2	1.9	7.0
1970s	12.0	6.7 (9.0)	6.0	9.1	3.6	12.7	11.0
1980s	2.6	1.3 (1.6)	0.0	1.0	3.3	15.0	5.7
1990s	7.0	5.0 (5.7)	3.7	6.0	2.8	7.4	4.7

TUNISIA

	Man	GDP	Agri	Serv	Pop	Inf	Ex
18th Century		0.2	0.1				
19th Century	1.0	0.8	0.5				
20th Century	4.4	3.1	2.1				
1900-49	2.2	1.7	1.1				
1950-99	6.6	4.5 (5.1)	3.0	5.5			
1950s	6.5	5.0	3.0	6.0			
1960s	7.8	3.8 (4.7)	2.0	4.5	1.9	3.7	4.2
1970s	9.6	6.5 (7.6)	5.1	8.1	2.1	7.5	13.0
1980s	4.0	3.0 (3.4)	2.8	3.5	2.5	7.5	4.0
1990s	5.0	4.2 (4.6)	2.1	5.3	1.6	4.0	5.1

TURKEY

	Man	GDP	Agri	Serv	Pop	Inf	Ex
18th Century	0.4	0.3	0.2				
19th Century	1.4	1.1	0.8				
20th Century	5.5	3.3	2.2				
1900-49	3.1	2.1	1.6				
1950-99	7.9	4.5 (5.8)	2.8	6.4			9.5
1950s	9.9	5.0 (7.1)	4.5	9.0			12.0
1960s	9.5	4.5 (6.0)	2.5	6.9	2.5	5.6	10.6
1970s	7.7	4.6 (6.6)	3.7	7.5	2.5	24.6	1.7
1980s	7.6	4.0 (5.4)	1.5	4.4	2.3	41.4	11.4
1990s	4.8	3.5 (4.1)	1.6	4.3	1.5	80.0	11.9

145

United Arab Emirates

	Man	GDP	Agri	Serv	Pop	Inf	Ex
18th Century		0.1					
19th Century	0.4	0.3					
20th Century	6.4	5.4					
1900-49	0.9	0.7					
1950-99	11.8	10.0			5.0		
1950s	1.4	1.1					
1960s	7.4	6.0					
1970s	27.0	24.0					
1980s	18.4	14.9					
1990s	5.0	4.0					

Yemen

	Man	GDP	Agri	Serv	Pop	Inf	Ex
18th Century							
19th Century	0.3	0.2					
20th Century	2.0	1.0					
1900-49	0.5	0.4					
1950-99	3.5	1.6 (2.2)					
1950s	1.4	0.7 (1.0)					
1960s	2.6	1.4 (2.0)			1.8		
1970s	6.0	2.6 (3.4)			1.8		
1980s	2.4	1.0 (1.5)			3.3		
1990s	5.0	2.5 (3.0)			4.0		

All figures up to the 1980s are just for North Yemen. The figures for the 1990s include the territory comprising North and South Yemen.

CHAPTER 6. NORTH AMERICA

CANADA

	Man	GDP	Agri	Serv	Pop	Inf	Ex
18th Century	0.3	0.2	0.2				
19th Century	3.0	2.6	1.7				
20th Century	4.4	3.9	2.0	4.0			
1900-49	4.0	3.5	1.9	3.7			
1950-99	4.7	4.3	2.0	4.3	1.4		
1950s	6.1	5.4	3.2	6.0	2.0		
1960s	6.8	5.6	2.5	5.5	1.8	3.1	10.0
1970s	4.4	4.2	2.2	4.7	1.1	9.1	4.6
1980s	3.6	3.3	1.2	3.6	1.2	4.6	6.1
1990s	2.5	2.3	1.1	1.9	1.1	3.0	7.0

THE UNITED STATES OF AMERICA

	Man	GDP	Agri	Serv	Pop	Inf	Ex	Unem
16th Century	0.0	0.0	0.0		0.0	0.0		
17th Century	0.1	0.1	0.1			0.0		
18th Century	0.4	0.3	0.2		5.5	0.0		
19th Century	5.4	4.5	2.4		5.1	0.0		
20th Century	4.2	3.5	1.7	3.9	1.3	2.5		6.5
1800-49	3.3	2.7	1.8		5.9	0.0		
1850-99	7.5	6.3	3.0		4.2	0.0		
1900-49	4.2	3.5	1.6	4.1	1.4	1.2		7.6
1950-99	4.1	3.4	1.7	3.7	1.2	3.8	5.7	5.3
1800s	2.3	1.8	1.4			0.1		
1810s	2.0	1.6	1.6			0.1		
1820s	3.7	3.0	1.6			0.0		
1830s	4.2	3.5	2.0			0.0		
1840s	4.7	3.8	2.2			0.0		
1850s	5.5	4.5	2.3			0.0		
1860s	6.0	4.7	2.0			0.7		

1870s	8.0	6.9	3.5	6.6		-0.9		
1880s	9.4	7.8	4.0	8.0		0.0		
1890s	8.6	7.5	3.0	7.7		0.0		
1900s	5.8	5.2	3.0	5.5		0.4		4.0
1910s	3.7	3.0	1.6	4.0		1.3		5.2
1920s	4.7	4.0	0.8	4.9		1.1		5.1
1930s	0.8	0.6	0.1	1.2		0.4		18.0
1940s	6.0	4.8	2.5	5.0		3.0		6.1
1950s	5.3	4.3	3.0	5.2	1.8	2.3	6.4	4.3
1960s	5.5	4.4	0.3	4.3	1.3	2.8	6.1	4.0
1970s	3.4	3.0	0.9	3.4	1.0	6.9	6.9	6.3
1980s	2.9	2.5	3.2	3.3	1.0	4.0	3.4	6.5
1990s	3.2	2.9	1.1	2.1	1.0	3.0	5.8	5.6

CHAPTER 7. OCEANIA

AUSTRALIA

	Man	GDP	Agri	Serv	Pop	Inf	Ex
18th Century	0.0	0.0	0.0				
19th Century	3.0	2.5	1.6				3.0
20th Century	4.2	3.7	1.9	4.0			4.4
1900-49	3.6	3.1	1.4	3.6			3.8
1950-99	4.8	4.3	2.2	4.4			5.0
1950s	6.7	5.8	3.3	6.0			7.0
1960s	5.9	5.5	2.7	4.0	2.0	3.1	6.5
1970s	3.5	3.2	1.8	3.8	1.5	11.7	4.2
1980s	3.6	3.4	3.2	3.6	1.4	7.8	4.1
1990s	4.1	3.8	1.1	4.4	1.2	2.8	3.3

NAURU

	Man	GDP	Agri	Serv	Pop	Inf	Ex
19th Century		0.0					
20th Century	6.3	5.2					
1900-49	0.9	0.7					
1950-99	11.6	9.6					
1950s	1.8	1.3					
1960s	5.0	4.0		6.0			
1970s	35.0	30.0		23.0			
1980s	18.8	15.0		13.3			
1990s	-2.7	-2.2		-1.7			

New Zealand

	Man	GDP	Agri	Serv	Pop	Inf	Ex
18th Century		0.0					
19th Century	2.7	2.2	1.4				
20th Century	3.7	3.2	2.3				4.0
1900-49	3.8	3.3	2.0				3.4
1950-99	3.6	3.0	2.6	3.6			4.5
1950s	5.0	4.2	2.5	5.1			5.0
1960s	4.8	3.9	2.4	4.9	1.7	3.3	4.6
1970s	3.0	2.4	1.5	3.0	1.5	12.3	3.4
1980s	1.9	1.7	3.8	1.8	1.0	11.4	4.0
1990s	3.5	2.9	2.6	3.4	1.2	1.5	5.4

Papua New Guinea

	Man	GDP	Agri	Serv	Pop	Inf	Ex
18th Century							
19th Century		0.1					
20th Century	3.2	2.5	1.7				
1900-49	1.4	1.0	0.8				
1950-99	5.0	4.0	2.5	3.9			
1950s	6.6	5.0	3.4	6.0			
1960s	7.0	6.5	3.6	6.0	2.1	3.6	18.0
1970s	2.7	2.2	1.5	2.5	2.3	9.5	9.0
1980s	2.6	2.0	1.8	2.0	2.2	5.6	4.0
1990s	6.0	4.2	2.3	2.8	2.3	8.0	9.5

Chapter 8. South Asia

Bangladesh

	Man	GDP	Agri	Serv	Pop	Inf	Ex
18th Century		0.0					
19th Century	0.1	0.1	0.1		0.2		
20th Century	2.4	1.4	1.0		1.3		2.8
1900-49	0.3	0.2	0.2		0.4		0.4
1950-99	4.5	2.6 (3.2)	1.8	4.4	2.2	6.9	5.1
1950s	1.1	0.6 (0.8)	0.6	1.6	1.1	0.3	0.8
1960s	5.3	2.9 (3.6)	2.7	3.8	2.4	3.7	6.5
1970s	4.4	2.0 (3.2)	1.9	4.9	3.0	15.8	-4.1
1980s	4.3	3.0 (3.5)	2.1	5.2	2.6	10.6	7.6
1990s	7.2	4.4 (5.0)	1.5	6.3	1.9	3.9	14.6

Bhutan

	Man	GDP	Agri	Serv	Pop	Inf	Ex
18th Century							
19th Century		0.1	0.1				
20th Century	2.3	1.3	1.2				
1900-49	0.3	0.2	0.1				
1950-99	4.2	2.4 (3.0)	2.3				
1950s	3.0	1.5 (2.0)	2.0				
1960s	2.8	1.5 (2.0)	1.7		2.0		
1970s	2.7	1.5 (2.0)	1.5		2.1		
1980s	6.0	3.4 (4.1)	3.0		2.1		
1990s	6.4	4.0 (5.0)	3.2		2.3	9.5	

INDIA

	Man	GDP	Agri	Serv	Pop	Inf	Ex
16th Century	0.2	0.1	0.1		0.1	0.0	
17th Century	0.3	0.2	0.2		0.1	0.0	
18th Century	0.0	0.0	0.0		0.0	0.0	
19th Century	0.4	0.3	0.2		0.3	0.2	
20th Century	3.7	2.0	1.6		1.4	5.7	4.0
1800-49	0.1	0.1	0.1		0.1	0.3	
1850-99	0.7	0.5	0.4		0.5	0.1	
1900-49	1.3	1.0	0.7		0.8	4.4	1.8
1950-99	6.1	3.0 (4.3)	2.5	5.3	1.9	6.9	6.2
1800s	0.0	0.0	0.0		0.0	0.0	
1810s	0.1	0.1	0.0		0.0	0.0	
1820s	0.2	0.1	0.1		0.1	0.2	
1830s	0.3	0.2	0.2		0.1	0.6	
1840s	0.3	0.2	0.2		0.2	0.7	
1850s	0.4	0.3	0.2		0.3	0.5	
1860s	0.6	0.4	0.3		0.4	0.1	
1870s	0.7	0.5	0.4		0.5	0.0	
1880s	0.9	0.7	0.5		0.7	0.0	
1890s	1.0	0.7	0.5		0.7	0.0	
1900s	0.6	0.4	0.5		0.6	0.3	1.1
1910s	1.2	0.9	0.6		0.4	0.9	1.4
1920s	1.5	1.0	0.5		0.9	0.5	2.3
1930s	1.7	1.3	0.7		1.1	0.2	1.8
1940s	2.1	1.6	1.1		0.9	20.2	2.4
1950s	6.0	2.4 (3.8)	2.8	4.4	1.5	1.3	0.9
1960s	4.6	1.5 (3.0)	1.6	4.6	2.3	6.9	3.2
1970s	5.0	2.3 (3.6)	2.3	4.5	2.1	8.1	6.8
1980s	7.1	4.0 (5.4)	2.9	6.5	2.1	8.7	7.4
1990s	7.8	5.0 (5.8)	3.1	6.6	1.7	9.5	12.5

NEPAL

	Man	GDP	Agri	Serv	Pop	Inf	Ex
18th Century							
19th Century		0.1					
20th Century	2.4	1.5	1.1				
1900-49	0.2	0.2	0.1				
1950-99	4.6	2.8 (3.0)	2.0	3.2			
1950s	1.4	1.0	0.8	1.0			
1960s	3.5	2.0 (2.5)	2.0	3.0	2.0	7.7	
1970s	3.0	1.6 (2.1)	0.8	2.0	2.2	8.7	
1980s	8.0	4.0 (4.6)	4.0	3.9	2.6	9.1	
1990s	7.0	4.5 (4.8)	2.3	6.0	2.4	6.0	

PAKISTAN

	Man	GDP	Agri	Serv	Pop	Inf	Ex
18th Century	0.0	0.0	0.0				
19th Century	0.1	0.1	0.1		0.2		
20th Century	3.6	2.1	1.8		1.7		
1900-49	0.6	0.4	0.3		0.6		
1950-99	6.5	3.8 (4.8)	3.4	6.0	2.7	8.1	4.4
1950s	5.2	2.8 (3.8)	1.8	5.1	2.4	6.4	3.1
1960s	9.0	5.0 (6.4)	5.0	7.0	2.8	3.3	8.2
1970s	5.1	2.5 (4.0)	2.1	6.3	3.1	13.9	-0.9
1980s	8.2	5.4 (6.2)	4.4	6.8	3.2	6.7	8.5
1990s	5.0	3.3 (3.7)	3.8	4.6	2.8	10.2	3.2

SRI LANKA

	Man	GDP	Agri	Serv	Pop	Inf	Ex
18th Century	0.1	0.1					
19th Century	0.4	0.3	0.3				
20th Century	3.4	2.4	1.6				
1900-49	1.0	0.8	0.7				
1950-99	5.7	3.9 (4.4)	2.5	4.9	1.8		
1950s	6.0	4.0 (4.2)	3.0	5.0	2.4		
1960s	6.3	4.0 (4.6)	3.0	4.6	2.4	1.8	4.7
1970s	4.3	2.8 (3.8)	2.6	4.5	1.7	12.3	-3.0
1980s	4.6	3.6 (4.0)	2.2	4.7	1.4	10.9	6.0
1990s	7.4	5.0 (5.3)	1.5	5.6	1.2	9.8	8.4

CHAPTER 9. SOUTHEAST ASIA

BRUNEI

	Man	GDP	Agri	Serv	Pop	Inf	Ex
18th Century							
19th Century		0.4					
20th Century	6.2	5.0					
1900-49	2.4	2.0					
1950-99	9.9	8.0					
1950s	12.0	10.0					
1960s	15.8	12.5					
1970s	18.0	15.0					
1980s	1.5	1.0				4.0	
1990s	2.0	1.5				2.1	

BURMA (MYANMAR)

	Man	GDP	Agri	Serv	Pop	Inf	Ex
18th Century							
19th Century		0.2	0.1				
20th Century	2.6	1.2	1.7				
1900-49	0.3	0.2	0.2				
1950-99	4.9	2.2 (3.6)	3.3	3.7	1.9		0.5
1950s	5.4	2.2 (4.0)	3.0	5.4	2.0		3.4
1960s	3.5	1.3 (2.6)	4.1	1.5	2.2	2.7	-10.0
1970s	5.6	2.1 (4.3)	3.9	4.3	2.2	12.1	-0.3
1980s	0.7	0.3 (0.6)	0.5	0.8	1.8		1.9
1990s	9.1	5.0 (6.3)	4.9	6.6	1.2	30.0	7.5

CAMBODIA

	Man	GDP	Agri	Serv	Pop	Inf	Ex
18th Century							
19th Century	0.1	0.1					
20th Century	2.7	1.7	1.1				
1900-49	1.0	0.7	0.6				
1950-99	4.2	2.1 (2.8)	1.6				
1950s	6.6	4.0 (5.0)	3.5				
1960s	4.0	2.0 (3.1)	2.0		2.7	3.8	
1970s	-1.5	-0.9 (-1.0)	-0.6				
1980s	4.0	1.2 (2.0)	1.0		2.9		
1990s	8.0	4.0 (4.8)	2.1	6.9	2.8	33.0	

INDONESIA

	Man	GDP	Agri	Serv	Pop	Inf	Ex
16th Century	0.0	0.0	0.0		0.0		
17th Century	0.0	0.0	0.1		0.1		
18th Century	0.1	0.1	0.1		0.1		
19th Century	0.6	0.4	0.3		0.4		
20th Century	3.6	2.2 (2.7)	1.6		1.2		2.4
1800-49	0.3	0.2	0.2		0.2		
1850-99	0.8	0.6	0.4		0.5		
1900-49	1.4	1.1	0.7		0.7		0.8
1950-99	5.7	3.4 (4.3)	2.5	5.5	1.7		4.0
1900s	1.0	0.8	0.6		0.5		0.7
1910s	1.3	1.1	0.6		0.6		0.4
1920s	1.9	1.6	1.0		0.9		1.7
1930s	1.5	1.2	0.8		0.8		1.0
1940s	1.1	0.8	0.5		0.7		0.3
1950s	1.4	0.8 (1.1)	0.7	1.4	0.6		0.5
1960s	4.6	2.2 (3.3)	2.4	4.5	1.9	115.0	3.7
1970s	9.6	5.4 (7.4)	3.6	9.2	2.6	20.1	6.7
1980s	7.0	4.6 (5.3)	3.2	6.8	1.9	8.3	2.4
1990s	6.0	4.2 (4.6)	2.6	5.4	1.7	15.4	6.6

LAOS

	Man	GDP	Agri	Serv	Pop	Inf	Ex
18th Century							
19th Century							
20th Century	2.9	1.6	1.5				
1900-49	0.8	0.6	0.5				
1950-99	4.9	2.6 (3.5)	2.4		2.2		
1950s	3.6	2.5 (3.0)	2.0		2.2		
1960s	1.9	1.0 (1.3)	0.8		1.4		
1970s	4.0	2.0 (2.9)	0.9		2.7		
1980s	6.1	2.2 (4.0)	3.5	3.3	2.3		
1990s	9.0	5.3 (6.4)	4.6	7.4	2.6	20.0	

MALAYSIA

	Man	GDP	Agri	Serv	Pop	Inf	Ex
18th Century		0.0					
19th Century	0.5	0.4	0.3				
20th Century	5.5	4.1	2.6				
1900-49	2.9	2.2	1.7				
1950-99	8.1	6.0	3.5	7.1	2.6		8.2
1950s	6.7	5.0	3.5	6.7	2.8		7.5
1960s	8.4	6.0	4.2	8.6	2.9	-0.3	5.8
1970s	10.0	7.7	5.0	8.4	2.2	7.3	6.5
1980s	6.8	5.0	3.8	4.2	2.7	1.5	10.1
1990s	8.6	6.5	1.1	7.6	2.5	4.4	11.0

PHILIPPINES

	Man	GDP	Agri	Serv	Pop	Inf	Ex
18th Century	0.1	0.1	0.1				
19th Century	0.8	0.6	0.5				
20th Century	3.7	2.7	2.2				2.8
1900-49	1.7	1.4	1.1				1.5
1950-99	5.6	4.0 (4.6)	3.2	5.2	2.7	9.5	4.1
1950s	8.5	5.9 (6.7)	4.5	8.8	3.0	1.2	6.0
1960s	6.7	4.7 (5.3)	4.2	5.2	3.0	5.8	2.2
1970s	8.0	5.6 (6.5)	5.0	5.4	2.6	13.3	6.2
1980s	1.2	0.9 (1.1)	1.0	2.8	2.5	14.8	1.3
1990s	3.4	3.0 (3.2)	1.5	3.9	2.3	12.2	5.0

SINGAPORE

	Man	GDP	Agri	Serv	Pop	Inf	Ex	Unem
18th Century	0.0	0.0	0.0					
19th Century	1.8	1.4	0.7					
20th Century	7.0	5.7	1.3	6.8			6.2	
1800-49	0.7	0.5	0.3					
1850-99	2.8	2.3	1.1					
1900-49	4.4	3.5	1.9	4.5			3.1	
1950-99	9.5	7.8	0.7	9.1	2.3	2.4	9.2	7.7
1900s	4.3	3.6	2.3	4.3				
1910s	5.0	3.8	2.0	5.0				
1920s	5.1	4.0	2.2	5.0				
1930s	3.4	2.6	1.4	3.7				
1940s	4.4	3.6	1.6	4.5				
1950s	6.3	5.4	2.5	6.0	4.0		3.1	16.2
1960s	12.0	9.3	5.0	12.2	2.4	1.1	4.2	10.1
1970s	11.8	9.4	1.7	11.0	1.4	5.7	11.0	5.8
1980s	8.4	7.0	-6.2	8.1	1.7	1.7	11.9	4.0
1990s	8.8	7.8	0.4	8.0	1.9	1.9	16.0	2.2

THAILAND

	Man	GDP	Agri	Serv	Pop	Inf	Ex
18th Century	0.2	0.1	0.1				
19th Century	0.7	0.5	0.4				
20th Century	5.3	3.5	2.6				
1900-49	2.0	1.6	1.1				
1950-99	8.4	5.4 (6.3)	4.1	7.0	2.0		8.6
1950s	5.3	3.0 (4.0)	2.8	5.5	2.0		3.5
1960s	10.0	6.0 (7.5)	5.5	9.0	2.9	1.8	5.2
1970s	10.5	6.7 (7.7)	5.4	7.7	2.4	9.5	12.0
1980s	9.8	7.0 (7.6)	4.0	7.4	1.7	3.2	12.8
1990s	6.7	4.5 (4.7)	2.7	5.5	1.2	8.9	9.4

VIETNAM

	Man	GDP	Agri	Serv	Pop	Inf	Ex
18th Century	0.2	0.1	0.1				
19th Century	0.3	0.2	0.2				
20th Century	3.4	1.8	1.7				
1900-49	1.0	0.8	0.5				
1950-99	5.8	2.8 (4.1)	2.6				
1950s	3.4	2.0 (2.6)	1.7				
1960s	5.2	3.0 (4.4)	2.0		3.1		
1970s	2.0	0.6 (1.2)	0.6		2.9		
1980s	6.4	2.6 (4.2)	4.0	6.0	2.1		
1990s	12.0	6.0 (8.1)	4.6	8.6	1.8	20.0	27.7

CHAPTER 10. SUB-SAHARAN AFRICA

ANGOLA

	Man	GDP	Agri	Serv	Pop	Inf	Ex
18th Century							
19th Century		0.0	0.0				
20th Century	1.0	0.8	0.2				
1900-49	0.5	0.4	0.2				
1950-99	1.4	1.2	0.1				
1950s	4.0	3.0	4.0				
1960s	6.0	4.8	5.0	4.2	1.5	3.3	9.0
1970s	-7.0	-5.0 (-6.2)	-6.2	-5.0	2.3	21.6	-7.9
1980s	5.4	2.4 (3.4)	0.8	1.8	2.6		2.2
1990s	1.6	0.7 (0.8)	-3.1	-3.4	3.2	790.0	8.2

BENIN

	Man	GDP	Agri	Serv	Pop	Inf	Ex
18th Century							
19th Century		0.0					
20th Century	2.3	1.4	1.6				
1900-49	0.5	0.4	0.3				
1950-99	4.0	2.4 (3.0)	2.8	2.9			
1950s	4.0	3.0	2.5	3.0			
1960s	3.0	2.0 (2.2)	1.0	2.5	2.6	1.9	5.0
1970s	4.6	1.8 (3.0)	1.0	4.0	2.9	9.2	-11.0
1980s	3.4	1.4 (2.3)	4.2	0.7	3.1	7.5	-2.4
1990s	5.0	4.0 (4.7)	5.3	4.4	2.8	6.0	1.9

BOTSWANA

	Man	GDP	Agri	Serv	Pop	Inf	Ex
18th Century		0.0					
19th Century	0.0	0.0	0.0		0.1		
20th Century	4.9	3.8	1.9		1.4		
1900-49	0.3	0.2	0.2		0.2		
1950-99	9.4	7.5	3.6	7.8	2.6		
1950s	2.3	1.8	1.1	2.5	1.2		
1960s	6.0	5.0	3.0	4.0	2.3	4.1	
1970s	19.4	15.1	10.4	14.7	3.8	10.2	
1980s	14.0	11.3	3.1	11.6	3.4	12.0	10.1
1990s	5.0	4.3	0.3	6.3	2.4	8.5	2.5

BURKINA FASO

	Man	GDP	Agri	Serv	Pop	Inf	Ex
18th Century		0.0					
19th Century	0.0	0.0	0.0				
20th Century	1.9	1.3	1.0				
1900-49	0.5	0.4	0.2				
1950-99	3.3	2.2 (2.7)	1.8				
1950s	4.0	3.0	2.8				
1960s	4.3	2.4 (3.0)	2.6	2.0	1.6	1.3	15.0
1970s	0.3	0.0 (0.1)	-3.0	2.9	1.6	9.8	3.1
1980s	4.0	2.5 (3.6)	3.1	4.6	2.4	4.6	-0.4
1990s	4.0	3.3 (3.8)	3.5	3.5	2.4	6.0	0.4

BURUNDI

	Man	GDP	Agri	Serv	Pop	Inf	Ex
18th Century							
19th Century		0.0	0.0				
20th Century	1.9	1.2	1.2				
1900-49	0.5	0.4	0.3				
1950-99	3.2	2.0 (2.6)	2.0				
1950s	2.6	2.0	2.0				
1960s	5.3	3.0 (4.4)	3.0	2.0	1.6	2.8	
1970s	7.0	4.0 (5.0)	4.0	3.0	2.0	11.2	
1980s	4.8	3.3 (4.3)	3.1	5.6	2.8	3.7	3.4
1990s	-3.7	-2.4 (-2.9)	-2.0	-2.5	2.2	14.0	2.4

CAMEROON

	Man	GDP	Agri	Serv	Pop	Inf	Ex
18th Century							
19th Century		0.0	0.0				
20th Century	2.6	1.8	1.9				
1900-49	0.7	0.5	0.4				
1950-99	4.5	3.0 (3.7)	3.4	3.6			
1950s	5.5	4.5	3.0	5.0			
1960s	5.0	2.8 (3.7)	3.0	4.4	1.8	4.2	7.1
1970s	6.0	4.0 (5.4)	3.5	6.0	2.2	10.3	2.4
1980s	4.6	2.8 (3.4)	2.2	2.0	2.8	6.6	3.0
1990s	1.5	1.0 (1.3)	5.3	0.4	2.7	6.0	2.7

CENTRAL AFRICAN REPUBLIC

	Man	GDP	Agri	Serv	Pop	Inf	Ex
18th Century							
19th Century		0.0					
20th Century	2.0	1.5	1.3				
1900-49	0.5	0.4	0.3				
1950-99	3.4	2.5 (2.7)	2.3				
1950s	5.0	4.0	3.0				
1960s	3.3	1.9 (2.2)	0.8	1.8	2.2	4.1	8.1
1970s	5.0	3.3 (3.9)	2.4	3.3	2.2	9.1	-0.5
1980s	1.9	1.4 (1.6)	1.6	1.0	2.4	6.5	-1.2
1990s	2.0	1.8 (2.0)	3.7	-0.7	2.1	6.0	6.7

CHAD

	Man	GDP	Agri	Serv	Pop	Inf	Ex
18th Century							
19th Century		0.0					
20th Century	1.9	1.3	1.1				
1900-49	0.4	0.3	0.2				
1950-99	3.3	2.3	2.0				
1950s	5.0	4.0	2.6				
1960s	0.8	0.4 (0.5)	0.0		1.8	4.6	5.9
1970s	0.2	0.0	0.7	-2.6	2.0	7.9	-3.4
1980s	8.0	5.0 (6.1)	2.3	6.7	2.4	1.5	6.5
1990s	2.6	2.0 (2.3)	4.9	0.8	2.9	6.0	5.0

CONGO

	Man	GDP	Agri	Serv	Pop	Inf	Ex
18th Century							
19th Century		0.0					
20th Century	2.4	1.4	1.3				
1900-49	0.5	0.4	0.3				
1950-99	4.2	2.4 (3.0)	2.3				
1950s	5.2	4.0	2.8				
1960s	4.0	1.6 (2.7)	1.0	2.1	2.1	5.4	5.1
1970s	5.8	2.5 (4.0)	3.0	0.0	2.5	10.9	8.2
1980s	5.0	3.0 (3.3)	3.2	2.1	2.9	0.3	5.1
1990s	1.0	0.8 (0.9)	1.7	1.5	2.8	6.0	4.3

DEMOCRATIC REPUBLIC OF CONGO (ZAIRE)

	Man	GDP	Agri	Serv	Pop	Inf	Ex
18th Century		0.0					
19th Century	0.0	0.0	0.0		0.0		
20th Century	1.2	0.9	1.1		1.5		
1900-49	0.5	0.4	0.3		0.4		
1950-99	1.9	1.4 (1.6)	2.0		2.6		
1950s	8.0	6.4	4.1		2.2		
1960s	5.7	3.5 (4.9)	2.3	6.0	2.0	30.0	-1.0
1970s	1.1	0.5 (0.7)	1.2	1.4	2.7	37.4	-1.1
1980s	2.8	1.6 (2.0)	2.6	1.8	3.1	60.5	0.6
1990s	-8.3	-5.0 (-5.9)	-0.3	-11.2	3.2	2,092.0	-5.5

165

EQUATORIAL GUINEA

	Man	GDP	Agri	Serv	Pop	Inf	Ex
18th Century		0.0					
19th Century	0.0	0.0	0.0				
20th Century	3.1	2.4	1.4				
1900-49	0.2	0.1	0.1				
1950-99	5.9	4.9	2.6				
1950s	3.7	3.0	2.2				
1960s	4.0	3.3	2.5	3.5			
1970s	-4.0	-3.0	-2.0	-3.0			
1980s	2.6	2.0	0.7	2.3			
1990s	23.3	18.2	9.6	16.4	2.5	9.3	34.5

ETHIOPIA

	Man	GDP	Agri	Serv	Pop	Inf	Ex
18th Century							
19th Century		0.0	0.0				
20th Century	2.0	1.1	0.8				
1900-49	0.3	0.2	0.2				
1950-99	3.6	1.9 (2.7)	1.3				
1950s	2.5	1.5 (2.0)	1.0				
1960s	6.0	2.8 (4.0)	2.2	4.8	2.4	2.1	3.6
1970s	2.0	0.8 (1.5)	0.4	1.6	2.1	4.3	-2.7
1980s	1.3	0.6 (1.1)	0.2	3.1	3.0	2.0	2.4
1990s	6.3	4.0 (4.8)	2.5	6.7	2.8	3.0	9.3

GHANA

	Man	GDP	Agri	Serv	Pop	Inf	Ex
18th Century	0.0	0.0	0.0				
19th Century	0.1	0.1	0.1				
20th Century	2.7	2.0	1.4				
1900-49	1.0	0.8	0.6				
1950-99	4.4	3.2 (3.5)	2.1	3.8			
1950s	7.4	6.0	3.7	6.0			
1960s	4.3	2.5 (3.1)	1.7	1.3	2.4	7.6	0.2
1970s	1.5	0.7 (1.0)	0.6	1.0	3.0	20.2	-4.0
1980s	4.0	2.6 (3.0)	1.0	5.7	3.4	43.6	5.0
1990s	4.8	4.0 (4.3)	3.4	5.0	2.7	30.0	10.8

GUINEA

	Man	GDP	Agri	Serv	Pop	Inf	Ex
18th Century							
19th Century	0.1	0.1					
20th Century	2.8	1.9	1.7				
1900-49	0.7	0.5	0.4				
1950-99	4.9	3.2 (3.8)	2.9				
1950s	6.0	5.0	3.5				
1960s	7.5	3.8 (5.0)	3.4	6.0	2.8	1.5	
1970s	6.0	3.0 (4.4)	3.0	5.0	2.9	4.4	
1980s	0.1	0.0 (0.1)	0.0	0.0	2.5		
1990s	4.8	4.2 (4.5)	4.5	3.2	2.6	6.0	4.7

IVORY COAST

	Man	GDP	Agri	Serv	Pop	Inf	Ex
18th Century	0.0	0.0	0.0				
19th Century	0.0	0.0	0.0				
20th Century	3.1	2.1	1.3				
1900-49	0.5	0.4	0.3				
1950-99	5.7	3.8 (4.5)	2.3	4.7			
1950s	2.6	2.0	1.6	2.8			
1960s	11.6	9.0 (10.0)	4.2	9.7	3.7	2.8	8.8
1970s	7.8	4.5 (6.0)	3.4	7.0	5.5	13.5	5.2
1980s	1.4	0.5 (0.7)	0.3	0.0	3.5	3.1	2.5
1990s	5.0	3.0 (3.7)	1.8	3.9	2.6	10.0	4.4

KENYA

	Man	GDP	Agri	Serv	Pop	Inf	Ex
18th Century	0.0	0.0	0.0				
19th Century	0.0	0.0	0.0				
20th Century	3.0	2.0	1.8				
1900-49	0.5	0.4	0.3				
1950-99	5.5	3.6	3.3	5.1			
1950s	4.3	3.5	2.4	4.3			
1960s	8.0	4.3 (5.5)	4.0	7.0	3.2	1.5	7.2
1970s	8.2	4.7 (6.0)	5.4	5.8	3.4	11.1	-0.5
1980s	4.8	3.3 (4.2)	3.2	4.9	3.5	9.0	4.4
1990s	2.4	2.0 (2.2)	1.4	3.3	2.7	20.0	0.4

LIBERIA

	Man	GDP	Agri	Serv	Pop	Inf	Ex
18th Century							
19th Century		0.3	0.2				
20th Century	2.0	1.3	1.3				
1900-49	1.1	0.8	0.5				
1950-99	2.9	1.8 (2.2)	2.0				
1950s	5.0	3.0 (3.6)	2.5				
1960s	6.0	4.3 (5.1)	4.0		3.1	1.9	18.4
1970s	3.0	1.5 (1.8)	4.0		3.3	9.4	2.3
1980s	0.2	0.1 (0.1)	0.0		3.2		0.3
1990s	0.3	0.1 (0.2)	-0.3				

MADAGASCAR

	Man	GDP	Agri	Serv	Pop	Inf	Ex
18th Century		0.0					
19th Century	0.0	0.0					
20th Century	1.4	1.1	1.0				
1900-49	0.5	0.4	0.3				
1950-99	2.3	1.7 (1.9)	1.7		2.4		
1950s	4.2	3.6	2.7		2.0		
1960s	3.5	2.4 (2.7)	1.8	3.5	2.1	3.2	5.3
1970s	0.6	0.2 (0.3)	0.1	0.1	2.5	10.1	-1.0
1980s	1.3	0.8 (1.1)	2.5	0.3	2.7	17.8	-1.7
1990s	2.0	1.5 (1.7)	1.5	1.9	2.9	20.0	3.6

MALAWI

	Man	GDP	Agri	Serv	Pop	Inf	Ex
18th Century		0.0					
19th Century		0.0	0.0				
20th Century	2.3	1.6	2.1				
1900-49	0.4	0.3	0.3				
1950-99	4.2	2.9 (3.5)	3.9				
1950s	2.5	2.0	1.3				
1960s	5.5	3.2 (4.0)	3.4	5.0	2.8	2.4	11.6
1970s	7.0	3.6 (5.0)	4.0	9.0	2.8	9.1	4.6
1980s	3.1	2.0 (2.5)	2.0	3.6	3.2	14.6	2.5
1990s	3.0	3.5 (4.0)	9.0	0.7	2.6	28.0	4.9

MALI

	Man	GDP	Agri	Serv	Pop	Inf	Ex
18th Century							
19th Century	0.0	0.0					
20th Century	2.2	1.2	1.2				
1900-49	0.3	0.2	0.1				
1950-99	4.1	2.2	2.3				
1950s	4.0	3.0	2.0				
1960s	4.8	1.6 (3.0)	1.0	3.0	2.4	5.0	4.0
1970s	6.0	3.5 (5.0)	4.0	6.1	2.6	9.7	6.7
1980s	1.8	0.6 (0.8)	1.5	1.9	2.5	3.6	4.8
1990s	4.0	2.5 (3.0)	2.8	2.7	2.8	7.0	9.6

MAURITANIA

	Man	GDP	Agri	Serv	Pop	Inf	Ex
18th Century							
19th Century	0.2	0.2					
20th Century	2.5	1.8	0.9				
1900-49	0.4	0.3	0.2				
1950-99	4.6	3.3 (3.6)	1.6	4.9			
1950s	3.2	2.5	1.5	3.0			
1960s	9.3	8.0	3.0	9.0	2.5	1.6	20.2
1970s	2.5	1.2 (1.8)	-1.4	7.2	2.7	10.1	-1.1
1980s	3.0	1.3 (1.8)	1.7	0.4	2.7	9.4	2.1
1990s	5.0	3.5 (4.1)	3.2	4.8	2.8	10.0	1.6

MOZAMBIQUE

	Man	GDP	Agri	Serv	Pop	Inf	Ex
18th Century							
19th Century	0.0	0.0					
20th Century	1.8	1.3	1.1				
1900-49	0.4	0.3	0.2				
1950-99	3.1	2.3	1.9				
1950s	4.7	3.7	3.0				
1960s	6.6	4.6	2.1		2.2	2.8	6.0
1970s	-4.8	-2.0 (-2.9)	-1.8		2.5	11.0	-6.6
1980s	-0.7	0.0	0.8		2.0	34.9	-1.8
1990s	9.9	5.4 (6.3)	5.2	5.5	2.2	25.0	13.4

171

NAMIBIA

	Man	GDP	Agri	Serv	Pop	Inf	Ex
18th Century							
19th Century		0.2	0.1				
20th Century	4.7	3.8	2.8				
1900-49	3.8	3.0	2.0				
1950-99	5.6	4.6 (5.0)	3.5	4.9			
1950s	8.0	6.4 (6.8)	4.0	7.0			
1960s	9.0	7.0 (7.5)	5.0	8.0			
1970s	5.5	5.0 (5.6)	3.0	4.0			
1980s	1.4	1.3 (1.5)	1.9	2.3	2.7		0.7
1990s	4.3	3.4 (3.7)	3.8	3.4	2.6	7.0	4.3

NIGER

	Man	GDP	Agri	Serv	Pop	Inf	Ex
18th Century							
19th Century			0.0				
20th Century	2.0	1.1	1.0				
1900-49	0.4	0.3	0.2				
1950-99	3.5	1.9	1.8				
1950s	4.0	3.0	2.0				
1960s	4.5	2.0 (2.7)	3.3	4.0	3.3	2.1	6.0
1970s	5.0	2.5 (3.3)	-1.5	4.6	2.8	10.8	11.7
1980s	0.0	0.0	1.8	-0.7	3.2	3.4	-2.9
1990s	3.0	2.0 (2.5)	3.3	1.9	3.4	6.0	1.7

172

NIGERIA

	Man	GDP	Agri	Serv	Pop	Inf	Ex
16th Century	0.0	0.0	0.0		0.0		
17th Century	0.0	0.0	0.0		0.0		
18th Century	0.0	0.0	0.0		0.0		
19th Century	0.1	0.1	0.1		0.1		
20th Century	2.6	1.7	1.3	2.2	1.6		3.4
1800-49	0.0	0.0	0.0		0.0		
1850-99	0.2	0.1	0.1		0.2		
1900-49	0.7	0.5	0.4	0.5	0.5		0.8
1950-99	4.5	2.8 (3.5)	2.1	3.8	2.6		6.0
1900s	0.3	0.2	0.2		0.2		
1910s	0.5	0.4	0.3		0.4		
1920s	0.3	0.2	0.4		0.4		
1930s	0.7	0.5	0.4		0.6		
1940s	1.5	1.2	0.7		0.9		
1950s	5.2	4.0	2.6	2.5	2.3		6.0
1960s	4.0	2.0 (2.6)	0.0	3.9	2.5	2.5	6.6
1970s	9.0	5.1 (7.4)	3.8	8.0	2.5	19.0	15.4
1980s	1.5	0.8 (1.3)	1.6	1.3	3.0	14.2	-0.3
1990s	2.7	2.0 (2.4)	2.5	3.1	2.8	27.1	2.5

RWANDA

	Man	GDP	Agri	Serv	Pop	Inf	Ex
18th Century							
19th Century		0.0	0.0				
20th Century	1.9	1.4	0.7				
1900-49	0.6	0.5	0.4				
1950-99	3.2	2.2 (2.5)	0.9				
1950s	4.0	3.0	3.0				
1960s	5.5	3.6 (4.0)	3.0	4.0	2.8	13.1	15.8
1970s	5.0	4.0 (4.6)	2.0	4.0	2.8	14.6	3.2
1980s	2.5	1.9 (2.2)	0.5	5.5	3.0	4.0	3.0
1990s	-1.1	-1.3 (-1.5)	-3.9	-1.2	2.0	17.3	-6.0

SENEGAL

	Man	GDP	Agri	Serv	Pop	Inf	Ex
18th Century	0.0	0.0	0.0				
19th Century	0.1	0.1	0.1				
20th Century	2.5	1.7	1.4				
1900-49	0.8	0.6	0.4				
1950-99	4.2	2.7 (3.1)	2.3	2.7			
1950s	5.0	4.0	3.0	4.0			
1960s	4.0	2.0 (2.5)	2.9	1.7	2.4	1.7	1.2
1970s	3.5	2.0 (2.5)	1.1	1.6	2.6	7.6	3.0
1980s	4.0	2.7 (3.1)	2.9	2.8	2.8	7.3	3.0
1990s	4.3	3.0 (3.2)	1.6	3.4	2.6	6.0	2.6

SIERRA LEONE

	Man	GDP	Agri	Serv	Pop	Inf	Ex
18th Century							
19th Century	0.1	0.1					
20th Century	1.2	0.9	1.6				
1900-49	0.7	0.5	0.4				
1950-99	1.6	1.2 (1.3)	2.8				
1950s	5.0	4.0	3.0				
1960s	5.5	4.0 (4.3)	4.0	4.5	2.2	2.9	0.3
1970s	2.0	1.2 (1.6)	2.3	4.4	2.5	11.3	-6.0
1980s	1.7	0.9 (1.2)	3.1	-2.0	2.4	54.1	0.2
1990s	-6.1	-4.0 (-4.8)	1.6	-5.3	2.4	45.0	-12.2

SOUTH AFRICA

	Man	GDP	Agri	Serv	Pop	Inf	Ex
16th Century	0.0	0.0	0.0				
17th Century	0.1	0.1	0.0				
18th Century	0.2	0.2	0.1				
19th Century	1.7	1.4	0.8				
20th Century	4.8	3.6	2.3	4.8			
1800-49	0.8	0.6	0.4				
1850-99	2.6	2.2	1.2				
1900-49	5.1	3.7	2.5	4.9			
1950-99	4.4	3.5 (3.8)	2.2	4.6	2.4		
1900s	3.3	2.6	1.7	3.0			
1910s	4.5	3.5	2.2	4.0			
1920s	4.6	3.3	2.8	5.7			
1930s	5.8	4.2 (4.8)	2.6	5.5			
1940s	7.0	5.0 (5.9)	3.0	6.3	2.1		
1950s	6.5	4.6 (5.1)	3.6	6.6	2.3		
1960s	8.0	6.4 (6.8)	1.7	7.3	2.6	3.0	5.4
1970s	4.0	3.2 (3.6)	2.0	4.0	2.7	11.8	8.1
1980s	1.7	1.3 (1.5)	2.7	2.5	2.4	14.1	-8.0
1990s	2.0	1.8 (1.9)	1.0	2.4	2.0	10.2	2.2

SUDAN

	Man	GDP	Agri	Serv	Pop	Inf	Ex
18th Century	0.0	0.0					
19th Century	0.0	0.0					
20th Century	2.3	1.5	1.6				
1900-49	0.3	0.2	0.1				
1950-99	4.3	2.7 (3.2)	3.1		2.4		
1950s	5.5	3.5 (4.0)	3.0		2.3		
1960s	2.0	1.0 (1.3)	2.4	3.0	2.2	3.7	0.1
1970s	4.5	3.0 (4.3)	2.7	6.9	2.6	12.4	-0.7
1980s	1.1	0.3 (0.4)	0.0	0.3	2.8		0.0
1990s	8.3	5.5 (6.0)	7.2	9.0	2.3	75.0	

175

TANZANIA

	Man	GDP	Agri	Serv	Pop	Inf	Ex
18th Century							
19th Century			0.0				
20th Century	2.0	1.3	1.3	1.9			
1900-49	0.3	0.2	0.1	0.2			
1950-99	3.7	2.4	2.5	3.6			
1950s	3.4	2.7	1.5	3.0			
1960s	6.0	3.0 (4.5)	2.5	5.0	2.7	1.8	3.4
1970s	3.6	2.2 (3.0)	1.0	5.9	3.4	13.0	-6.0
1980s	2.5	1.6 (2.3)	4.0	1.5	3.1	26.1	-8.0
1990s	3.0	2.4 (3.0)	3.6	2.5	2.9	16.0	9.0

TOGO

	Man	GDP	Agri	Serv	Pop	Inf	Ex
18th Century							
19th Century		0.0	0.0				
20th Century	2.8	1.9	1.8				
1900-49	0.4	0.3	0.2				
1950-99	5.2	3.4 (4.3)	3.5				
1950s	5.0	4.0	3.5				
1960s	10.8	7.4 (8.5)	4.0	5.6	2.7	1.1	10.0
1970s	5.0	2.3 (3.6)	1.3	4.0	3.0	10.3	-2.0
1980s	2.1	1.2 (1.7)	5.0	0.0	2.9		0.1
1990s	3.0	2.0 (2.5)	3.5	0.9	2.9	11.0	1.5

UGANDA

	Man	GDP	Agri	Serv	Pop	Inf	Ex
18th Century		0.0					
19th Century	0.0	0.0					
20th Century	3.0	1.9	1.3				
1900-49	0.4	0.3	0.3				
1950-99	5.5	3.4 (3.8)	2.3	4.6	2.5		
1950s	4.5	3.6	2.2	4.5	2.4		
1960s	7.6	4.5 (5.7)	2.7	7.7	2.6	3.0	5.0
1970s	-0.8	-0.3 (-0.4)	0.8	0.1	2.2	28.3	-5.0
1980s	4.4	2.3 (2.9)	2.1	2.8	2.4	108.1	2.0
1990s	11.7	7.0 (7.2)	3.7	8.1	3.0	14.0	16.3

ZAMBIA

	Man	GDP	Agri	Serv	Pop	Inf	Ex
18th Century							
19th Century		0.0	0.0				
20th Century	1.8	1.3	0.9				
1900-49	0.4	0.3	0.2				
1950-99	3.1	2.2	1.5	3.1			
1950s	5.0	4.0	2.5	4.5			
1960s	6.4	4.5 (5.0)	2.5	2.0	2.8	7.6	2.2
1970s	1.6	1.1 (1.4)	2.3	1.2	3.0	6.8	-0.7
1980s	1.3	0.7 (1.0)	4.0	-1.0	3.0	38.3	-3.0
1990s	1.0	0.8 (1.0)	-4.0	9.0	2.7	70.0	2.0

177

ZIMBABWE

	Man	GDP	Agri	Serv	Pop	Inf	Ex
18th Century							
19th Century	0.1	0.1					
20th Century	3.3	2.6	2.0				
1900-49	2.2	1.7	1.3				
1950-99	4.4	3.5	2.7	4.1			
1950s	8.0	6.0	4.0	7.0			
1960s	5.2	4.3	2.8	5.0	3.9	1.3	
1970s	2.5	2.0	-0.5	2.1	3.3	8.4	3.1
1980s	4.0	3.0 (3.5)	3.0	3.0	3.5	11.0	4.3
1990s	2.4	2.1 (2.4)	4.3	3.6	2.2	25.9	11.0

CHAPTER 11. WESTERN EUROPE

AUSTRIA

	Man	GDP	Agri	Serv	Pop	Inf	Ex	Unem
18th Century	0.6	0.5	0.3					
19th Century	2.7	2.1	1.4					
20th Century	4.4	3.8	1.9	4.2				
1900-49	4.2	3.5	2.1	3.9				
1950-99	4.6	4.1	1.7	4.5	0.5			
1950s	9.4	8.0	5.0	9.0	0.9			
1960s	5.0	4.5	1.2	4.5	0.6	3.7	9.6	
1970s	4.0	3.7	2.0	4.2	0.1	6.5	7.2	
1980s	2.5	2.2	1.1	2.5	0.2	3.8	5.1	
1990s	2.3	2.0	-0.7	2.2	0.5	2.0	4.5	

BELGIUM

	Man	GDP	Agri	Serv	Pop	Inf	Ex	Unem
18th Century	0.7	0.5	0.4					
19th Century	3.4	2.9	1.6					
20th Century	3.6	3.0	1.5	2.9				
1900-49	3.4	2.8	1.9	2.8				
1950-99	3.8	3.2	1.1	3.0	0.4			
1950s	5.0	4.0	3.0	4.0	0.7			
1960s	6.0	5.2	-0.5	4.6	0.5	3.6	10.9	
1970s	3.5	3.2	-0.7	3.3	0.2	8.1	5.2	
1980s	2.3	1.9	2.0	1.9	0.1	4.5	4.7	
1990s	2.1	1.7	1.7	1.4	0.3	2.0	4.0	

179

DENMARK

	Man	GDP	Agri	Serv	Pop	Inf	Ex	Unem
18th Century	0.7	0.5	0.4					
19th Century	3.1	2.5	1.8					
20th Century	4.4	3.7	2.2	4.0				
1900-49	4.3	3.5	2.3	4.1				
1950-99	4.4	3.8	2.1	3.9	0.5			
1950s	7.7	6.3	4.0	8.0	1.0			
1960s	5.4	4.7	0.2	4.9	0.7	5.5	7.1	
1970s	3.3	2.8	1.4	2.8	0.4	9.8	4.4	
1980s	2.6	2.2	3.1	2.3	0.0	6.0	5.3	
1990s	2.9	2.8	1.7	1.5	0.4	3.0	3.8	

FINLAND

	Man	GDP	Agri	Serv	Pop	Inf	Ex	Unem
18th Century	0.5	0.4	0.3					
19th Century	2.3	1.8	1.3					
20th Century	4.8	4.0	1.7	4.1				
1900-49	4.9	4.0	2.3	4.2				
1950-99	4.6	4.0	1.1	4.0	0.5			
1950s	7.0	6.0	5.0	7.0	0.7			
1960s	6.0	4.6	0.6	5.3	0.4	5.6	6.8	
1970s	3.8	3.5	-0.2	3.9	0.5	12.9	3.9	
1980s	3.5	3.3	-0.2	3.7	0.4	7.0	3.2	
1990s	2.7	2.5	0.2	0.1	0.4	4.0	9.6	

FRANCE

	Man	GDP	Agri	Serv	Pop	Inf	Ex	Unem
16th Century	0.2	0.2	0.1		0.1			
17th Century	0.4	0.3	0.2		0.2			
18th Century	0.8	0.6	0.4		0.3			
19th Century	3.0	2.4	1.0		0.5			
20th Century	4.0	3.3	1.2	2.9	0.4			
1800-49	2.6	2.2	0.9		0.4			
1850-99	3.3	2.6	1.1		0.6			
1900-49	3.4	2.6	0.8	1.8	0.1			
1950-99	4.6	3.9	1.6	4.0	0.7	5.9	6.3	5.0
1800s	2.3	1.9						
1810s	2.0	1.7						
1820s	2.6	2.0						
1830s	3.3	2.8						
1840s	3.0	2.6						
1850s	4.6	3.8						
1860s	3.5	2.8						
1870s	3.3	2.4						
1880s	2.4	1.8						
1890s	2.8	2.0						
1900s	4.1	3.3						
1910s	6.7	5.1						
1920s	4.8	3.9						
1930s	0.3	0.2						
1940s	1.0	0.7						
1950s	7.2	6.0	2.7	5.6	0.9	6.0	9.0	5.0
1960s	7.5	6.4	2.0	5.8	1.0	4.0	8.3	1.2
1970s	4.0	3.3	0.2	4.3	0.6	9.6	7.1	3.3
1980s	2.5	2.3	2.4	2.7	0.5	6.5	3.3	6.1
1990s	1.9	1.7	0.5	1.7	0.5	3.0	3.7	9.4

GERMANY

	Man	GDP	Agri	Serv	Pop	Inf	Ex	Unem
16th Century	0.3	0.2	0.1		0.2			
17th Century	0.3	0.2	0.1		-0.1			
18th Century	0.6	0.4	0.3		0.2			
19th Century	3.4	2.7	1.6		1.2			
20th Century	4.6	3.7	2.0	4.3	0.4			
1800-49	2.0	1.5	0.8		0.7			
1850-99	4.8	3.9	2.3		1.7			
1900-49	4.7	3.6	1.9	4.6	0.3			
1950-99	4.5	3.8	2.1	4.0	0.5	3.1	7.5	5.6 (Western Germany)
1800-39	1.8	1.4	0.7					
1840s	2.6	2.0	1.2					
1850s	3.0	2.5	1.6					
1860s	3.7	3.0	2.0					
1870s	4.4	3.6	2.0					
1880s	6.6	5.4	3.0	6.6				
1890s	6.2	5.1	2.8	6.0				
1900s	4.5	3.8	2.2	4.4				
1910s	1.9	1.2	0.3	2.2				
1920s	5.2	4.4	2.7	5.0				
1930s	6.8	5.0	2.4	6.9				
1940s	5.1	3.5	2.3	4.7				
1950s	9.3	8.0	4.0	9.4	1.2	2.2	15.0	8.1 (Western Germany)
1960s	5.7	4.6	1.7	4.2	0.9	2.7	10.1	1.2 (Western Germany)
1970s	3.2	2.6	1.5	1.7	0.1	5.3	6.0	3.0 (Western Germany)
1980s	2.4	2.0	1.6	2.9	0.0	2.7	4.4	6.1 (Western Germany)
1990s	2.0	1.6	1.2	1.8	0.4	2.8	2.2	9.6 (Western Germany)

GERMAN DEMOCRATIC REPUBLIC (EASTERN GERMANY)

	Man	GDP	Agri	Unem
1950s	12.2	5.1(10)	3.6	
1960s	5.1	2.0 (4)	2.0	
1970s	6.3	2.4 (5)	2.1	
1980s	3.9	1.7 (3)	1.8	
1990s	1.4	2.0		17.0

GREAT BRITAIN

	Man	GDP	Agri	Serv	Pop	Inf	Ex	Unem
16th Century	0.4	0.3	0.2		0.2	1.7		
17th Century	0.4	0.3	0.2		0.2	0.4		
18th Century	1.1	0.8	0.5		0.6	0.9		
19th Century	3.2	2.7	1.2		1.4	0.1		
20th Century	3.5	3.0	0.8	3.4	0.5	4.0		7.5
1700-59	0.7	0.7	0.6		0.4			
1760-79	1.3	0.6	0.1		0.5			
1780-99	2.0	1.4	0.8		0.9			
1800-49	3.6	2.9	1.3		1.6	0.2		
1850-99	2.8	2.4	1.1		1.2	0.0		
1900-49	4.0	3.3	1.8	3.6	0.7	1.8		8.6
1950-99	2.9	2.7	-0.3	3.1	0.3	6.3	4.7	6.5
1800s	2.7	2.3	0.7		1.2	0.4		
1810s	3.4	2.7	1.2		1.5	0.3		
1820s	3.9	3.4	1.6		1.7	0.2		
1830s	4.0	3.3	1.7		1.8	0.1		
1840s	3.8	3.0	1.4		1.7	0.0		
1850s	3.0	2.8	1.3		1.4	0.0		
1860s	3.0	2.6	1.2		1.3	0.0		
1870s	2.9	2.5	1.0	2.2	1.2	0.0		
1880s	2.7	2.2	0.9	2.1	1.1	0.0		
1890s	2.4	2.0	0.9	1.9	1.0	0.0		
1900s	2.5	2.0	0.6	2.4	1.0	0.0		6.8
1910s	4.2	3.5	1.1	3.1	0.6	0.1		5.2
1920s	2.9	2.5	0.9	3.5	0.9	1.9		12.1
1930s	4.2	3.5	1.2	3.8	0.8	2.1	-4.0	15.4
1940s	6.3	5.0	5.0	5.0	0.4	5.0		3.6
1950s	3.4	3.0	2.7	3.0	0.5	3.0	5.1	4.7
1960s	3.5	3.1	2.4	2.7	0.4	4.1	4.8	5.1
1970s	2.3	2.3	1.0	2.4	0.3	14.2	8.2	6.7
1980s	3.0	2.6	-7.2	4.8	0.3	6.1	3.0	8.3
1990s	2.5	2.3	0.4	2.5	0.2	3.9	2.2	7.4

GREECE

	Man	GDP	Agri	Serv	Pop	Inf	Ex	Unem
18th Century	0.4	0.3	0.2					
19th Century	2.6	2.0	1.3					
20th Century	4.2	3.4	1.9					
1900-49	2.9	2.3	1.6					
1950-99	5.5	4.5	2.2	5.1	0.5			
1950s	8.4	7.0	4.0	8.0	0.7			
1960s	9.0	6.9	3.5	7.1	0.5	3.2	10.8	
1970s	6.0	4.9	1.4	5.7	0.6	14.1	12.3	
1980s	2.1	1.8	0.0	2.7	0.5	18.2	4.1	
1990s	2.0	1.9	2.0	1.8	0.4	10.0	3.3	

ICELAND

	Man	GDP	Agri	Serv	Pop	Inf	Ex	Unem
18th Century								
19th Century	3.5	2.8						
20th Century	5.0	4.2						
1900-49	5.0	4.1						
1950-99	5.0	4.3						
1950s	8.0	6.6						
1960s	6.4	6.0						
1970s	5.0	4.0						
1980s	2.7	2.3			1.1			
1990s	2.8	2.4			1.0	3.0		

IRELAND

	Man	GDP	Agri	Serv	Pop	Inf	Ex	Unem
18th Century	0.5	0.4	0.3					
19th Century	2.2	1.9	1.2					
20th Century	4.5	3.7	1.6	4.2				
1900-49	3.4	2.9	1.4	3.3				
1950-99	5.6	4.5	1.8	5.1				
1950s	5.8	4.5	3.0	5.8				
1960s	5.7	4.3	0.9	4.3	0.5	5.0	7.0	
1970s	4.9	3.7	2.5	4.5	1.1	14.6	8.4	
1980s	2.5	2.0	1.4	3.4	0.4	7.8	7.4	
1990s	9.0	7.9	1.1	7.6	0.7	3.3	9.8	

ITALY

	Man	GDP	Agri	Serv	Pop	Inf	Ex	Unem
16th Century	0.3	0.2						
17th Century	0.2	0.2						
18th Century	0.5	0.4	0.3					
19th Century	2.1	1.7	1.1					
20th Century	4.1	3.5	1.6	3.4	0.6			
1800-49	1.5	1.1	0.7					
1850-99	2.7	2.3	1.4	1.4	0.8			
1900-49	3.4	2.8	1.5	3.0	0.7			
1950-99	4.8	4.1	1.7	3.8	0.5	7.5	8.8	7.1
1850s	1.7	1.4						
1860s	2.2	1.8						
1870s	2.6	2.2						
1880s	3.1	2.6						
1890s	4.0	3.4						
1900s	6.2	5.0						
1910s	3.6	3.0						
1920s	3.3	2.8						
1930s	3.0	2.4						

1940s	0.8	0.6	0.4					
1950s	8.2	6.6	3.3	6.4	0.6	2.5	15.0	7.0
1960s	7.9	6.5	3.0	5.3	0.8	4.1	13.8	2.2
1970s	4.2	3.8	0.8	3.3	0.6	15.6	7.3	4.4
1980s	2.3	2.4	0.4	2.8	0.2	10.3	3.7	9.6
1990s	1.2	1.2	1.1	1.2	0.2	5.0	4.4	12.3

LUXEMBOURG

	Man	GDP	Agri	Serv	Pop	Inf	Ex	Unem
18th Century	0.6	0.4						
19th Century	4.9	4.1						
20th Century	5.1	4.3						
1800-49	2.1	1.7						
1850-99	7.7	6.5						
1900-49	4.0	3.4						
1950-99	6.1	5.1						
1900s	9.8	8.4						
1910s	0.3	0.2						
1920s	6.0	5.1						
1930s	0.5	0.4						
1940s	3.3	2.8						
1950s	7.9	6.6						
1960s	8.3	7.0						
1970s	3.4	2.7						
1980s	4.2	3.6		4.8	0.4	4.4		3.5
1990s	6.6	5.4		5.9	0.8	2.3		2.0

MALTA

	Man	GDP	Agri	Serv	Pop	Inf	Ex	Unem
1990s	6.8	5.4		6.6	0.4	3.3		4.1

NETHERLANDS

	Man	GDP	Agri	Serv	Pop	Inf	Ex	Unem
18th Century	0.5	0.4	0.3					
19th Century	3.2	2.7	2.0					
20th Century	4.4	3.7	3.0	3.7				
1900-49	4.1	3.5	2.7	3.5				
1950-99	4.6	3.9	3.3	3.9	0.9			
1950s	6.6	5.2	3.0	6.0	1.3			
1960s	7.4	6.0	2.9	5.1	1.3	5.4	9.9	
1970s	3.3	3.1	3.7	3.3	0.8	8.3	5.7	
1980s	2.6	2.3	3.4	2.6	0.5	1.9	4.5	
1990s	2.9	2.7	3.7	2.3	0.6	1.3	4.8	

NORWAY

	Man	GDP	Agri	Serv	Pop	Inf	Ex	Unem
18th Century	0.7	0.5	0.3					
19th Century	3.4	2.8	1.7					
20th Century	5.1	4.2	2.2	4.5				
1900-49	5.0	4.0	2.3	4.3				
1950-99	5.2	4.4	2.1	4.7	0.7			
1950s	7.4	6.0	4.0	8.0	1.1			
1960s	5.6	4.9	0.1	5.0	0.8	4.3	9.1	
1970s	5.0	4.8	2.1	4.6	0.5	8.2	7.2	
1980s	3.3	2.8	0.0	2.7	0.4	5.6	6.8	
1990s	4.5	3.7	4.1	3.2	0.5	3.0	6.0	

PORTUGAL

	Man	GDP	Agri	Serv	Pop	Inf	Ex	Unem
18th Century	0.4	0.3	0.2					
19th Century	2.1	1.6	1.2					
20th Century	4.6	3.8	1.7					
1900-49	3.6	2.9	1.9					
1950-99	5.6	4.7	1.5	5.1				
1950s	9.0	7.0	6.0	8.0				
1960s	8.0	6.2	2.3	6.0	0.0	3.0	9.6	
1970s	4.8	4.5	-1.5	6.3	1.4	16.1	-0.3	
1980s	3.6	3.1	1.0	3.0	0.1	19.1	11.7	
1990s	2.7	2.5	-0.4	2.2	0.1	4.0	5.6	

SPAIN

	Man	GDP	Agri	Serv	Pop	Inf	Ex	Unem
18th Century	0.6	0.4	0.3					
19th Century	2.2	1.6	1.1					
20th Century	4.6	3.6	1.5	4.2				
1900-49	2.7	2.3	1.4	2.7				
1950-99	6.4	4.9	1.6	5.6	0.8		9.7	
1950s	9.4	8.0	3.7	8.0	1.5		11.4	
1960s	9.1	7.0	4.0	7.8	1.1	8.0	11.6	
1970s	6.6	4.4	2.5	4.9	1.0	15.9	10.8	
1980s	4.0	3.1	0.5	4.2	0.4	9.4	7.0	
1990s	2.7	2.2	-2.5	3.1	0.2	4.1	7.7	18.5

SWEDEN

	Man	GDP	Agri	Serv	Pop	Inf	Ex	Unem
18th Century	0.8	0.6	0.4					
19th Century	3.3	2.6	1.5					
20th Century	3.9	3.1	1.5	2.9				
1900-49	4.1	3.2	2.0	2.8				
1950-99	3.7	3.0	1.0	3.0	0.5			
1950s	5.4	4.1	3.0	4.0	0.7			
1960s	6.3	5.0	0.6	3.9	0.7	4.4	7.7	
1970s	2.4	2.0	-1.3	2.8	0.3	9.8	2.6	
1980s	2.8	2.3	1.5	2.2	0.3	7.4	4.9	
1990s	1.8	1.5	1.0	2.0	0.4	4.0	8.3	

SWITZERLAND

	Man	GDP	Agri	Serv	Pop	Inf	Ex	Unem
18th Century	1.0	0.8						
19th Century	4.0	3.3						
20th Century	4.5	3.7		4.2				
1900-49	4.3	3.6		4.0				
1950-99	4.7	3.8		4.4				
1950s	7.4	6.0		7.0				
1960s	6.0	5.0		5.0	1.6	4.4	8.5	
1970s	7.0	5.5		7.0	0.3	4.0	6.0	
1980s	2.5	2.1		2.3	0.6	3.6	3.8	1.3
1990s	0.7	0.5		0.6	0.7	1.4	2.2	4.0

189

CONCLUSION

During World War II, the economies of most developed and middle-income nations were extremely regulated. With the war over, the most prominent economists in the world argued that liberalization and privatization were necessary to provide better economic performance. Most governments followed their advice. With the attainment of independence or self-rule, most developing countries considerably increased the level of regulation in the after-war years, but over time they too moved in the direction of liberalization. In most developed countries, deregulation began in the 1950s, in most middle-income countries in the 1960s, and in developing countries it began in the 1970s.

Although the degree and the speed of liberalization varied from country to country, the vast majority did progressively liberalize their economies during the second half of the century; and with the demise of communism in 1991, the liberalization program abruptly accelerated. However, as the century ended, the policy came under increasing criticism.

By then, even liberal economists were questioning the usefulness of these policies; but the arguments against it were disorganized, frequently inconsistent, and usually offered alternatives that had already proven to be ineffective. The debate that had polarized free-market intellectuals and central-planning advocates was over, and the major schools of thought that had questioned the free market policies had largely disappeared. It was hard to understand why a growing share of the world population was against "globalization," as economists termed the accelerated efforts of liberalization since the early 1990s.

A big picture analysis based on the statistical record, however, suddenly shows why the anti-globalization movement is so vociferous. During the 1950s and 1960s, the world economy averaged a growth rate of about 4.7% annually. In the 1970s, the figure slowed to 4.1%; in the 1980s it slid further to 3.2%, and in the 1990s it was just 2.5%. Even the most developed nations need a minimum of about 3% over at least a decade to avoid increases in unemployment, while developing countries need a much faster rate in order to drive back unemployment, underemployment and poverty.

Only with such statistical information is it possible to see that, as the economy of the nations of the world was increasingly liberalized, the rate of GDP growth progressively went down for the large majority of countries, and to a level that caused a rise in unemployment. These figures make it evident that the fundamental claim of mainstream economics is weak and that there is something intrinsically awry.

There are different ways to measure market distortions: the level of trade barriers, the amount of internal competition, the share of state enterprises to GDP, the flexibility of labor markets, the flexibility of currency markets and of financial markets. Individually, each of these factors significantly affects the market but it is hard to determine which affects it more. There is, nonetheless, one factor that individually is most important in determining the level of market distortion. That is the share of government expenditure in the total economy.

Where government expenditure is about one-third of GDP, the nation that practices free trade, has no state companies, has a flexible exchange rate, and allows no monopolies is surely more market driven than a nation whose government spends the same one-third of GDP but is highly protectionist, has numerous state firms, has a fixed exchange rate, and allows industrial monopolies. However, if government expenditure (the sum of central, state and local government) approaches 50% of GDP, as was the case for most countries in northwestern Europe in the 1990s, then the market forces in those countries are far more distorted than they would be in any scenario involving a government expenditure of only 1% of GDP.

By the 1990s, even the countries with the lowest government expenditure in the world set the figure at about 20% of GDP. During the 20th century, that proportion varied from country to country and also over time, but on average for the whole world it was about 14%. The world average for the 19th century was much lower, more like 4%, and the further back we go in time, the lower the figure might be.

In the 20th century the world economy grew on average by about 3.0% per year, in the 19th by about 1.2%, in the 18th it is likely to have grown by 0.2%, in the 17th and 16th by 0.1%, and during the 6th to 15th century period it was close to stagnation (0.0%).

Government expenditure does not tell the whole story of market distortion in an economy, but sometimes it is the largest part of the story. Interestingly enough, as we go back in time, most if not all of the other factors that distort market forces are also less present (when seen the world as a whole). High trade barriers, for example, which are usually seen as a very important factor, were decreed at various moments in history but most of the time they were difficult to enforce. In general terms, the farther back we go, the lower was the capacity of governments to enforce trade regulations — or regulations of any other kind. There were fewer public officials relative to the total population. There was more petty corruption, and public officials were easier to bribe. State companies were practically non-existent; they are largely a phenomenon of the 20th century.

During the thousand-year period of the 6th to the 15th century, prices and exchange rates were almost entirely determined by supply and demand. There was no institution, administrative or otherwise, that was capable of determining anything on the matter. On top of that, government expenditure was close to zero. This economic environment seems to fulfill all or almost all of the conditions liberal economists have identified as essential for the attainment of fast and sustained economic growth. Nonetheless, stagnation prevailed and living conditions rarely improved beyond survival.

What the record actually shows is that the more the economy is left to the effect of market forces, the worse it will perform; and in an environment where supply and demand are totally unrestrained, the end result is stagnation and misery. That does not mean that increasing government intervention in the economy necessarily delivers fast growth; but it does mean that the central thesis of mainstream economics rests on a very shaky foundation.

The reason the world economy progressively slowed down during the second half of the 20th century is that the academic and political elite ignored the real causes of economic growth. Paul Romer, professor of Economics at the University of Berkeley and a reputed expert in growth theory, repeatedly admits that he and his colleagues are unsure what truly drives economic growth. That is why economics is called "the dismal science." Nations that have managed to get out of poverty did so without knowing how. That leaves it in the realm of luck, and luck is hard to sustain — or replicate.

During the 20th century and in particular the last decades, economists have struggled to calibrate the basic tenets of the theories they endorsed. Economics, however, is not in need of calibration with sophisticated mathematical models. So long as the basic tenets are false, the conclusions will continue to be worthless. Economists need first to develop a clear understanding of the causes of growth. They need to see the big picture before moving on to analyze the details. For that, they need well-organized, concise statistics, and that is what this book supplies.

REFERENCES

Books

Abel, Christopher & Lewis, Colin (ed): *Latin America, Economic Imperialism and the State*, The Athlone Press, London, 1985.

Abreu, Marcelo & Verner, Dorte: *Long-Term Brazilian Economic Growth 1930-94*, OECD, Paris, 1997.

A Case of Successful Adjustment-Korea's Experience During 1980-84, International Monetary Fund, Washington D.C., August 1985.

A Handbook of Korea, Korean Overseas Information Service, Seoul, 1993.

Aberbach, Joel, Dollar, David & Sokoloff, Kenneth (ed): *The Role of the State in Taiwan's Development*, M.E. Sharpe, Armonk-London, 1994.

Adams, D.: *America in the 20th Century*, Cambridge University Press, London, 1967.

Adshead, S. A.: *China in World History*, St. Martin's Press, New York, 1995.

Africa South of the Sahara 2001, Europa Publications, London, 2001.

Africa South of the Sahara 2002, Europa Publications, London, 2002.

Ahmad, Sultan: *Regression Estimates of Per Capita GDP Based on Purchasing Power Parities*, World Bank, Washington D.C., 1992.

Ahmad, Sultan: *Improving Inter-Spatial and Inter-Temporal Comparability of National Accounts*, Journal of Development Economics 4, 1994.

Albert, Bill: *South America and the World Economy from Independence to 1930*, The Macmillan Press Ltd., London, 1983.

Alexander, Robert: *An Introduction to Argentina*, Pall Mall Press, London, 1969.

Alford, B.: *British Economic Performance 1945-1975*, Cambridge University Press, Cambridge, 1995.

Aldcroft, D. & Fearron, P.(ed): *British Fluctuations 1790-1939*, Macmillan St. Martin Press, London, 1972.

Aldcroft, Derek & Richardson, Harry. *The British Economy 1870-1939*, Macmillan & Co. Ltd., London, 1969.

Aldcroft, Derek: *The British Economy Vol. I*, Wheatsheaf Books Ltd., London, 1986.

Allen, G.: *The British Disease*, The Institute of Economic Affairs, London, 1979.

Allen, G. C.: *A Short Economic History of Modern Japan*, George Allen & Unwin Ltd., London, 1972.

Allen, J. & Massey, D.(ed): *The Economy in Question*, SAGE Publications Ltd., London, 1988.

Allen, Kevin & Stevenson, Andrew: *An Introduction to the Italian Economy*, Martin Robertson, London, 1974.

Allen, N. J. (ed): *Oxford University Papers on India Part 2*, Oxford University Press, Oxford, 1987.

Almanach der Schweiz, Verlag Peter Lang AG, Schweiz, 1978.

Amaral, Samuel: *The Rise of Capitalism on the Pampas*, Cambridge University Press, Cambridge, 1998.

Ambrose, Stephen & Brinkley, Douglas: *Rise to Globalism*, Penguin Books, New York, 1997.

Ashworth, William: *An Economic History of England 1870-1939*, Methuen & Co. Ltd., London, 1965.

Aslund, Anders: *Gorbachev's Struggle for Economic Reform*, Pinter Publishers, London, 1991.

Axtell, James: *Beyond 1492-Encounters in Colonial North America*, Oxford University Press, Oxford, 1992.

Baer, Werner: *Industrialization and Economic Development in Brazil*, Richard Irwin Inc., Homewood-Illinois, 1965.

Bagwell, Philip & Mingay, G.: *Britain and America 1850-1939*, Routledge Kegan Paul Ltd., London, 1970.

Bayly, Susan: *Caste, Society and Politics in India from the 18th Century to the Modern Age*, The New Cambridge *History of India*, Cambridge University Press, Cambridge, 1999.

Bhagwati, Jagdish: *India in Transition*, Oxford University Press, Oxford, 1993.

Bailyn, Bernard: *The Ideological Origins of the American Revolution*, Harvard University Press, Cambridge-MA, 1992.

Bairoch, Paul: *Economics and World History*, Harvester Wheatsheaf, London, 1993.

Barber, William: *From New Era to New Deal*, Cambridge University Press, Cambridge, 1988.

Barnes, Gina: *The Rise of Civilization in East Asia*, Thames and Hudson, London, 1999.

Barraclough, Geoffrey: *Mediaeval Germany Vol. I*, Basil Blackwell, Oxford, 1979.

Batta, Paul: *Le Grand Maghreb*, Editions La Decouverte, Paris, 1990.

Beauvois, Daniel : *Histoire de la Pologne*, Hatier, France, 1995.

Befu, Harumi (ed): *Cultural Nationalism in East Asia*, Institute of East Asian Studies-University of California, Berkeley-CA, 1993.

Behari, Madhuri: *Indian Economy since Independence*, D. K. Publications, Delhi, 1983.

Beinart, Williams: *20th century South Africa*, Oxford University Press, Oxford, 1994.

Bergere, M. Bianco, L. & Domes, J.: *La Chine au XXe Siecle*, Fayard, Paris, 1989.

Berghahn, V.: *Modern Germany*, Cambridge University Press, Cambridge, 1985.

Bergier, Jean: *Naissance et Croissance de la Suisse Industrielle*, Francke Editions, Suisse, 1974.

Berkowitz, Edward: *America's Welfare State*, The John Hopkins University Press, Baltimore, 1991.

Bermant, Chaim: *Israel*, Thames and Hudson, London, 1967.

Berosman, Joel : *Brazil-Industrialization and Trade Policies*, Oxford University Press, London, 1970.

Berry, Laverle (ed): *Ghana-A Country Study*, Library of Congress, Washington D. C., 1995.

Bethel, Leslie (ed): *Brazil-Empire and Republic 1822-1930*, Cambridge University Press, Cambridge, 1989.

Bethel, Leslie (ed): *Spanish America after Independence 1820-1870*, Cambridge University Press, Cambridge, 1987.

Bethel, Leslie (ed): *The Cambridge History of Latin America Vol. I*, Cambridge University Press, Cambridge, 1984.

Bethel, Leslie (ed): *The Cambridge History of Latin America Vol. II*, Cambridge University Press, Cambridge, 1984.

Bethel, Leslie (ed): *The Independence of Latin America*, Cambridge University Press, Cambridge, 1987.

Bettelheim, Charles: *L'Economie Allemande sous le Nazisme Vol. I & II*, François Maspero, Paris, 1971.

Bharier, Julian : *Economic Development in Iran 1900-1970*, Oxford University Press, London, 1971.

Bhattacharya, Sabya sachi (ed) : *Situating Indian History*, Oxford University Press, Oxford, 1986.

Birmingham, David & Martin, Phyllis (ed): *History of Central Africa—The Contemporary Years since 1960*, Longman, London, 1998.

Bix, Herbert: *Peasant Protest in Japan 1590-1884*, Yale University Press, New Haven-US, 1986.

Blackwell, William: *The Beginnings of Russian Industrialization*, Princeton University Press, Princeton, 1968.

Blackwell, William: *The Industrialization of Russia*, Thomas Crowell Co., New York, 1970.

Blaug, Mark: *La Pensée économique*, Economica, Paris, 1996.

Blazant, Jan: *A Concise History of Mexico from Hidalgo to Cardenas*, Cambridge University Press, Cambridge, 1977.

Bogart, Ernest & Kemmerer, Donald: *Economic History of the American People*, Longmans Green & Co., New York, 1947.

Bolton, J. L.: *The Medieval English Economy 1150-1500*, The Garden City Press Ltd., London, 1980.

Bonilla, Heraclio (ed): *El Sistema Colonial en la América Española*, Editorial Critica, Barcelona, 1991.

Boorstin, Daniel: *Histoire des Americaines-Naissance d'une nation*, Armand Collin, Paris, 1981.

Boulding, Kenneth: *The Structure of a Modern Economy*, Macmillan Press, London, 1993.

Boyle, John: *Persia—History and Heritage*, Henry Melland, London, 1978.

Bramsted, Ernest: *Germany*, Prentice-Hall Inc., New York, 1972.

Brass, Paul: *The Politics of India since Independence*, The New Cambridge History of India, Cambridge University Press, Cambridge, 1990.

Breach, R. & Hartwell, R. (ed): *British Economy and Society 1870-1970*, Oxford University Press, Oxford, 1972.

Bremond, J., Chalaye, C. & Loeb, M.: *L'Economie du Japon*, Hatier, Paris, 1987.

Brenner, Y.: *A Short History of Economic Progress*, Frank Cass & Co. Ltd., London, 1969.

Britain 1984, The Central Office of Information, London, 1984.

Brown, Judith: *Modern India—The origins of an Asian Democracy*, Oxford University Press, Oxford, 1985.

Brown Richard: *Society and Economy in Modern Britain 1700-1850*, Routledge, London, 1991.

Bruno, M. & Sachs, J.: *Economics of Worldwide Stagflation*, Harvard University Press, Cambridge, Mass., 1985.

Buckley, Patricia: *The Cambridge Illustrated History of China*, Cambridge University Press, Cambridge, 1996.

Bulmer, Victor: *The Economic History of Latin America since Independence*, Cambridge University Press, Cambridge, 1994.

Burnett, John: *Plenty and Want*, Routledge, London, 1989.

Burns, Arthur: *Production Trends in the United States since 1870*, National Bureau of Economic Research, US, 1934.

Bushnell, David & Macaulay, Neill: *The Emergence of Latin America in the 19th century*, Oxford University Press, Oxford, 1988.

Byrnes, Rita (ed): *Uganda-A Country Study*, Library of Congress, Washington D. C., 1992.

Byrnes, Rita (ed): *South Africa-A Country Study*, Library of Congress, Washington D. C., 1997.

Cain, P. J.: *Economic Foundations of British Overseas Expansion 1815-1914*, The Macmillan Press Ltd., London, 1980.

Cameron, Rondo (ed): *Essays in French Economic History*, Richard D. Irwin, Homewood-Illinois, 1970.

Campbell, Robert: *Soviet Economic Power*, Macmillan & Co., London, 1967.

Carpentier, Jean & Lebrun, François (ed): *Histoire de la Méditerranée*, Editions du Seuil, Paris, 1998.

Carter, Gwendolen & O'Meara, Patrick (ed): *Southern Africa—The Continuing Crisis*, Indiana University Press, Bloomington-US, 1982.

Chambers, J. D.: *The Workshop of the World*, Oxford University Press, Oxford, 1961.

Chandavarkar, Rajinarayan: *The Origins of Industrial Capitalism In India*, Cambridge University Press, Cambridge, 1994.

Chandler, Lester: *America's Greatest Depression*, Harper & Row, New York, 1970.

Chang, Chun-shu & Chang, Hsueh-lun: *Crisis and Transformation in 17th Century China*, University of Michigan Press, Ann Arbor, 1992.

Chaplin, Helen (ed): *Nigeria-A Country Study*, Library of Congress, Washington D. C., 1992.

Chaplin, Helen (ed): *Turkey-A Country Study*, Library of Congress, Washington D. C., 1996.

Chatterji, Joya: *Bengal Divided*, Cambridge University Press, Cambridge, 1994.

Chaudhuri, K.: *Asia Before Europe*, Cambridge University Press, Cambridge, 1990.

Cheney, L.J.: *A History of the Western World*, George Allen & Unwin, London, 1961.

Chevalier, François: *L'Amérique Latine*, Presses Universitaires de France, Paris, 1993.

China at the Threshold of a Market Economy, International Monetary Fund, Washington D.C., September 1993.

Chou, Chin-sheng: *An Economic History of China*, Western Washington State College, US, 1974.

Chung, Chai-sik: *A Korean Confucian Encounter with the Modern World*, Institute of East Asian Studies-University of California, Berkeley-CA, 1995.

Clapham, John: *A Concise Economic History of Britain*, Cambridge University Press, Cambridge, 1949.

Chambers, J. D.: *Population, Economy and Society in Pre-Industrial England*, Oxford University Press, Oxford, 1972.

Cipolla, Carlo: *Before the Industrial Revolution*, Routledge, London, 1993.

Cipolla, Carlo (ed): *The Fontana Economic History of Europe—Contemporary Economies Part I*, William Collins Sons & Co., Glasgow, 1976.

Cipolla, Carlo (ed): *The Fontana Economic History of Europe—The Emergence of Industrial Societies Part I*, William Collins Sons & Co., Glasgow, 1975.

Clark, George: *The Wealth of England from 1496 to 1760*, Oxford University Press, Oxford, 1946.

Clark, Peter & Slack, Paul: *English Towns in Transition 1500-1700*, Oxford University Press, Oxford, 1976.

Clarke, Roger: *Soviet Economic Facts 1917-70*, Macmillan, London, 1972.

Clarke, Roger & Matko, Dubravko: *Soviet Economic Facts 1917-81*, Macmillan, London, 1983.

Clarkson, Leslie: *Death, Disease and Famine in Pre-Industrial England*, Gill and Macmillan Ltd., London, 1975.

Cleere, Henry & Crossley, David: *The Iron Industry of the Weald*, Leicester University Press, London, 1985.

Clough, Shepard: *Histoire Economique des Etas Unis*, Presses Universitaires de France, Paris, 1953.

Clough, Shepard: *European Economic History—The Economic Development of Western Civilization*, McGraw-Hill, New York, 1968.

Clough, S. B.: *Grandeur et Décadence des Civilisations*, Payot, Paris, 1954.

Coates, David (ed): *Economic and Industrial Performance in Europe*, Edward Elgar, Aldershot UK, 1995.

Cohen, Paul: *Discovering History in China*, Columbia University Press, New York, 1984.

Cohen, Stephen; *Rethinking the Soviet Experience*, Oxford University Press, Oxford, 1985.

Coleman, D. C.: *The Economy of England 1415-1750*, Oxford University Press, Oxford, 1977.

Cook, Chris & Paxton, John: *European Political Facts 1848-1918*, Macmillan, London, 1978.

Cook, M. A.(ed): *Studies in the Economic History of the Middle East*, Oxford University Press, London, 1970.

Cooley, John: *Libyan Sandstorm*, Holt-Rhnehart and Winston, New York, 1982.

Cornell, Hamelin, Oullet, Trudel: *Canada—Unite et diversite*, Holt, Rinehart et Winston, Quebec, 1971.

Costa, Emilia: *The Brazilian Empire-Myths and Histories*, The University of Chicago Press, Chicago, 1985.

Cotler, Julio & Fagen, Richard (ed): *Latin America and the United States—The Changing Political Realities*, Stanford University Press, Stanford, 1974.

Cotterel, Arthur: *East Asia-From Chinese Predominance to the Rise of the Pacific Rim*, Oxford University Press, Oxford, 1993.

Council of Europe-various years, *Recent Demographic Developments in Europe and North America*, Strasbourg, Council of Europe Press.

Cowan, C. D.(ed): *The Economic Development of China and Japan*, George Allen & Unwin Ltd., London, 1964.

Crisis in Governance-A Review of Bangladesh's Development 1997, The University Press Ltd., Dhaka, 1998.

Crowder, Michael (ed): *The Cambridge History of Africa Vol. 8*, Cambridge University Press, Cambridge, 1984.

Cullen, L. & Smout, T.(ed): *Comparative Aspects of Scottish and Irish Economic and Social History 1600-1900*, John Donald Publishers Ltd., Edinburgh, 1976.

Cumings, Bruce: *Korea's Place in the Sun-A Modern History*, W. W. Norton & Co., New York, 1997.

Daniel, Elton: *The History of Iran*, Greenwood Press, Westport-London, 2001.

Davies, Norman: *Europe—A History*, Oxford University Press, Oxford, 1996.

Davis, Eric: *Challenging Colonialism-Bank Misr and Egyptian Industrialization 1920-1941*, Princeton University Press, Princeton, 1983.

Davis, Lance, Easterlin, Richard & Parker William (ed): *American Economic Growth*, Harper & Row Publishers, New York, 1972.

Davis, Lance & Huttenback, Robert: *Mammom and the Pursuit of Empire*, Cambridge University Press, Cambridge, 1988.

Davis, L., Hughes, J. & McDougall, D.: *American Economic History*, Richard Irwin Inc., New York, 1969.

De Crespigny, Rafe: *China this Century*, Oxford University Press, Oxford, 1992.

Deane, Phyllis: *The First Industrial Revolution*, Cambridge University Press, Cambridge, 1979.

Deiss, Joseph: *Economie Politique et Politique Economique de la Suisse*, Editions Fragniere, Suisse, 1979.

Delouche, Ffrederic : *L'Europe-Histoire de ses peuples*, Perrin, Germany, 1990.

Deuchler, Martina: *The Confucian Transformation of Korea*, Harvard University Press, Cambridge-MA, 1992.

Deutsche Bundesbank Annual Report 1992-95, Frankfurt.

Devin, J. & Dickson, D.(ed): *Ireland and Scotland 1600-1850*, John Donald Publishers Ltd., Edinburgh, 1983.

Dictionnaire Geopolitique des Etats, Flammarion, Paris, 1994.

Dobb, Maurice: *Soviet Economic Development since 1917*, Routledge, London, 1960.

Dolan, Roland (ed): *Philippines-A Country Study*, Library of Congress, Washington D. C., 1993.

Dore, R.: *Structural Adjustment in Japan 1970-82*, International Labor Organization, Geneva, 1986.

Dornbusch, Rudiger & Edwards, Sebastian (ed): *The Macroeconomics of Populism in Latin America*, The University of Chicago Press, Chicago, 1991.

Dower, John: *Japan in War and Peace*, Harper Collins, London, 1995.

Drèze, Jacques: *Pour l'emploi, la croissance et l'Europe*, Balises, Bruxelles, 1995.

Duchene, Gerard: *l'Economie de l'URSS*, Editions La Decouvert, Paris, 1987.

Dukes, Paul. *A History of Europe 1648-1948*: The Arrival, The Rise, The Fall, Macmillan, London, 1985.

Duroselle, Jean-Baptiste : *L'Europe—Histoire de ses peuples*, Perrin, 1990.

East, Roger & Pontin, Jolyon : *Revolution and Change in Central and Eastern Europe*, Pinter Publishers, London, 1997.

East Asian Miracle, Economic Growth and Public Policy, The World Bank, IBRD, 1993.

Easterbrook, W.T. & Aitken, Hugh: *Canadian Economic History*, The Macmillan Co., Toronto, 1970.

Eastern Europe and the Commonwealth of Independent States 1999, Europa Publications, London, 1999.

Eberhard Wolfram: *A History of China*, University of California Press, US, 1977.

Eck, Jean-François: *Histoire de l'Economie Française depuis 1945*, Armand Colin, Paris, 1990.

Eckert, Lee, Lew, Robinson, Wagner: *Korea-Old and New-A History*, Harvard University Press, Cambridge-MA, 1990.

Economic Development of Singapore 1960-91, Economic Development Board, Singapore, 1992.

Edelmayer, F., Hausberger, B. & Weinzierl, M. (Hrsg): *Die beiden Amerikas*, Brandes & Apsel, Frankfurt, 1996.

Eisenstadt, S. N.: *Japanese Civilization-A Comparative View*, University of Chicago Press, Chicago, 1995.

Ekundare, Olufem: *An Economic History of Nigeria 1860-1960*, Africana Publishing Co., New York, 1973.

Elbaum, Bernard & Lazonick William (ed): *The Decline of the British Economy*, Oxford University Press, Oxford-US, 1986.

Encyclopaedia of Asian History Vol. I, Macmillan Publishing Co., New York, 1988.

Encyclopaedia Universalis Vol. 1, Encyclopaedia Universalis France S. A., Paris, 1985.

Encyclopaedia Universalis Vol. 17, Encyclopaedia Universalis France S. A., Paris, 1985.

Encyclopaedia Universalis Vol. 21, Encyclopaedia Universalis France S. A., Paris, 1985.

Engerman, Stanley & Gallman, Robert (ed): *The Cambridge Economic History of the United States Vol. 1*, Cambridge University Press, Cambridge, 1996.

Etudes Economiques de l'OCDE-1996-Royaume-Uni, OCDE, Paris, 1996.

European Historical Statistics 1750-1970, B. R. Mitchell, Mcmillan Press Ltd., 1975.

Europe du Nord-Europe Mediane, Geographie Universelle, Belin-Reclus, Paris, 1996.

Eurostat (Statistical Office of the European Communities)-various years, Statistical Yearbook, Luxembourg.

Fage, J. D.: *A History of Africa*, Unwin Hyman, London, 1988.

Fairbank, John: *China-A New History*, Harvard University Press, Cambridge-Mass., 1992.

Fairbank, John & Goldman, Merle: *China-A New History*, Harvard University Press, Cambridge-MA, 1998.

Farley, Rawle: *The Economics of Latin America*, Harper & Row, New York, 1972.

Faulkner, Harold: *Histoire Economique des Etas Unis d'Amérique vol. IV*, Presses Universitaires de France, Paris, 1958.

Faulkner, Harold: *Histoire Economique des Etas Unis d'Amérique Vol. I*, Presses Universitaires de France, Paris, 1958.

Ferns, H. S.: *Argentina*, Ernest Benn Ltd., London, 1969.

Finzsch, Norbert: *Die Goldgräber Kaliforniens*, Vandenhoeck & Ruprecht, Göttingen, 1982.

Fisher, Douglas: *The Industrial Revolution*, St. Martin Press, London, 1992.

Fisher, H.A.L.: *A History of Europe*, Edward Arnold, London, 1961.

Fite, Gilbert & Reese, Jim: *An Economic History of the United States*, Houghton Mifflin Co., Boston, 1965.

Floud, Roderick & McCloskey, Donald (ed): *The Economic History of Britain since 1700 Vol. II* ,Cambridge University Press, Cambridge, 1981.

Floud, Roderick & McCloskey, Donald (ed): *The Economic History of Britain since 1700 Vol. I*, Cambridge University Press, Cambridge, 1994.

Food and Agriculture Organization of the United Nations-various years, Production Yearbook, FAO Statistics Series, Rome.

Fox, Robert & Guagnini, Anna (ed): *Education, Technology and Industrial Performance in Europe 1850-1939*, Cambridge University Press, Cambridge, 1993.

Fraser, J. & Gerstle, G.: *The Rise and Fall of the New Deal Order*, Princeton University Press, Princeton, 1989.

Frederick, William (ed): *Indonesia-A Country Study*, Library of Congress, Washington D. C., 1992.

Freund, Bill: *The Making of Contemporary Africa*, Lynne Rienner Publishers, Boulder-Colorado, 1998.

Frieden, Jefffrey: *Debt, Development and Democracy*, Princeton University Press, Princeton, 1991.

Furtado, Celso: *La Formation Economique du Bresil*, Publisud, France, 1998.

Furtado, Celso: *Economic Development of Latin America*, Cambridge University Press, Cambridge, 1970.

Fututake, Tadashi: *The Japanese Social Structure*, University of Tokyo Press, Tokyo, 1981.

Gadgil, D. R.: *The Industrial Evolution of India in Recent Times 1860-1939*, Oxford University Press, London, 1972.

Gagliardo, John: *Germany under the Old Regime 1600-1790*, Longman, London, 1991.

Galland, Xavier: *Histoire de la Thailande*, Presses Universitaires de France, Paris, 1998.

Gamble, Andrew: *Britain in Decline*, Macmillan Education Ltd., London, 1985.

Ganguli, B. N. (ed): *Readings in Indian Economic History*, Asian Publishing House, Bombay, 1964.

Garon, Sheldon: *Molding Japanese Minds*, Princeton University Press, Princeton-New Yersey, 1997.

Garon, Sheldon: *The State and Labor in Modern Japan*, University of California Press, Berkeley-CA, 1987.

Gatrell, Peter: *The Tsarist Economy 1850-1917*, B.T. Batsford Ltd., London, 1986.

Gaxotte, Pierre: *Histoire de l'Allemagne*, Flammarion, Paris, 1975.

George, Pierre: *l'Economie de l'URSS*, Presses Universitaires de France, Paris, 1965.

Germany-OECD-Economic Surveys, OECD, Paris, 1992.

Gernet, Jacques: *La Chine Ancienne*, Presses Universitaires de France, Paris, 1992.

Goodman, D. & Segal, G.: *China in the Nineties*, Oxford University Press, Oxford-US, 1991.

Gordon, Andrew: *The Evolution of Labor Relations in Japan*, Harvard University Press, Cambridge-MA, 1985.

Goubert, Pierre: *Initiation a L'Histoire de la France*, Fayard-Tallandier, France, 1984.

Grant, Alexander & Stringer, Keith (ed): *Uniting the Kingdom?* Routledge, London, 1995.

Grassby, Richard: *The Business Community of 17th Century England*, Cambridge University Press, Cambridge, 1995.

Gravereau, Jacques: *Le Japon-l'ere de Hirohito*, Imprimerie nationale, Paris, 1988.

Gray Jack: *Rebellions and Revolutions*, Oxford University Press, Oxford-US, 1990.

Gray, J. & White, G.(ed): *China's New Development Strategy*, Academic Press Ltd., London, 1982.

Greene, Jack & Pole, J. R. (ed): *The Blackwell Encyclopedia of the American Revolution*, Basil Blackwell, Cambridge-MA, 1991.

Greenough, Paul: *Prosperity and Misery in Modern Bengal*, Oxford University Press, New York-Oxford, 1982.

Grossman, James (ed): *The Frontier in American Culture*, University of California Press, Berkeley-Los Angeles, 1994.

Guroff, Gregory & Cartensen, Fred (ed): *Entrepreneurship in Imperial Russia and the Soviet Union*, Princeton University Press, Princeton, 1983.

Haber, Stephen: *Industry and Underdevelopment—The Industrialization of Mexico 1890-1940*, Stanford University Press, Stanford, 1989.

Hacker, Louis: *Major Documents in American Economic History Vol. I*, D. Van Norstrand Co., US, 1961.

Haggerty, Richard (ed): *Venezuela-A Country Study*, Library of Congress, Washington D. C., 1993.

Hansen, Bent: *Egypt and Turkey*, Oxford University Press, Oxford, 1991.

Hao, Yen-ping: *The Commercial Revolution in 19th century China*, University of California Press, Berkeley-CA, 1986.

Harberger, Arnold (ed): *World Economic Growth*, ICS Press, US, 1984.

Hardach, Karl: *Wirtschafts Geschichte Deutschlands im 20 Jahrhundert*, Vandenhoeck und Ruprecht, Deutschland, 1979.

Harding, Harry: *China's Second Revolution*, The Brookings Institution, Washington D.C., 1987.

Harris, Richard (ed): *The Political Economy of Africa*, Schenkman Publishing Co., Cambridge-MA, 1975.

Harris, Seymour: *American Economic History*, McGraw Hill, New York, 1961.

Hayward, Jack: *The State and the Market Economy*, Wheatsheaf Books, United Kingdom, 1986.

Heisenberg, Wolfgang (ed): *German Unification in European Perspective*, Brassey's, Bruxelles, 1991.

Henretta, James: *The Evolution of American Society 1700-1815*, D. C. Heath & Co., Lexington-MA, 1973.

Herail, Francine: *Histoire du Japon*, Publications Orientalistes de France, Paris, 1986,

Hernandez, Alicia (ed): *Las Inversiones Extranjeras en America Latina 1850-1930*, Fondo de Cultura Economica, Mexico, 1995.

Herring, Hubert: *A History of Latin America—From the Beginnings to the Present*, Alfred a. Knopf, New York, 1968.

Heywood, Colin: *The Development of the French Economy 1750-1914*, The Macmillan Press, 1992.

Hill, C. P.: *British Economic and Social History*, Edward Arnold Ltd., London, 1977.

Hobday, Michael: *Innovations in East Asia*, Edwar Elgar Publishing Ltd., Cheltenham, UK, 1997.

Hobsbawn, E. J.: *Industry and Empire*, Weidenfeld and Nicolson, London, 1968.

Hodges, Donald: *Argentina 1943-1976*, University of New Mexico Press, Albuquerque-US, 1976.

Hoffman, Mccusker & Menard, Albert (ed): *The Economy of Early America-The Revolutionary Period 1763-1790*, University Press of Virginia, Charlottesville, 1988.

Hoffmann, Walther: *Das Wachstum der Deutschen Wirtschaft seit der mitte 19. Jahrhunderts*, Springer Verlag, Berlin, 1965.

Holborn, Hajo: *A History of Modern Germany Vol. I*, Alfred A Knopf, New York, 1967.

Holderness, B. A.: *Pre-Industrial England*, J.M. Dent & Sons Ltd., London, 1976.

Hopkins, Keith (ed): *Hong Kong-The Industrial Colony*, Oxford University Press, London, 1971.

Hou, Chi-ming: *Foreign Investment and Economic Development in China 1840-1937*, Harvard University Press, Cambridge, Mass., 1965.

Houghton, Hobart & Dagut, Jennifer: *Source Material on the South African Economy Vol. 3*, Oxford University Press, Cape Town, 1973.

Howe, Christopher: *China's Economy*, Granada Publishing, London, 1978.

Huang, Ray: *China-A Macro History*, M. E. Sharpe Inc., Armonk-New York, 1988.

Hudson, Rex (ed): *Brazil-A Country Study*, Library of Congress, Washington D. C., 1998.

Hudson, Rex (ed): *Chile-A Country Study*, Library of Congress, Washington D. C., 1994.

Huff, W. G.: *The Economic Growth of Singapore*, Cambridge University Press, Cambridge, 1994.

Hughes, Jonathan: *American Economic History*, Scott Foresman & Co., Glenview, Illinois, 1987.

Human Development Report, United Nations Development Program (UNDP), Oxford University Press, Oxford. 2000.

Hunt, Michael: *Ideology and U. S. Foreign Policy*, Yale University Press, New Haven-London, 1987.

International Financial Statistics-various volumes, International Monetary Fund, Washington D.C.

ILO (International Labour Organization)-various years, Key Indicators of the Labour Market, Geneva.

Israel, J. J.: *Race, Class and Politics in Colonial Mexico 1610-1670*, Oxford University Press, London, 1975.

Issawi, Charles (ed): *The Economic History of the Middle East 1800-1914*, University of Chicago Press, Chicago, 1966.

Jack, Sybil: *Trade and Industry in Tudor and Stuart England*, George Allen & Unwin Ltd., London, 1977.

Jaffrelot, Christophe (ed): *Le Pakistan-Carrefour de Tensions Regionales*, Editions Complexe, 1999.

Jain, Purushottam Chandra: *Socio-Economic Exploration of Mediaeval India*, B. R. Publishing Corp. New Delhi, 1976.

Jalal, Ayesha: *The State of Martial Rule*, Cambridge University Press, Cambridge, 1990.

Jalan, Bimal: *India's Economic Crisis*, Oxford University Press, Oxford, 1991.

Jansen, Marius (ed): *The Emergence of Meiji Japan*, Cambridge University Press, Cambridge, 1995.

Jansen, Marius (ed): *Warrior Rule in Japan*, Cambridge University Press, Cambridge, 1995.

Jansen, Marius & Rozman, Gilbert (ed): *Japan in Transition-From Tokugawa to Meiji*, Princeton University Press, Princeton-New Yersey, 1986.

Jao, Hungdah Chiu & Wu, Yuan-li (ed): *The Future of Hong Kong*, Quorum Books, New York, 1987.

Jarausch, Konrad: *The Rush to German Unity*, Oxford University Press, Oxford, 1994.

Japan's Economy and Japan-U.S. Trade, The Japan Times, Tokyo, 1982.

Johnson, John (ed): *Continuity and Change in Latin America*, Stanford University Press, Stanford, 1964.

Jones, Geoffrey (ed): *Banking and Empire in Iran Vol. I*, Cambridge University Press, Cambridge, 1986.

Jones, Maldwyn: *The Limits of Liberty-American History 1607-1980*, Oxford University Press, Oxford, 1989.

Jones, E. L. (ed): *Agriculture and Economic Growth in England 1650-1815*, Methuen & Co. Ltd., London, 1967.

July, Robert: *Precolonial Africa-An Economic and Social History*, Division Publishing Ltd., England, 1976.

Kahan, Arcadius: *The Plow, the Hammer and the Knout*, University of Chicago Press, Chicago, p. 1985.

Kahan, Arcadius: *Russian Economic History*, University of Chicago Press, Chicago, 1989.

Kaldor, Nicholas: *Causes of Growth and Stagnation in the World Economy*, Cambridge University Press, Cambridge, 1996.

Kasar, Michael: *Soviet Economics*, Weidenfeld & Nicolson, London, 1970

Kaufman, Susan (ed): *Mexico in Transition*, Council on Foreign Relations, New York, 1988.

Kedourie, Elie: *The Middle Eastern Economy*, Frank Cass & Co., London, 1977.

Keeler, John & Schain, Martin (ed): *Chirac's Challenge*, Macmillan, London, 1996.

Keep, John: *Last of the Empires*, Oxford University Press, Oxford, 1995.

Kellenbenz, Herman: *The Rise of the European Economy*, Weidenfeld & Nicolson, London, 1976.

Keller, Henry: *Labour, Science and Technology in France 1500-1620*, Cambridge University Press, Cambridge, 1996.

Kennedy, Charles: *Bureaucracy in Pakistan*, Oxford University Press, Oxford, 1987.

Kenwood, A & Lougheed, A.: *The Growth of the International Economy 1820-1990*, Routledge, London, 1992.

Kerblay, Basile: *Modern Soviet Society*, Methuen & Co., London, 1983.

Kicza, John: *Colonial Entrepreneurs*, University of New Mexico Press, Albuquerque-US, 1983.

Kidron, Machel: *Foreign Investments in India*, Oxford University Press, London, 1965.

Kindermann, Gottfried: *Der Aufstieg Koreas in der Weltpolitik*, Olzog Verlag, München, 1994.

King, Frank: *Money and Monetary Policy in China*, Harvard University Press, Cambridge, Mass., 1965.

Kingston, Paul: *Britain and the Politics of Modernization in the Middle East 1945-1958*, Cambridge University Press, Cambridge, 1996.

Kirby, M. W.: *The Decline of British Economic Power since 1870*, George Allen & Unwin Ltd., London, 1981.

Kirchner, Walter: *History of Russia*, Barnes & Noble, New York, 1965.

Kitchen, Martin: *The Cambridge Illustrated History of Germany*, Cambridge University Press, Cambridge, 1997.

Kitchen, Martin: *The Political Economy of Germany 1815-1914*, McGill-Queen's University Press, Montreal, 1978.

Kneschaurek, Francesco: *La Suisse Face a une Nouvelle Phase de son Developpement*, Centre de Recherches Europeenes, Suisse, 1975.

Kolb, Albert : *Ostasien—China, Japan, Korea*, Quelle & Meyer Verlag, Heidelberg, 1963.

Kolko, Gabriel: *Main Currents in Modern American History*, Harper & Row, New York, p. 1976.

Konczacki, Z. & Konczaki, J. (ed): *An Economic History of Tropical Africa Vol. I*, Frank Cass, London, 1977.

Kort, Michael: *The Soviet Colossus*, Unwin Hyman Inc., New York, 1990.

Krisch, Henry: *The German Democratic Republic*, Westview Press, US, 1985.

Krout, John: *The United States to 1877*, Barnes & Noble, New York, 1966.

Krout, John: *The United States since 1865*, Barnes & Noble, New York, 1965.

Krugman, Paul: *The Age of Diminished Expectations*, The MIT Press, Boston, 1991.

Krugman, Paul: *Peddling Prosperity-Economic Sense and Nonsense in the Age of Diminished Expectations*, W.W. Norton, 1994.

Kulke, Hermann & Rothermund, Dietmar: *A History of India*, Croom Helm Ltd., Great Britain, 1986.

Kulick, Elliot & Wilson, Dick: *Thailand's Turn—Profile of a New Dragon*, Macmillan, London, 1992.

Kurian, George: *Encyclopaedia of the Third World*, Mansell Publishing Ltd., London, 1982.

Kuznets, Simon: *Modern Economic Growth*, Yale University Press, US, 1966.

Lacoste, Ives: *Dictionnaire Geopolitique des Etas*, Flammarion, Paris, 1994.

La Grande Bretagne à la Fin du XXe Siècle, Notes e Etudes Documentaires, Decembre 1994.

Lage und Probleme der Schweizerischen Wirtschaft, Schweizerische National bank, Bern, 1977.

Lal, Deepak: *Aspects of Indian Labour*, Oxford University Press, New York, 1989.

Lal, Deepak: *Cultural Stability and Economic Stagnation Vol. I*, Oxford University Press, Oxford, 1988.

Lampe, John & Jackson, Marvin: *Balkan Economic History 1550-1950*, Indiana University Press, Bloomington, 1982.

Landes, David: *The Wealth and Poverty of Nations*, W. W. Norton & Co., New York, 1998.

Larrabee, Stephen: *The Two German States and European Security*, Macmillan, London, 1989.

L'Afrique—Reforme et Croissance, OECD, Paris, 2000.

Le Japon d'Aujourd'hui, Ministère des Affaires Etrangères, Tokyo, 1971.

L'Economie Suisse 1946-1986, Union de Banque Suisses, Suisse, 1987.

Lee, C. H.: *The British Economy since 1700-A Macroeconomic Perspective*, Cambridge University Press, Cambridge, 1986.

Leslie, R.F. (ed): *The History of Poland since 1863*, Cambridge University Press, Cambridge, 1980.

L'etat du Monde-Annuaire Economique et Geopolitique, La Decouvert, Paris, 2002.

Levine, Salomon & Kawada, Hisashi: *Human Resources in Japanese Industrial Development*, Princeton University Press, Princeton, 1980.

Lewis, John: *The United States and the End of the Cold War*, Oxford University Press, Oxford, 1992.

Livet, Georges & Mousnier, Roland (ed): *Histoire Générale de l'Europe*, Presses Universitaires de France, Paris, 1980.

Lloyd, T. O.: *The British Empire 1558-1995*, Oxford University Press, Oxford, 1996.

Lockhart, James & Schwartz, Stuart: *Early Latin America-A History of Colonial Spanish America and Brazil*, Cambridge University Press, Cambridge, 1983.

Lockwood, William: *The Economic Development of Japan*, Princeton University Press, Princeton-New Yersey, 1968.

Lodge, George: *Engines of Change*, Alfred A. Knopf, New York, 1970.

Lombard, Denys: *La Chine Imperiale*, Presses Universitaires de France, Paris, 1967.

Lopez, Robert : *Naissance de l'Europe*, Librairie Armand Collin, France, 1962.

Lowe, Peter: *The Origins of the Korean War*, Longman, London, 1997.

Luck, Murray (ed): *Modern Switzerland*, Sposs Inc., US, 1978.

Mabro, Robert & Rodwan, Samir: *The Industrialization of Egypt 1939-1973-Policy and Performance*, Oxford University Press, Oxford, 1976.

Macpherson, W. J. (ed): *The Industrialization of Japan*, Blackwell Publishers, Oxford, 1994.

McGann, Thomas: *Argentina—The Divided Land*, D. Van Nostrand Co., Princeton-US, 1966.

McGuire, James: *Peronism without Peron*, Stanford University Press, Stanford, 1997.

Madison, Angus: *Economic Growth in Japan and the USSR*, George Allen & Unwin Ltd., London, 1969.

Madison, Angus: *L'Economie Chinoise-Une perspective historique*, OECD, Paris, 1998.

Madison, Angus: *Economic Growth in the West*, The 20th century Fund, New York, 1964.

Mafeje, Archie & Rodwan, Samir (ed): *Economic and Demographic Change in Africa*, Oxford University Press, Oxford, 1995.

Main Economic Indicators, Organisation for Economic Cooperation and Development, OECD, Paris.

Majd, Mohammad Ghuli: *Great Britain & Reza Shah*, University Press of Florida, Gainesville-US, 2001.

Major, J. & Kane, A.: *China Briefing 1987*, Westview Press, US, 1987.

Malik, Iftikhar: *State and Civil Society in Pakistan*, Macmillan Press Ltd., London, 1997.

Mann, Golo: *The History of Germany since 1789*, Chatto & Windus, London, 1968.

Marichal, Carlos: *A Century of Debt Crises in Latin America*, Princeton University Press, Princeton, 1989.

Martin, Janet: *Medieval Russia 980-1584*, Cambridge University Press, Cambridge, 1996.

Mason, R. H. & Caiger, J. G.: *A History of Japan*, Charles E. Tuttle Co., Australia, 1997.

Mass, Jeffrey & Hauser, William (ed): *The Bakufu in Japanese History*, Stanford University Press, Stanford-CA, 1985.

Mathias, Peter: *The First Industrial Nation*, Methuen & Co. Ltd., US, 1983.

Mathis, Franz: *Die Deutsche Wirtschaft im 16. Jahrhundert*, R. Oldenbourg Verlag, München, 1992.

Mauro, Frederic: *La Preindustrialisation du Bresil*, CNRC, Paris, 1984.

Mauro, Frederic (ed): *Transport et Commerce en Amerique Latine 1800-1970*, Editions L'Harmattan, Paris, 1990.

Mazrui, Ali (ed): *Histoire Generale de l'Afrique Vol. VIII*, Editions Unesco, Paris, 1998.

Mehta, F. A.: *Second India Studies—Economy*, Macmillan of India Ltd., Delhi, 1976.

McAuley, Mary: *Soviet Politics 1917-1991*, Oxford University Press, Oxford, 1992.

McCloskey, Donald (ed): *Essays on a Mature Economy-Britain After 1840*, Methuen & Co. Ltd., London, 1971.

Meditz, Sandra (ed): *Zaire-A Country Study*, Library of Congress, Washington D. C., 1994.

Merrick, Thomas & Graham, Douglas: *Population and Economic Development in Brazil*, John Hopkins University Press, Baltimore-London, 1979.

Merrill, Tim & Miro, Ramon (ed): *Mexico-A Country Study*, Library of Congress, Washington D. C., 1997.

Metclaf, Thomas: *Land, Landlords and the British Raj*, University of California Press, Los Angeles, 1979.

Metz, Helen (ed): *Algeria-A Country Study*, Library of Congress, Washington D. C., 1994.

Mexico-The Strategy to Achieve Sustained Economic Growth, International Monetary Fund, Washington D.C., September 1992.

Millward, R. & Singleton, J. (ed): *The Political Economy of Nationalization in Britain 1920-1950*, Cambridge University Press, Cambridge, 1995.

Milward, A. & Saul, S. B.: *The Development of the Economies of Continental Europe 1850-1914*, George Allen & Unwin Ltd., London, 1977.

Min, Tu-ki: *National Polity and Local Power*, Harvard University Press, Cambridge-MA, 1989.

Mitchell, B. R.: *European Historical Statistics 1750-1970*, Macmillan Press Ltd., 1975.

Moore, R. J.: *The Crisis of Indian Unity 1917-1940*, Oxford University Press, London, 1974.

More, Charles: *The Industrial Age*, Longman Inc., New York, 1989.

Moreland, W. H.: *From Akbar to Aurangzeb—A Study in Indian Economic History*, AMS Press, New York, 1975.

Morishima, Michio: *Why Has Japan Succeeded?* Cambridge University Press, Cambridge, 1982.

Morison, John (ed): *Eastern Europe and the West*, St. Martin's Press, 1992.

Mörner, Magnus: *Ensayos sobre Historia Latinoamericana*, Corporacion Editora Nacional, Quito-Ecuador, 1992.

Munro, Forbes: *Africa and the International Economy 1800-1960*, J. M. Dent & Sons Ltd., London, 1976.

Munting, Roger & Holderness, B.: *Crisis, Recovery and War*, St. Martin Press, US, 1991.

Murphy, Brian: *A History of the British Economy 1086-1740*, Longman Group Ltd., London, 1973.

Musson, A. E.: *The Growth of British Industry*, B.T. Batsford Ltd., London, 1978.

Nafziger, Wayne: *Learning from the Japanese*, M.E. Sharpe Inc., New York, 1995.

Naquin, Susan & Rawski, Evelyn: *Chinese Society in the 18th Century*, Yale Universi Press, New Haven-London, 1987.

Needham, Joseph: *Clerks and Craftsmen in China and the West*, Cambridge University Press, Cambridge, 1970.

Niemi, Albert: *U. S. Economic History*, Rand McNally College Publishing Co., US, 1975.

Nish, Ian: *Japan's Struggle with Internationalism*, Kegan Paul International, London, 1993.

Noman, Omar: *The Political Economy of Pakistan 1947-85*, KPI Limited, London, 1988.

North, Douglas: *The Growth of the US economy to 1860*, Harper & Row, New York, 1968.

Nove, Alec: *An Economic History of the USSR*, Penguin Press, London, 1969.

Nove, Alec: *Political Economy and Soviet Socialism*, George Allen & Unwin Ltd., London, 1979.

Nyrop, Richard, Benderly, Beryl, Cover, William, Englin, Darrel & Kirchner, Robert: *Area Handbook for Egypt*, US Government Printing Office, Washington D. C., 1976.

OECD Economic Outlook, OECD, Paris, 1990.

OECD Economic Surveys-Switzerland, OECD, Paris, 1992.

OECD Economic Surveys-Japan, OECD, Paris, 1992.

OECD, Main Economic Indicators-various years, Paris.

Ogilvie, Sheilagh (ed): *Germany-A New Social and Economic History Vol. 2*, Arnold, London, 1996.

Oliver, Roland & Mathew, Gervase (ed): *History of East Africa*, Oxford University Press, London 1963.

Ooms, Herman: *Tokugawa Ideology*, Princeton University Press, Princeton-New Yersey, 1985.

Orlovsky, Daniel: *The Limits of Reform-The Ministry of Internal Affairs in Imperial Russia 1802-1881*, Harvard University Press, Cambridge-MA, 1981.

Ortmann, Frank: *Revolutionäre im Exil*, Franz Steiner Verlag, Stuttgart, 1994.

Ortrowski, Donald: *Muscovy and the Mongols*, Cambridge University Press, Cambridge, 1998.

Osborne, Milton: *Southeast Asia*, Allen & Unwin, Sydney-London, 1987.

Palmier, Jean-Michel: *Lenine-l'art et la revolution*, Payot, Paris, 1975.

Parker, Geoffrey (ed): *The General Crisis of the 17th Century*, Routledge & Kegan Paul Ltd., London, 1978.

Parker, Richard: *North Africa-Regional Tensions and Strategic Concerns*, Praeger, 1984.

Parker, W. H.: *A Historical Geography of Russia*, University of London Press, London, 1968.

Pendle, George: *Argentina*, Oxford University Press, London, 1963.

Peres, Wilson: *L'investissement direct international et l'industrialisation Mexicaine*, OECD, Paris, 1990.

Perez, Louis: *The History of Japan*, Greenwood Press, Westport-US, 1998.

Perkins, Dwight (ed): *China's Modern Economy in Historical Perspective*, Stanford University Press, US, 1975.

Phongpaichit, Pasuk & Baker, Chris: *Thailand-Economy and Politics*, Oxford University Press, Oxford, 1995.

Pinson, Roppel: *Modern Germany*, The Macmillan Co., New York, 1966.

Pollard, Sidney: *The Development of the British Economy*, Routledge, London, 1992.

Pollard, Sidney & Holmes, Colin: *The End of the Old Europe 1914-1939*, Edward Arnold, 1973.

Pope, Rex (ed): *Atlas of British Social and Economic History since 1700*, Routledge, London, 1989.

Porter, Glenn (ed): *Encyclopedia of American Economic History Vol. I*, Charles Scribner's Sons, New York, 1980.

Porter, Michel: *The Competitive Advantage of Nations*, Macmillan Press Ltd., London, 1990.

Pottash, Robert: *The Army & Politics in Argentina 1928-1945*, Stanford University fPress, Stanford, 1969.

Powelson, John: *Latin America—Today's Economic and Social Revolution*, McGraw Hill, New York, 1964.

Prados, Leandro & Amaral, Samuel (ed): *La Independencia Americana-Consecuencias Economicas*, Alianza Editorial, Madrid, 1993.

Purcell, Victor: *South and East Asia since 1800*, Cambridge University Press, Cambridge, 1965.

Ramsey, Peter: *The Price Revolution in 16th Century England*, Methuen & Co. Ltd.,

London, 1971.

Rapp, Francis: *Les Origines Medievales de L'Allemagne Moderne*, Aubier, France, 1989.

Rawski, Thomas: *Economic Growth and Employment in China*, Oxford University Press,

Oxford-US, 1979.

Rawski, Thomas: *Economic Growth in Pre-War China*, University of California Press, US, 1989.

Rawski, Thomas & Li, Lillian (ed): *Chinese History in Economic Perspective*, University of California Press, Berkeley-Los Angeles, 1992.

Ray, Rajat Kanta (ed): *Entrepreneurship and Industry in India 1800-1947*, Oxford University Press, Oxford, 1992.

Realites d'Israel, Centre d'information d'Israel, Jerusalem, 1992.

Reischauer, Edwin: *Histoire du Japon et des Japonais Vol. 1*, Editions du Seuil, France, 1973.

Reischauer, Edwin & Craig, Albert: *Japan-Tradition and Transformation*, Allen & Unwin, Siydney, 1989.

Rey, Violette & Brunet, Roger : *Europes orientales, Russie, Asie central*, Belin-Reclus, Paris, 1996.

Reynaud, Alain: *Une Geohistoire-La Chine de Printemps et des Automnes*, Reclus, France, 1992.

Riado, Pierre: *L'Amérique Latine*, Presses Universitaires de France, Paris, 1993.

Riado, Pierre : *L'Amerique Latine de 1945 a nos jours*, Masson, Paris, 1992.

Ridings, Eugene: *Business Interest Groups in 19th century Brazil*, Cambridge University Press, Cambridge, 1994.

Robock, Stefan: *Brazil-A Study in Development Progress*, D.C. Heath & Co., Lexington-Mass., 1976.

Rock, David: *Argentina 1516-1987*, University of California Press, Berkeley, 1987.

Rock, David: *Authoritarian Argentina*, University of California Press, Berkeley, 1993.

Rock, David (ed): *Latin America in the 1940s*, University of California Press, Berkeley, 1994.

Rose, Caroline: *Interpreting History in Sino-Japanese Relations*, Routledge, London, 1998.

Rose, Michael: *The Relief of Poverty 1834-1914*, Macmillan Press Ltd., London, 1972.

Rosenberg, Nathan: *Technology and American Economic Growth*, Harper & Row, New York, 1972.

Ross, John (ed): *International Encyclopaedia of Population*, The Free Press, New York, 1982.

Rossabi, Morris (ed): *China Among Equals*, University of California Press, US, 1983.

Rostow, Walt: *The World Economy*, University of Texas Press, US, 1978.

Roth, Regina: *Staat und Wirtschaft im Ersten Weltkrieg*, Duncker & Humblot, Berlin, 1997.

Rothermund, Dietmar: *An Economic History of India*, Croom Helm Ltd., Australia, 1988.

Roustang, Guy: *Développement Economique de l'Allemagne Orientale*, Société d'Edition d'Enseignement Superieor, Paris, 1963.

Rovan, Joseph : *Histoire de l'Allemagne*, Editions du Seuil, 1994.

Rozman, Gilbert (ed): *The East Asian Region*, Princeton University Press, Princeton-New Yersey, 1991.

Rubistein, Murray (ed): *Taiwan-A New History*, M. E. Sharpe Inc., Armonk-New York, 1999.

Rudolph, Susan & Rudolph, Lloyd: *Gandhi-The Traditional Roots of Charisma*, The University of Chicago Press, Chicago, 1983.

Russell, A. J.: *Society and Government in Colonial Brazil 1500-1822*, Variorum, Great Britain, 1992.

Sabillon, Carlos: *Manufacturing, Technology*, and Economic Growth, M.E. Sharpe, New York, 2000.

Sagrera, Martin: *Los Racismos en las Américas*, IEPALA, Madrid, 1998.

Saletore, R. N.: *Early Indian Economic History*, Curzon Press, London, 1975.

San Martino, Ma. Laura: *Argentina Contemporànea-de Peron a Menem*, Ediciones Ciudad Argentina, Buenos Aires, 1996.

Sànchez-Albornoz, N.: *La Poblacion de América Latina*, Alianza Editorial, Madrid, 1994.

Sansom, George: *Histoire du Japon-Des Origines aux debuts du Japon moderne*, Fayard, Paris, 1988.

Sauvy, Alfred: *Histoire Economique de la France entre les deux Guerres*, Economica, Paris, 1984.

Schieder, Theodor (herausgegeben) : *Handbuch der Europäischen Geschichte*, Band 1-7, Union Verlag Stuttgart, 1968.

Scholl, Lars: *Ingenieure in der Frühindustrialisierung*, Vandenhoeck & Ruprecht, Göttingen, 1978.

Schulze, Hagen & Paul, Inal (herausgegeben): *Europäische Geschichte*, Bayerischer Schulbuch Verlag, München, 1994.

Schwartz, Stuart: *Slaves, Peasants and Rebels-Reconsidering Brazilian Slavery*, University of Illinois Press, Chicago, 1996.

Scobie, James. *Argentina—A City and a Nation*, Oxford University Press, New York, 1971.

Scott, James: *The Moral Economy of the Peasant*, Yale University Press, New Haven-London, 1976.

Scribner, Bob (ed): *Germany-A New Social and Economic History Vol. I*, Arnold, London, 1996.

Sen, Sunil Kumar: *Working Class Movements in India 1885-1975*, Oxford University Press, Oxford, 1994.

Sharma, Ram Sharan: *Light on Early Indian Society and Economy*, Manaktala & Sons, Bombay, 1966.

Shaw, Timothy (ed): *Alternatives Futures for Africa*, Westview Press, Boulder-Colorado, 1982.

Shepherd, Geoffrey, Duchene, François & Saunders, Christopher (ed): *Europe's Industries*, Frances Pinter, London, 1983.

Shumway, Nicolas: *The Invention of Argentina*, University of California Press, Berkeley, 1991.

Silver, Morris: *Economic Structures of the Ancient Near East*, Croom Helm, Sydney, 1985.

Singhal, D. P.: *A History of the Indian People*, Methuen, London, 1983.

Singapore in Brief 1991, Ministry of Trade and Industry, Singapore, 1992.

Smith, R. & Christian, D.: *Bread and Salt*, Cambridge University Press, Cambridge, 1984.

Smith, Thomas: *Native Sources of Japanese Industrialization 1750-1920*, University of California Press, Berkeley-Los Angeles, 1988.

South America, Central America and the Caribbean 2001, Europa Publications, London, 2001.

South America, Central America and the Caribbean 2002, Europa Publications, London, 2002.

Speake, Graham: *Cultural Atlas of Africa*, Facts on File Inc., New York, 1981.

Spear, Percival: *A History of India Vol. II*, Penguin Books, London, 1970.

Spear, Percival: *The Oxford History of Modern India 1740-1975*, Oxford University Press, Oxford, 1989.

Statistics de Base de la Communaute, Eurostat, Bruxelles, 1992.

Stein, J. & Stein, Barbara : *L'heritage colonial de l'Amerique Latine*, François Maspero, Paris, 1974.

Stepan, Alfred: *The Military in Politics-Changing Patterns in Brazil*, Princeton University Press, Princeton, 1971.

Stern, Robert: *Changing India*, Cambridge University Press, Cambridge, 1993.

Stiglitz, Joseph: *Where Global Markets are Going Wrong*, W.W. Norton, 2002.

Stirton, Frederick: *Class, State and Industrial Structure*, Greenwood Press, Westport-London, 1980.

Stokes, Eric: *The Peasant and the Raj*, Cambridge University Press, Cambridge, 1980.

Story, Jonathan (ed): *The New Europe-Politics*, Government and Economy since 1945, Blackwell, Oxford, 1993.

Stueck, William: *The Korean War*, Princeton University Press, Princeton-New Yersey, 1995.

Sub-Saharan Africa—From Crisis to Sustainable Growth, The World Bank, Washington D. C., 1989.

Supple, Barry (ed): *The Experience of Economic Growth*, Random House, New York, 1963.

Surveys of African Economies Vol. 6, International Monetary Fund, Washington D. C., 1975.

Suzuki, Tessa: *A History of Japanese Economic Thought*, Routledge, London, 1989.

Tabb, William: *The Postwar Japanese System*, Oxford University Press, Oxford-New York, 1995.

Takekoshi, Yoseburo: *The Economic Aspects of the History of the Civilization of Japan Vol. 3*,

Tames, Richard: *Economy and Society in 19th century Britain*, George Allen & Unwin Ltd., London, 1972.

Tanaka, Heizo: *Contemporary Japanese Economy and Economic Policy*, The University of Michigan Press, US, 1991.

Tanaka, Stefan: *Japan's Orient*, University of California Press, Berkeley-CA, 1993.

Tarling, Nicholas (ed): *The Cambridge History of Southeast Asia Vol. 11*, Cambridge University Press, Cambridge, 1994.

Taylor, Arthur: *Laissez-Faire and State Intervention in 19th century Britain*, The Macmillan Press Ltd., Hong Kong, 1972.

Taylor, Arthur (ed): *The Standard of Living in Britain in the Industrial Revolution*, Methuen & Co. Ltd., London, 1975.

Thailand-Adjusting for Success, International Monetary Fund, Washington D.C., August 1991.

Thane, Pat & Sutcliffe, Anthony (ed): *Essays in Social History*, Oxford University Press, Oxford-US, 1986.

Thapar, Romila: *A History of India Vol. I*, Penguin Books, London, 1966.

The Cambridge Economic History of Europe Vol. I, Cambridge University Press, Cambridge, 1971.

The Cambridge Economic History of Europe Vol. II, Cambridge University Press, Cambridge, 1987.

The Cambridge Economic History of Europe Vol. VII, Cambridge University Press, London, 1978.

The Cambridge Economic History of India Vol. II, Cambridge University Press, Cambridge, 1983.

The Cambridge Encyclopaedia of China, Cambridge University Press, Cambridge, 1991.

The Cambridge Encyclopaedia of Japan, Cambridge University Press, Cambridge, 1993.

The Cambridge Encyclopaedia of India, Pakistan, Bangladesh, Sri Lanka, Nepal, Bhutan and the Maldives, Cambridge University Press, Cambridge, 1989.

The Cambridge History of Africa Vol 5, 6, 7 and 8, Cambridge University Press, Cambridge, 1984.

The Cambridge History of China Vol. I, III, VII, Cambridge University Press, Cambridge, 1986.

The Cambridge History of Iran Vol. 7, Cambridge University Press, *Cambridge*, 1991.

The Cambridge History of Japan Vol. V-VI, Cambridge University Press, Cambridge, 1989.

The Cambridge History of Latin America Vol. II, III and IV, Cambridge University Press, Cambridge, 1984.

The Cambridge History of the United States Vol. I-II, Cambridge University Press, Cambridge, 2000.

The CIA Fact Book-various years, Central Intelligence Agency, US.

The Europa World Yearbook 1992 Vol. II, Europa Publications, London, 1992.

The Far East and Australasia 2001, Europa Publications, London, 2001.

The Far East and Australasia 2002, Europa Publications, London, 2002.

The Federal Republic of Germany, International Monetary Fund, Washington D.C., January 1991.

The Fontana Economic History of Europe-The Emergence of Industrial Societies, William Collins & Son Ltd., London, 1976.

The Fontana Economic History of Europe-Contemporary Economies, William Collins & Sons Ltd., London, 1976.

The Long Debate on Poverty, The Institute of Economic Affairs, London, 1972.

The Middle East and North Africa 2001, Europa Publications, London, 2001.

The Middle East and North Africa 2002, Europa Publications, London, 2002.

The New Encyclopaedia Britannica-Macropaedia Vol. I-XII, Encyclopaedia Britannica Inc., Chicago, 1988.

The US and Canada 1994, Europa Publications, London, 1994.

Thompson, Carol, Anderberg, Mary & Antel, Joan (ed): *The Current History-Encyclopaedia of Developing Nations*, McGraw Hill Inc., New York, 1982.

Thompson, F. (ed): *Landowners, Capitalists and Entrepreneurs*, Oxford University Press, Oxford, 1994.

Tiedemann, Arthur (ed): *An Introduction to Japanese Civilization*, Columbia University Press, New York, 1974.

Tolliday, Steven (ed): *The Economic Development of Modern Japan 1868-1945*, Elgar Reference Collection, Cheltenham-UK, 2001.

Tomlinson, B. R.: *The Economy of Modern India 1860-1970*, The New Cambridge History of India Vol. 3, Cambridge University Press, Cambridge, 1996.

Tomlinson, Jim: *Problems of British Economic Policy 1870-1945*, Methuen & Co. Ltd., London, 1981.

Trade Policy Review-Argentina, World Trade Organization, Geneva, 1999.

Trade Policy Review-Brazil Vol. I & II, GATT, Geneva, 1992.

Trade Policy Review-Brazil, World Trade Organization, Geneva, 1996.

Trade Policy Review-Egypt, World Trade Organization, Geneva, 1999.

Trade Policy Review-Nigeria, World Trade Organization, Geneva, 1998.

Trade Policy Review-South Africa, World Trade Organization, Geneva, 1999.

Trade Policy Review-Hong Kong, GATT, Geneva, 1990.

Trade Policy Review-Hong Kong, GATT, Geneva, 1994.

Trade Policy Review-Indonesia Vol. I & II, GATT, Geneva, 1991.

Trade Policy Review-Japan Vol. I & II, GATT, Geneva, 1992.

Trade Policy Review-Republic of Korea Vol. I & II, GATT, Geneva, 1992.

Trade Policy Review-Singapore, Vol. I & II, GATT, Geneva, 1992.

Trade Policy Review-Switzerland, Vol. I & II, GATT, Geneva, 1991.

Trausch, Gilbert: *Histoire du Luxembourg*, Hatier, Paris, 1992.

Trevelyan, G. M.: *A Shortened History of England*, Longmans Green & Co. Inc., New York, 1959.

Tsuru, Shigeto: *Japan's Capitalism*, Cambridge University Press, Cambridge, 1993.

Turnock, David: *A Historical Geography of Railways in Great Britain and Ireland*, Ashgate, England, 1998.

Ungar, Sanford: *Africa—The People and Politics of an Emerging Continent*, Simon & Schuster Inc., 1986.

United Nations-various years, *World Population Prospects*, New York.

United Nations Conference on Trade and Development-various years, *Handbook of International Trade and Development Statistics*, Geneva.

United Nations Development Program-various years, *Human Development Report*, Oxford University Press, Oxford.

United Nations Industrial Development Organization-various years, *International Yearbook of Industrial Statistics*, Vienna.

Van Zanden, Jan Luiten (ed): *The Economic Development of The Netherlands since 1870*, Elgar Reference Collection, Cheltenham-UK, 1996.

Vie, Michael: *Le Japon Contemporain*, Presses Universitaires de France, Paris, 1971.

Vilar, Pierre : *Crecimiento y Desarrollo*, Ediciones Ariel, Barcelona, 1964.

Vincent, Bernard (ed): *Histoire des Etas Unis*, Presses Universitaires de Nancy, France, 1994.

Vogel, Erza: *Japan as No. 1*, Harvard University Press, Cambridge, Mass., 1979.

Wade, Robert: *Governing the Market*, Princeton University Press, Princeton, 1990.

Waldron, Arthur: *From War to Nationalism*, Cambridge University Press, Cambridge, 1995.

Walter, Richard: *Politics and Urban Growth in Buenos Aires 1910-1942*, Cambridge University Press, Cambridge, 1993.

Watson, Francis: *A Concise History of India*, Thames & Hudson, Great Britain, 1979.

Wang, Nora: *L'Asie Orientale du milieu du XIXe siècle à nos jours*, Armand Colin, Paris, 1993.

Webster, Daniel: *The History of Ireland*, Greenwood Press, Westport-CT, 2001.

Wegel, Oskar: *China im Aufbruch*, Verlag C. H. Beck, München, 1997.

Wehler, Hans: *Deutsch Gesellschaftsgeschichte 1700-1815*, Verlag C. H. Beck, München, 1987.

Westwood, J.: *Endurance and Endeavor*, Oxford University Press, Oxford, 1993.

Western Europe 2002, Europa Publications, London, 2002.

Wickins, Peter: *Africa 1880-1980—An Economic History*, Oxford University Press, Oxford, 1986.

Wilber, Donald: *Iran—Past and Present*, Princeton University Press, Princeton, 1976.

Wilkie, James: *The Mexican Revolution-Federal Expenditure and Social Change since 1910*, University of California Press, Berkeley, 1967.

Wirth, John: *The Politics of Brazilian Development 1930-1954*, Stanford University Press, Stanford, 1970.

Whitaker, Arthur: *Argentina*, Prentice-Hall Inc., Englewood Cliffs-US, 1964.

White, Lynn: *Policies of Chaos*, Princeton University Press, Princeton-New Yersey, 1989.

Whitney Hall, John (ed): *The Cambridge History of Japan-Early Modern Japan*, Cambridge University Press, Cambridge, 1991.

Will, Pierre: *Bureaucratie et Famine en Chine au 18e Siecle*, Mouton Editeur, Paris, 1980.

Wolpert, Stanley: *Jinnah of Pakistan*, Oxford University Press, New York-Oxford, 1984.

Wolpert, Stanley : *A New History of India*, Oxford University Press, New York, 1982.

Wolpert, Stanley: *Zulfi Bhutto of Pakistan*, Oxford University Press, Oxford, 1993.

Woodward, C. Vann (ed): *The Comparative Approach to American History*, Oxford University Press, Oxford, 1997.

World Bank, World Development Report-various years, Washington.

World Trade Organization-various years, Annual Report, Geneva.

Woronoff, Denis: *Histoire de l'Industrie en France*, Editions du Seuil, Paris, 1994.

Woronoff, Jon: *Hong Kong-Capitalist Paradise*, Heinemann Educational Books Ltd., Hong Kong, 1980.

Wright, Chester: *Economic History of the United States*, McGraw Hill, New York, 1941.

Wrigley, E.: *Continuity, Chance and Change*, Cambridge University Press, Cambridge, 1988.

Yamamura, Kozo (ed): *The Cambridge History of Japan-Medieval Japan*, Cambridge University Press, Cambridge, 1990.

Yarnell, Allen (ed): *The American People-Creating a Nation and Society*, Harper & Row, New York, 1986.

Yapp, M. E.: *The Near East since the First World War-A History to 1995*, Longman, London, 1996.

Yearbook of Statistics Singapore 1991, Department of Statistics, Singapore, 1992.

Xiang, Lanxin: *Recasting the Imperial Far East*, M. E. Sharpe Inc., Armonk-New York, 1995.

Zorrilla, Rubén: *Estructurl Social y Caudillismo 1810-1870*, Grupo Editorial Latinoamericano, Buenos Aires, 1994.

Zysman, John & Cohen, Stephen: *Manufacturing Matters*, Basic Books, New York, 1987.

Periodicals

Asiaweek, Hong Kong
Bilan, Switzerland
Businessweek, New York
Cambio, Madrid
Comercio Exterior, Mexico D.F.
Der Spiegel, Frankfurt
EU Magazin, Germany

Focus-WTO, Geneva
Fortune, New York
Harvard Business Review, Cambridge-MA
Jeune Afrique-L'intelligent, Paris
Le Monde Diplomatique, Paris
Le Nouvel Afrique-Asie, Paris
Le Nouvel Economist, Paris
L'Hebdo, Switzerland
National Geographic, Washington D.C.
Newsweek, New York
Scientific American, New York
Spektrum der Wissenschaft, Deutschland
The Economist, London
The Far Eastern Economic Review, Hong Kong
The Middle East, London
Time, New York

Printed in the United States
27142LVS00001B/168

9 780875 863535